SON OF MY FATHER
Me, My Dad and Derby County FC

SON OF MY FATHER

Me, My Dad and Derby County FC

CRAIG TREMBIRTH

First published in Great Britain in 2012 by The Derby Books Publishing Company Limited, 3 The Parker Centre, Derby, DE21 4SZ.

ISBN 978-1-78091-098-7

CONTENTS

ACKNOWLEDGEMENTS

None of the fond memories contained within this book would have been possible if my Dad had not taken me to that first match in 1979, and so I am indebted to him. I am also thankful to my brothers, Ian and Daniel, and Uncle Paul, and to the friends who have added to the stories within, and to my Mum for the supportive home I always came back to.

I also owe a great deal of gratitude to my wife, Emma, for giving me the encouragement and the confidence to realise this book could be published.

NOTE:

When I started attending football matches in 1979, the top four divisions in England were run by the Football League and simply known as Division One, Division Two, Division Three and Division Four.

At the start of the 1992–93 season, the teams in Division One resigned en masse from the Football League to form the Premier League. What had been the Football League's second division the season before then became the Football League's first division, and was renamed Division One. The top four divisions from 1992–93 were therefore known as the Premier League, Division One, Division Two and Division Three.

As this novel spans the change it may get confusing as to which divisions are being mentioned.

When a division is referred to with the initial letters in lower case, this means the place in the League structure where it sits. For example, 'the second division' will always indicate the second tier, be that Division Two before 1992–93 or Division One from 1992–93 onwards.

When a division is referred to with the initial letters in upper case, this means the name of the division at the time. For example, 'Division One' before 1992–93 indicates the top-flight, whereas 'Division One' from 1992–93 onwards indicates the second tier.

At the start of the 2004–05 season the divisions changed again, with the Football League Division One rebranded as the Championship. Subsequently the third tier became Division One and the fourth tier became Division Two.

Somebody somewhere won't rest until Rochdale are Division One champions.

1979–80

Derby County 4 Nottingham Forest 1
Saturday 24 November 1979
When the people stood up and cheered the lights changed.

I was only four years old when my Dad took me to my first football match. My brother, Ian, came as well but he was seven. He was old enough to like The Boomtown Rats, while I preferred the Village People as they dressed like Red Indians and the policemen from *CHiPs*. Meanwhile Dad spent most of November 1979 serenading Mum with Dr Hook's, *When You're In Love With a Beautiful Woman*. Despite this it still reached Number One that year.

The three of us must have slipped out of the back door when my Mum wasn't watching, as football seems to have been a different beast back then. These days, certainly in England's top two divisions, every supporter gets their own seat and so can wander into the ground within five minutes of the kick-off. Men form orderly queues into the toilets and there are cubicles with paper to alleviate the most anxious of pre-match nerves. There are toilets for the ladies too, while in the concourses polite caterers serve from a wide menu of fast-food from pristine kitchens.

Back in the late 1970s football was in the grip of hooliganism. Comics like Jimmy Tarbuck and Cannon and Ball would joke that they, '…went to watch a fight and a football match broke out'. Horror stories of Chelsea Smiles and people throwing darts at opposition fans have become folklore. Supporters packed the terraces from one o'clock in the afternoon, urinating in each other's pockets rather than marching back to the bogs and losing their place. Meanwhile attempting any of the stadium food rendered your health insurance invalid.

I'm sure it wasn't that terrible. It couldn't have been or Dad wouldn't have taken us. And I know Mum would have been waving us out of the door rather than turning round bewildered halfway through that Saturday afternoon to wonder where her three boys had disappeared to. But history records the exciting exceptions rather than the norm, wars and tragedies rather than common acts of simply living, and so according to the record books we spent the afternoon ripping out seats and throwing them at the police.

The Baseball Ground, the home of Derby County until 1997, was a cauldron wedged between rows of terraced houses and the foundries that flanked the railway line. You could be a street away and not know the stadium existed, but once within sight it dominated the area.

The mist created by 27,279 spectators on that cold November afternoon seemed to seep out like steam beneath the floodlights, while inside passions brewed as subplots bubbled in the melting pot. The visitors, Nottingham Forest, were the local adversary, built on a rivalry sprung from the coalminers who lived in the towns and villages of Nottinghamshire and Derbyshire situated along the county border. Places like Annesley, Eastwood and Hucknall; Alfreton, Selston and Ripley.

Every club has its rival but this is not always based on location, as beneath the surface of inner or inter-city squabbles there can lay deeper reasons for hatred. Contention between Liverpool and Manchester United dates back to the 19th century and the building of the Manchester Ship Canal, which took work away from the Merseyside docks. Meanwhile the two biggest teams in Glasgow, Celtic and Rangers, share a rivalry based on the former's mass contingent of Irish Catholic workers and the Protestant communities of the city who follow the latter. The two clubs first met in 1888, while the two divisions of Christianity have been at each other's throats for over 300 years.

That afternoon Forest arrived in Derby as football's European Champions, having beaten German club, Hamburg, in the Cup Final in the summer of 1979. At the time they were one of the best club sides in Europe, and probably the world, with their victory being the second time in as many years that the club captain, John McGovern, had claimed the iconic trophy. To me and my Dad, watching him parade the Cup via grainy televised pictures from Munich was like seeing a neighbour parking his Porsche on the driveway next to your Austin Allegro.

Forest had won the English Division One title in 1977–78 in their first season after being promoted from Division Two. It was an incredible feat that would have been hard for those hemmed into the ground that afternoon to believe, had the Forest manager, Brian Clough, not achieved a similar domestic rise to success with Derby earlier in the decade. Clough had taken Derby to their first League title in 1972 just four years after the side had finished 18th in the second tier of English football.

In the changing rooms of our local park, where we played in the paddling pool and ate ice lollies in summer, and rode our bikes among the trees in winter, there is a plaque commemorating its opening;

WEST PARK
NEW CHANGING ROOMS
OPENED BY
BRIAN CLOUGH ESQ.
MANAGER OF DERBY COUNTY F.C.
10TH AUGUST 1972

but I didn't see the plaque until some years after that first match, only realising at the age of 10 that Clough had also managed Derby. Having joined Nottingham Forest six days after I was born in 1975 I could be forgiven for believing that the great man had always been their manager.

History back then was alien to me. At four years old all I was interested in were the red bits of pepper in our Bird's Eye chicken pies, being petrified of the Crowman on *Worzel Gummidge* and what Willis was talkin' about in *Diff'rent Strokes*. Meanwhile Ian was enthralled with *Voyager 1* reaching the rings of Jupiter.

Today the school playing fields of our hometown are littered with boys and girls in the shirts of Manchester United, Liverpool, Arsenal and more recently Chelsea. The plague of Newcastle United shirts died out in 2008. The colours of Derby and Nottingham Forest form a shared and healthy split among the menagerie, while Notts County and Leicester fans play a bit-part.

Back in 1979 Forest had painted the town red, helped by the inclusion of local boy Garry Birtles in their squad. He'd made his debut in March 1977 after signing from Long Eaton United, going on to play in both of the club's European Cup successes. A picture of him still hangs in the Tiger Inn on Tamworth Road in town, opposite the old Grammar school, as part of the pub's winning darts team of the mid-1970s.

Ian didn't stand a chance. One day he came home from his primary school to have a quiet word with my father.

'Dad,' he asked, 'why do you support Derby…they're rubbish?'

It was too late for him but at four I had yet to be turned by taunts on the schoolyard. I had no peers to tell me that Derby County had been on the slide, slipping from Champions of England for the second time in 1975 to fourth and then 15th in the following seasons. Finishing 12th in the 1977–78 campaign was just a tease. While Forest were on cloud nine, a cumulonimbus of gloom was descending upon our club and in our home.

On 24 November 1979 my brother and I sat either side of our Dad in the middle tier of the Baseball Ground's Normanton End. Wrapped in dark blue parkers, worn jeans and scuffed brown shoes, we were 15 years behind the Mods who had made the look fashionable and 15 years ahead of Oasis who were behind its renaissance. This meant we were about as unfashionable as you could get.

Watching the match was like being at the cinema, with strangers huddled in darkness while the main feature played out brightly in front of us all. It was Mum who used to take Ian and I to the Ritz picture house in Long Eaton though, stopping first at the small shop on the Market Place to buy candy alphabet sweets before queuing up to see films like *Superman the Movie* and *Star Trek the Motion Picture*, or to watch James Bond defeat Hugo Drax in *Moonraker*.

If you made a noise at the cinema an usher would come with a red torch and tell you to keep quiet but here everything was animated and alive. The roof stooped low above our heads and the thunderous roar of feet and voice, around and within, echoed through the wooden frame. People were out of their seats and shouting with bitter anger and spiteful venom, but also with great passion, excitement and will. Dad had warned us both before the game, 'Boys, you may hear words at the match today that you've never heard before – don't ask me what they mean and for Heaven's sake don't ask your mother!'

Despite only being an average 5ft 8in, to me my Dad was huge in stature and with his arms wrapped around the pair of us like Mr Tickle I never once felt threatened by the grown men shouting obscenities just yards away.

I was beginning to get accustomed to these new surroundings when, without warning, the ground was suddenly transformed. On the crest of a huge roar wild limbs started fighting the air in celebration, with men jumping on their seats, joined by the rest of the supporters in the stadium who I had been watching just moments before.

I looked up to my Dad who had turned to me in celebration while simultaneously consoling my brother among the furore.

'We've scored Craigy!' he yelled, and as the jumping and celebrating seemed so much fun, I joined in.

Time and again that afternoon the stadium united in joy. Individuals in the crowd offered their own instructions, agitated and moving against the flow before becoming one voice in celebration. Every time it filled me with an excitement that I always wanted repeating until eventually I started to anticipate it, becoming a part of it and jumping in time with the crowd and yelling my own words of congratulations every time a goal was scored.

As the game neared its end I looked up at my Dad. His kind face always gave an air of assured confidence, resting beneath a thatch of dark hair perfect for insulation at away matches in Hartlepool. When things were going his way he owned a grin that advertised the happiness within him and even when they weren't it was never far away from his mouth. Despite the darkness in the stand his vivid blue eyes seemed more piercing than ever and as he looked back at me I tried to match his smile.

'I think we might win this.' I told him excitedly, and he laughed and pulled me right into the warmth of his jacket.

'I think you're right.' he replied.

My infant memory of that afternoon remembers little more. Snippets of recall enter like cuttings on an editor's floor but whether these are of this match or of the many more me and my Dad were to attend, I don't know. What I am certain of is that there was a scoreboard to my left, although I didn't know it was my left, and when the people stood up and cheered the lights changed.

In the year of the underdog, when Rocky Balboa knocked-out Apollo Creed to become the Heavyweight Champion of the World, Derby County beat the European Champions by four goals to one. John Duncan, probably more famous for guiding Chesterfield to the FA Cup semi-finals in 1997 scored twice, while Stephen Emery and Gerry Daly got the other two.

Often the three points earned for the win, or two points as it was back in the 1979–80 season, are vital to secure promotion or stave off relegation. Sometimes the points are secondary, as a victory against a bitter rival or an old manager burns itself into the memory of even a four-year-old kid. But when it's your first match, your maiden voyage through the steady click of the turnstiles and into the dark wooden stands that trap your eager voice, a win takes an afternoon out and turns it into the first of a string of future events and occasions that will punctuate your lifetime. This was one of those occasions, and on that afternoon at least two of the Trembirth family walked away from the ground happy. Thanks to my Dad, I was a Derby fan.

*****

Unfortunately this was a brief period of rejoicing. By the end of the season Derby finished 21st in the League and were relegated. Thirty-two players had represented the club throughout the year whereas when the Rams won the Championship in both 1972 and 1975, Brian Clough and Dave Mackay had used 16 each. Those included the eight: Colin Boulton, Ron Webster, Colin Todd, Archie Gemmill, Kevin Hector, Alan Hinton, Roy McFarland and Steve Powell who played in both of the Championship winning sides.

Just five years after being crowned Champions of England for the second time in the decade, and four years after beating the mighty Real Madrid by four goals to one in the first leg of a European Cup tie, Derby County would be playing their football in Division Two.

English First Division 1979–80

Pos		Pl	W	D	L	F	A	GD	Pts
1	Liverpool	42	25	10	7	81	30	51	60
2	Manchester United	42	24	10	8	65	35	30	58
3	Ipswich Town	42	22	9	11	68	39	29	53
19	Everton	42	9	17	16	43	51	-8	35
20	Bristol City	42	9	13	20	37	66	-29	31
21	**Derby County**	**42**	**11**	**8**	**23**	**47**	**67**	**-20**	**30**
22	Bolton Wanderers	42	5	15	22	38	73	-35	25

1980–81

I was born on 1 January and so while most children are sent to bed the night before their birthday too excited to sleep, I could always be found wide awake and celebrating the New Year. One of my Great Aunts and Uncles held the annual party and it seemed like our whole extended family crammed into their compact semi-detached home in the nearby village of Breaston. I spent the evenings alternating between playing games of Musical Chairs and Bird's Fly in the living room, orchestrated by my Uncle, and waiting to see the cuckoo clock signal each hour in the dining room, which was dominated by my Auntie Dot's huge collection of porcelain dogs.

1980 became 1981 and after forming a circle to sing *Auld Lang Syne* we sat listening to the soundtrack of a tribute to John Lennon who had been shot and killed that December.

I never knew when it stopped being the New Year and when it came to being my birthday but that year it seemed to arrive quicker than usual. Instead of the usual boxed gift to open Dad handed me an envelope with my name typed in small font across the front. He looked down at me with his familiar grin as I peeled it open, while the eyes of my relatives looking my way made me feel like I was unwrapping a Wonka Bar in *Charlie and the Chocolate Factory*.

The paper inside was unusually thin, not like that upon which I misspelled 'dolly mixters' and 'skelenton' on at school, but before I could take it out fully Dad announced my present to all, ruining my surprise with his eagerness.

While most kids in 1981 got a Rubik's Cube or an Action Man for their birthday, when I was six I got to be the mascot of Derby County.

The letter described how on the morning of the game the postman would deliver instructions to follow and a voucher to get the club strip from the Co-op department store in Derby city centre. Further directions on what to do when we arrived at the ground were included but I was so excited I could no longer read, as was everyone else, even my Dad's sister's family who didn't support Derby. I felt like a champion.

The fixture was not scheduled until 21 February, which was a long time to wait for a six-year-old. Eventually though the day arrived and as promised the letterbox clattered to the arrival of the postman. Again the letter was like tracing paper and it crumpled in my eager hands as I read the words typed by the actual club secretary of Derby County Football Club.

Derby County 1 Orient 1

Saturday 21 February 1981

The opposition were exotically named Orient, who I thought were based in the Far East of Asia but later found to be from the far East London borough of Leyton. Some say their name derives from a past player who asked for the unusual moniker as he worked for the Orient Shipping Company, while others think that the club's founders simply made it up on a particularly slow night in the Birckbeck Tavern.

At the time of the match Mum was three-months pregnant with my younger brother, Daniel, and was ill and confined to bed. Instead of coming to the match she would have to spend the day at home. There was still a chance for her to witness my moment of glory though, as despite being in the second division the match was to be featured on that night's *Match of the Day*.

Like most families in 1981 we only owned one television and Sky+ was yet to be invented. It would still be a few years before portable television sets and home video cassette recorders became commonplace, so instead we had to move the box up from the living room for Mum to witness my five minutes of fame. The situation didn't please my brother, Ian, as he always watched *Tiswas* on Saturday mornings, but Dad carried the hulking television up the stairs regardless, before rigging an elaborate device to get the aerial lead up the side of the house, through the window and into the bedroom.

Once his mind was set on something, Dad would achieve that goal no matter how hard the task or how long it took, and eventually we got everything in place just in time to see Sally James, Chris Tarrant, a Phantom Flan Flinger and Adam Ant bid farewell. Ian was livid.

After a lunch of scrambled egg on toast, me and my Dad walked briskly to the railway station in Long Eaton, and whereas I used to have to race to keep up with his long legs, that morning I was striding out the pace. It was a bitterly cold day but under a blue and white woolly hat, and wrapped in a parker jacket and my excitement, I felt as warm as the toast and tea that we always had for breakfast on Saturday mornings.

Dad had never learned to drive and so the two of us usually travelled by train to matches. He bought our train tickets and we headed under the bridge to the steep ramp that led up to the platform, taking photographs all the way of inconsequential things like me standing by the ticket office, me under the shelter at the railway station, me about to get into the carriage and even one of the train-driver. Once aboard though Dad put his camera away as we moved smoothly beneath the motorway bridge, over the level crossing between the breaker's yard and the riding school, past the huge reservoir and into the fields of Breaston and Draycott.

At the town of Spondon, a town on the edge of Derby, the train ran parallel to the River Derwent. Dad asked me if I knew what it was called, but being six years old geography was not my strong point. Over the course of many journeys we would take though I learned its name, as well as the details and history of every village and building that lined that route.

As we neared our destination I anxiously felt among the many pockets of my parker for the letter that had arrived that morning, along with a picture I had drawn for the team to put up in the dressing room. Being a creative child I had also sent a drawing to the Gallery on *Take Hart*, although it didn't get shown. I often wonder whether the team displayed my picture or whether they were as critical as Tony Hart.

Usually me and my Dad walked up Midland Road, took a left along London Road, up Osmaston Road, Douglas Street and then walked along Cambridge Street to get to the Baseball Ground. That day, however, we had to collect the kit and so headed out of the station and straight into the city centre.

Today the Co-op is dwarfed by the clinical Westfield Centre, but in 1981 the department store held a regal grandeur that made me subconsciously wipe my feet as I walked in. Replica kits weren't as fashionable as they are now but there were still plenty on sale. The strip was beautiful, with shiny navy blue shorts and a pristine white shirt, which included collars that looked like something out of *Saturday Night Fever*. You could glide all the way to France on them, which was quite appropriate as the sponsor's name, Fly British Midland, was printed across the front. As she placed the kit in a brown paper bag, Dad proudly told the cashier that I was going to be the mascot at Derby, which was something he told everyone along the way to the stadium that day. As we left the store there was just enough time for another photograph before we made our way to the Baseball Ground.

The gentleman on the door of the players' entrance, which was simply a gate cut into a piece of fence at the end of the A, B and C Stand, seemed a little confused when we arrived. At first he was reluctant to let us in but Dad had a certain charm with people, which was instantly likeable and persuasive. After he explained what I would be doing and showing the steward the letter we were through the fence and into the belly of the stadium. We found the changing rooms, with a separate area for the mascot to get changed in, and I peeled the famous white shirt onto my tiny frame.

By this time Dad had already got through one roll of film and was delving into his bag for another. It was long before the advent of digital cameras though and the film had wrapped around inside its casing and so there was no end to pull out and insert into the camera's mechanism. With Dad's usual determined streak though he went in search of a woman who might have a pair of tweezers with which he could get the film out.

It took him five minutes to come back, along with that familiar grin and the tweezers, during which time I had been diligently tying the laces on my Mitre trainers. The night before I'd had visions of tripping over them and causing the rest of the team to stumble ignominiously onto the pitch like some bizarre clip on *Hi-De-Hi*, and I had no intention of doing it for real.

The clock in my changing room barely seemed to move but after what seemed like an age a bell rang from beneath the ground. It was the referee's signal to the players that the match was about to start, and having left my drawing with our chaperone for the day I walked out of my own dressing room and waited in the thin corridor beneath the stands to see the team.

The player I was most eager to meet was Alan Biley, the centre-forward who had signed the previous season from Cambridge United for £350,000. I liked him because he played with his shirt hanging out and had a long blonde mullet a bit like Rod Stewart, which is strange as I don't really like Rod Stewart or mullets. When I saw him I couldn't breathe, but he looked at me coolly, looked at my shirt, smiled and said, 'The cameraman's gonna love you, kid!'

At this time shirt sponsors were something relatively new in the game but Derby County were leading the way. They were the first English team to have sponsored shirts in 1978, although these were never worn after the pre-season photo shoot. In 1979 Liverpool were the first club to display sponsors on their shirts in the Football League, but the BBC and ITV were less innovative and refused to broadcast matches featuring branded shirts until 1983. Thirty years on and shirt sponsors have now become as much a part of the football kit as the club badge, but it was Derby County who paved the way for the iconic Liverpool Hitachi design, Chelsea's Commodore kit and Sheffield Wednesday's 2002–03 shirt sponsored by Chupa Chups.

My own shirt that day, emblazoned with the Fly British Midland slogan, contravened the BBC and ITV rules and so the *Match of the Day* cameraman spent the pre-game warm-up desperately trying to avoid the young mascot who was in his element and running rings into the Baseball Ground mud. Despite the best efforts of my Dad to get our television up the stairs so my Mum could see her son on television, she would have to wait for the album of photographs that Dad had taken to capture me leading our team out.

Roy McFarland, who played 28 times for England and featured in both of the Ram's Championship winning sides, scored the only Derby goal in a 1–1 draw that afternoon. Kevin Hector, who also played in both of those teams, was there too. It was a pairing that in Derby was as evocative as Torville and Dean and Charles and Di. Meanwhile, leading them out onto the pitch was me, with my laces tied tight, running as fast as my legs could carry me and a grin as wide as that of my Dad's.

*****

In spite of relegation from Division One the season before, and a heavy 3–0 defeat in the first match of the season away at Cambridge United, over 20,000 supporters had attended Derby's first home game of the 1980–81 season to see the Rams record a 3–2 win against Chelsea. A penalty by Barry Powell, who went on to play in more exotic locations for Portland Timbers in the USA, Bulova in Hong Kong, and Burnley in Lancashire, opened the scoring. My mate Alan Biley grabbed the second and Martin Chivers put the ball into his own net for Derby's third. As the season wore on though, so did the patience of the fans and by the time Newcastle United arrived at the Baseball Ground on 18 April for the penultimate home game of the season, only 13,846 supporters turned up.

At our first attempt we had failed to get out of the division by just five points, finishing the season in sixth place. This was a long time before the introduction of the Play-offs though and so Derby were never in with a chance of a swift return to the top-flight. While we were disheartened though, heartbreak must have been deeper at Blackburn Rovers who missed out on promotion that season on goal difference alone.

The results didn't seem to matter to me though. Along with those who continued their pilgrimage to the Baseball Ground I was developing my own blind faith, based solely on ifs and maybes. I had led the team out onto the Baseball Ground pitch and in doing so the infamous mud had further cemented the spirit of the club within me and my Dad.

English Second Division 1980–81

Pos		Pl	W	D	L	F	A	GD	Pts
1	West Ham United	42	28	10	4	79	29	50	66
2	Notts County	42	18	17	7	49	38	11	53
3	Swansea City	42	18	14	10	64	44	20	50
4	Blackburn Rovers	42	16	18	8	42	29	13	50
5	Luton Town	42	18	12	12	61	46	15	48
6	**Derby County**	42	15	15	12	57	52	5	45

1981–82

In 1982, to a collective sigh of anticlimax, the nation turned to its television sets to see Henry VIII's rotten and whelk encrusted flagship, the *Mary Rose*, raised from the bottom of the English Channel. Elsewhere Argentina invaded the Falkland Islands, prompting an all-out war with the South Americans although Margaret Thatcher, not known for her pacifism abroad or at home, insisted it was nothing more than a conflict.

1982 was also the year that E.T. smashed box office records and scientists first found that the Earth had a hole in its ozone layer, long before most of us knew what ozone was, what it did and whether a hole was a good thing, like in a polo mint, or a bad thing, like in a sweater.

Despite these events there was only one thing on my seven-year-old mind. By the last game of the 1981–82 season Derby County needed to beat Watford at home to avoid relegation to Division Three. The slide from Division One champions did not look like abating.

Watford were riding high and had already secured promotion to the top-flight by the time they arrived at the Baseball Ground that season. On 6 January we had been thrashed 6–1 at Vicarage Road and so the pressure was firmly on us – it was no longer me and Derby County, I was as much a part of the team as they were a part of me.

We had started the 1981–82 season by selling my favourite player, Alan Biley, to Everton for £350,000. My Dad had understandably kept the news quiet from me, not wishing to break the news that a Derby player who I told Ian continually since the previous February, 'Had actually spoken to me, with his own voice, from his own mouth!' had moved elsewhere.

Dad didn't have to worry too much though as I was never one to pay a great deal of attention to arrivals and departures, being more infatuated with those 11 on the pitch to worry about anyone off it. The same could be said for a pet goldfish that I owned at the time, which I had won at Ilkeston Fair. In the summer of 1981 we had gone on holiday to Lowestoft, the most easterly point of the country, and left the fish with my auntie to look after. Unfortunately it wasn't until one Sunday dinner late in November that I noticed the disappearance when, with a forkful of mashed potato inches from my mouth, I bellowed out of nowhere, 'Hey, where's my goldfish?'

Feelings that I had only witnessed at the Baseball Ground coursed through my hurt body, first the sense of utter loss, and then betrayal, but ultimately I was left embarrassed as Mum explained, 'Craigy, it's been at your auntie's house since July!'

In the season where the number of points awarded for a win had increased from two to three, Derby struggled throughout. By January the manager, Colin Addison, had been replaced by John Newman, who enjoyed his first match in charge, beating Oldham Athletic by a single goal at home but was brought back down to earth by that crunching 6–1 defeat away at Watford. The club then won only four more matches before the last match of that torrid season.

Derby County 3 Watford 2

Saturday 15 May 1982

Instead of taking the train to the Watford match, me and my Dad got a lift with a friend of his called Ron. Sharing the journey were Ron's wife and their son, Gary, who was a little older than me and probably Ian's age. I barely spoke for the entirety of the trip, which Dad mistook as my concern over the match, whereas in fact I was more worried about looking like a prat in front of Gary. He'd already sung all the words perfectly to The Jam's, *A Town Called Malice* when it had been played on the radio, which made me glad I had kept my mouth shut as I'd thought the lyrics were, 'a 10 foot mallet'.

Peer pressure was moulding me even then. I was already in trouble at my Infant school with a lad called Mark Archer who, together with Frankie Middleton and I had formed the core of a Derby County supporters' club. Mark was cool because his Dad was a fireman, while I liked Frankie because he was friendly and would always be the first to greet me at the start of the day with a smile and an unfeasibly fluorescent bogey wedged in his left nostril.

Mark had found out that I had gone to see a Forest match with Ian and my Dad and he was not happy.

Dad had got tickets for the executive boxes at the City Ground for a night match against Ipswich Town. I should have taken the hint and gone home when the train overshot the platform at Long Eaton station by 200 metres, only to reverse back down the line for us to get on, but the three of us boarded and went anyway.

Despite being in a house with two Derby fans and his experience in 1979, my older brother was admirably sticking to his team, and even with Dad's own allegiance to Derby he occasionally took Ian to see Forest. There was never any danger of me thinking that Dad had turned though as even away from matchdays he was Derby through and through.

As well as watching the games me and my Dad were part of the South East Derbyshire branch of the team's supporters' club, which had a slightly larger membership than what we had going on at Infant school. We used to hold what I called 'dos' in the function room upstairs at the White Lion on Tamworth Road in Old Sawley, just across the road from the church, where we drank flat coke, ate salty crisps and played table skittles. One time a guest appearance by Steve Powell, who played in both of Derby's Championship winning sides was cut short when I swung the ball round too hard and hit him directly on the head.

Larger events were held every year at the Assembly Rooms in Derby for all branches of the supporters' club. At one of these I was given a commemorative piece of soil from the Baseball Ground, apparently dug from beneath the centre circle, which was a cake of mud encased in plastic, attached to a piece of card explaining the historical significance of the relic. That was until Ian and I were playing in one of the sheds in our back garden and he ripped it open and spilt the contents onto the floor.

Our various journeys ignited memories such as this, and the trip to the see us play out our fate against Watford was no different.

With the five of us wedged into Ron's car we headed into the city along the A6 from Shardlow and found ourselves behind a yellow Datsun, but being 1982 it was far too early to be Scott Robinson's from *Neighbours*. Hands were out of the windows on either side of the vehicle and banging on the roof.

'Watford singing along…' came the chant from within.

Ron's wife bellowed out, 'We'll thrash you Watford!' which I thought seemed quite bold, partly because of the 6–1 reverse earlier in the season and partly because she was a lady.

Ron parked on the other side of the ground to that which me and my Dad approached from the train station, which made it feel like we were visiting another stadium. Not knowing quite where we were I was reticent to leave the front seat of the car, which was where I usually sat because I was always travel-sick. Dad didn't seem too eager either and instead of getting out he handed me a brown paper bag to open, similar to the one that the shop assistant in the Co-op had packed my mascot's kit in the season before.

Inside the bag was a blue and white scarf with our team's name emblazoned across it, with, 'Come On You Ram's' printed grammatically incorrect along the top. It would be a few years before I heard on the BBC School's *Words and Pictures* though that, 'I am apostrophe, to shorten what you say to me, I'm not a comma, I'm not a full stop, don't put me at the end…I go at the top!'

To me it seemed to be the most amazing piece of material I had ever seen, at least since I walked along the shelf of Derby strips lined up in Co-op, and a wave of excitement burst through me as it was placed round my neck.

Me and my Dad got out of the car and joined the others as they walked along Elton Road, past the Rolls-Royce buildings that have since been demolished and merged into the steady flow of supporters. I was desperate not to lose those in front, but almost did when they took a sharp turn left off the pavement and into an alleyway by the side of a row of shops. Along the wall was a huge mural painted on the stark brickwork of the newsagent depicting a Derby goal and I knew it was a good omen.

The click of the turnstiles welcomed me into the ground once more and I clung onto the scarf that Dad had draped around my neck like an Olympian's medal. Even at that tender age I sensed how important the fixture was, with a win as vital to me as the rest of the 14,945 supporters there that afternoon who, by the end of the match had even spilled out onto the thin edge of grass between the hoardings and the flank. Nerves were overflowing and literally spilled out onto the turf.

The tension on the terraces and in the ground was incredible, especially when the Rams went behind and it looked like our worst fears were about to be realised. But just like in the mural Derby equalised and a massive, massive roar erupted in the stands. Even though I could barely see above the adult heads around me, I knew exactly what it meant and when an even greater sound followed, the crowd turned into a wave of moving bodies and arms that threw me against my Dad who was squeezing me breathless. I was ecstatic, he was euphoric and Ron's wife was bellowing again, 'I told you we'd thrash you, Watford!'

There was still time for more drama though, as with five minutes remaining the linesman to our left signalled an off-side. When the referee blew his whistle the supporters thought it was the end of the match and ran out onto the pitch creating bedlam, with police and the public address pleading for the fans to return to the terraces, which in the end they did.

Kevin Hector's last goal for the club had won the game, and at the time appeared to have saved us from a relegation that would have financially crippled the club.

Hector made more appearances than anybody else in a Derby shirt, scoring 201 goals in 581 games, playing for the club at the highest level and then returning to help us out in later years. He was the sort of player you name your pets after, which Uncle Paul, my Dad's brother, did. Unlike Hector the player though, Hector the cat was a vicious black thing that used to bite and scratch everyone when my Grandma wasn't looking.

Dad had taken his brother to his first match in 1965, which was a home game against Newcastle United. Instead of travelling by train though they had caught the bus from the stop at the top of Hills Road in Breaston, by the factory that makes fairground parts. Fourteen years before me and my Dad had done they set off on their own adventure, travelling past Draycott Village Green, over the railway line that used to carry the train to Derby and out into the swathes of open farmland.

These were the fields where my Dad grew up, spending hours in the open air and making up games with whatever came to hand. Once he told me that while one of his mates had climbed a tree, another had stolen the lad's shoe and sailed it out across a large puddle. I could never decide whether, in fact, Dad was the lad who had climbed the tree or indeed if he had been the sailor.

After the farms the bus route takes a sharp right-hand bend just before Borrowash. It was on this corner that my Dad and Mum both fell from his moped just months after they had got married, forcing them to spend their first Christmas as a married couple apart. Dad was holed up in the grim surroundings of hospital when they should have been celebrating together in their first home.

Once into Borrowash the route passes the turning down to Elvaston Castle, where as a family we spent many afternoons looking for squirrels, eating picnics and playing hide-and-seek among the shrubs and trees. Further on and into Spondon, the Courtaulds factory stands as a testament to why our family were in Derby at all.

My Grandma was born in Newcastle-upon-Tyne, an area hit hardest by the economic crisis between World War One and Two. Her Dad was out of work and so headed to London to find a job but got as far as Derby before finding a motorist who had broken down by the side of the road. After fixing the stranger's car the driver remarked on my Great-Grandad's accent and asked him why he was so far south. He told the motorist he was heading to London to look for work but the driver told him that he didn't need to bother. Being one of the Directors at Courtaulds he would make sure that if my Great-Grandad went there the following Monday there would be a job waiting for him.

During World War Two Grandma, then Edna Beadling, had been stationed in London to work on the huge spotlights that illuminated enemy aircraft during the Blitz. On her very first attempt controlling the lights she was overjoyed to find an aircraft in her line of sight, but her euphoria soon diminished when she heard her commanding officer shout, 'For Christ's sake Beadling, that's one of ours!'

It was there that she met my Granddad and was immediately attracted to his unfamiliar accent.

'It's French Canadian.' Granddad had told her, when in effect he came from Devon. Always one to bend the truth, he also used to tell us that he'd driven through the centre of Berlin in a Chieftan Tank.

After the war the couple moved back to Breaston as my Granddad, a bricklayer by trade, reasoned that there were no walls needed to be built in Devon. My Grandma later reasoned that maybe he should have stayed in Berlin.

Just as he had handed me that scarf on Saturday 15 May in 1982, Dad had bought my Uncle Paul a rosette on Saturday 3 April 1965, for 2s 6d. Dad had introduced Derby County to his brother and they had gone on to witness the promotion in 1969, the Championships of 1972 and 1975, and the incredible nights of European football at the Baseball Ground. All I had so far were relegation and another fight too close to mention, but strangely this didn't bother me. I was starting to discover that it wasn't success and trophies that caught the imagination and hooked you into supporting a football team, it was something to do with standing up and being counted and a sense of taking your place in history. It was pushing your way in against the cold heavy metal of the turnstile and feel it pull you in towards something special, and whether you were in the stands or on the school playground, as long as you were with people who felt the same as you did, with your team's name written boldly on the scarf around your neck, the score didn't matter.

*****

Records show that Derby finished the season four points clear of the relegation zone, three places above the relegated teams of Cardiff City and Wrexham from Wales, and Orient who most people still thought came from China. Only those who were there can attest to the drama and anxiety that accompanied that final match, and appreciate the buzz it created that kept me and my Dad eagerly awaiting the next season.

English Second Division 1981–82

Pos		Pl	W	D	L	F	A	GD	Pts
1	Luton Town	42	25	13	4	86	46	40	88
2	Watford	42	23	11	8	76	42	34	80
3	Norwich City	42	22	5	15	64	50	14	71
14	Cambridge United	42	13	9	20	48	53	-5	48
15	Crystal Palace	42	13	9	20	34	45	-11	48
16	**Derby County**	**42**	**12**	**12**	**18**	**53**	**68**	**-15**	**48**
17	Grimsby Town	42	11	13	18	53	65	-12	46
18	Shrewsbury Town	42	11	13	18	37	57	-20	46
20	Cardiff City	42	12	8	22	45	61	-16	44
21	Wrexham	42	11	11	20	46	56	-16	44
22	Orient	42	10	9	23	36	61	-25	39

1982–83

As the 1982–83 season dawned I moved up from Infant school to the Juniors. In the second week my first year teacher, Ms Jones, asked me if I was a Derby fan, whether my Dad bought the green Saturday evening edition of the *Derby Evening Telegraph* and, if so, could I bring the copies to her on a Monday morning and so I thought that Mark Archer, Frankie Middleton and I could expand our Derby County Supporters Club to four.

Having a teacher that supported Derby left me feeling uneasy. Back then I didn't see school staff as normal people and it was bad enough when Mrs Allen, my first year teacher in Infant school who lived around the corner from us, walked past our house. I believed that when home-time came at quarter to four the teachers went into a period of suspended animation for the night. How they could then support a football team was a mystery to me. Football was about jumping around and cheering, singing chants and clapping and this did not seem possible for someone who spent most of the time catatonic at the back of some dusty school classroom like a laboratory skeleton.

All was revealed during the last week of our final term, however, when we were told that we would be making Paper Mache masks. Each pupil was given a balloon, which we were told to inflate and start covering in newspaper dipped in paste. Then, with great theatrical pomp, Ms Jones walked out of the storeroom saddled with nine month's worth of the green papers and announced to the class that we would be able to see the preceding layer if we alternated them with torn pieces of Craig's Dad's newspapers.

Most of my classmates had never heard of green newspaper and it was as exotic as post-war bananas to the evacuees. Suddenly I became something of a wonder in the eyes of my peers, while Ms Jones went back to being like the rest of the teachers who returned to standby at the end of each day. My new status in class was also soon reverted back to normality though when I was told off, or as we said back then, 'got done', for cutting round the players and sticking them to my balloon like it was a scrapbook rather than just ripping the green paper into squares.

At this time my Dad was Treasurer of the Long Eaton Sunday League which, as the name suggests, is a football league in Long Eaton for teams who play on a Sunday morning. By non-League standards it is a very well run organisation, typified by the time when the League were requested to provide all receipts and records of financial affairs dating back five years in order to disprove financial irregularities. The gentleman making the request knew that it was a foregone conclusion and that nobody would keep such records for a Sunday League, but as the Treasurer Dad knew different. He went up to our loft, and from among the few suitcases, Christmas decorations and a Big Trak, he brought down the financial records dating back to 1975.

One of my Dad's roles as Treasurer was to collate the results from Sunday's matches and so Ian and I used to take it in turns answering the phone, acting like Dad's personal assistants to the people reporting their scores.

Dad also refereed matches in that League and had a reputation as a fair man, and in that respect he was offered slightly more leeway by players than most officials when it came to making errors. He was known as a genuine and honest guy with great integrity and if he ever made a mistake it was simply that, with no dishonest intention.

One Sunday evening it was my turn to answer the phone for Dad and after handing him the receiver I waited patiently for him to finish so I could ask the score of the game being reported. The call lasted longer than usual though and soon, even though I could only hear one side to the conversation, and certainly not the majority of it, it was clear that there was some sort of dispute. After a time Dad lost patience.

'If you speak to me with those words again, I will put the phone down.' he said.

There was silence, after which Dad said, 'Now, tell me what's wrong.'

The tone changed, Dad listened without trying to interject and eventually he could explain that the whole matter had been a misunderstanding.

Kids on Sunday mornings in 1983 were usually playing with Cabbage Patch Kids and Care Bears, or in their back gardens pretending to be the A-Team, whereas Ian and I were often at a park in the area playing on swings and slides while Dad was refereeing. In winter months, when the early morning mist saw grown men reluctant to leave the dressing rooms that stank heavily of last night's ale and Deep Heat, we would eagerly run out and have the playgrounds to ourselves.

One particular Sunday Dad was allocated a match in Duffield, which lies about five miles the other side of Derby, and we had to catch a train there which added further excitement and mystique to the trip. The track leading out of Derby was being used to test the new Inter City trains and as both Ian and I liked trains a lot we spent the morning standing on the small footbridge that spanned the railway, daring each other to stay on the bridge while the high-speed trains went underneath.

We followed Dad all over to watch the games he refereed, from across Derbyshire and into Nottingham and as he had still not learnt to drive the journeys often required us to travel by public transport. One evening on board an old Barton bus to Nottingham, Dad, Ian and I were chatting as the early evening sky burned red as it welcomed the night.

'Red sky at night, shepherd's warning.' Dad told us, knowing that we'd fall for the bait.

'No, Dad, it's red sky at night, shepherd's delight.' both Ian and I responded.

'No boys,' Dad continued, with mock authority, 'Red sky at night, shepherd's warning.'

'It's red sky at night, shepherd's delight!' we continued, starting to giggle in our exasperation.

This went on for much of the journey, and as we came to our stop we rose from our seats, only for some chap behind us to pull Dad to one side and say, 'Actually mate, it is shepherd's delight.'

That evening the match was being played at a ground that Ian and I had never been to before, and when we arrived we were naturally delighted to see a huge grass bank to one side of the pitch. Our excitement was soon cut short though when Dad warned us that, as it had been a damp evening, we weren't allowed to roll down the bank as we'd get wet and be too cold to run and catch the bus after the game.

Ian and I managed the entirety of the first half before thinking that the grass would be dry, but it was not. As Dad had predicted we got wet and too cold to run and catch the bus after the game.

I thought Dad would go crazy but instead he took us to a newsagent and bought us Nestle Crunch chocolate bars instead. These were more expensive than other sweets and so were usually off-limits, but on this occasion we were treated.

After the Sunday matches we'd arrive home to the familiar smell of a roast dinner that Mum had prepared, and then watch Nelson Piquet and Keke Rosberg in the Grand Prix while potatoes and vegetables boiled on the hob. After dinner we'd often walk to my Grandma and Granddad's house three miles away in Breaston, taking it in turns to push Daniel in his pushchair, who by this time was 18 months old.

At that time, like most families, we certainly did not enjoy the levels of disposable income that we see today but we were never poor. We always had food to eat, we went on holiday every year, Ian had piano lessons, I was supporting Derby and Mum still took me and Ian to the cinema, especially when *Return of the Jedi* was released in the summer of 1983. Dad would also be looking to give us that extra special surprise, and so when he managed to persuade someone who he knew through the Sunday League that I should be mascot again for an away fixture, he jumped at the opportunity to make his son smile.

Oldham Athletic 2 Derby County 2
Saturday 1 January 1983

Oldham Athletic started life as Pine Villa in 1895 but changed their name from sounding like a kitchen cleaner after taking residence at the town's athletics stadium in 1899.

The club originally took to the field in red and white hooped shirts and blue shorts, which possibly resembled the uniform I would later wear at a food outlet at the American Adventure Theme Park near Ilkeston. A period of relative fashion sense involving blue and white hoops, and then white shirts with a blue stripe down the middle then followed before being changed to tangerine shirts and blue shorts. It wasn't until the mid 1970s that Oldham started wearing the present day all-blue, presumably when supporters started considering buying replica shirts and complained that they didn't want to look like the lad who had been told to take whatever was in the school laundry basket after forgetting his PE kit.

Me, my Dad and Uncle Paul embarked on the epic journey from Derby early on that New Year's Day, which at one stage involved us driving through clouds over the Peak District to get to our final destination. Ian had come along for the ride but was far from impressed as he spent a large portion of the journey, like me, with his head out of the window being travel-sick.

I had never heard of Oldham and didn't know how far it was, or indeed how to get there. Neither did Uncle Paul, but he drove his red Ford Cortina doggedly and got as far as the outskirts of the town before the Oldham manager, Joe Royle, pointed us in the right direction after seeing us drive around the same roundabout four times.

One of the conditions for allowing me to be mascot again was that I had to have my own kit and so there would be no pre-match visits to the Co-op this time.

Despite getting lost we pulled up with plenty of time for me to get changed into Derby's away strip of orange shirt and blue shorts, which must have had some home supporters fearing they were having a relapse to the pre-70s.

Just as I had done against Orient I pulled on the Ram's shirt proudly, and with television restrictions on sponsorship now lifted I could run out with the club's sponsor, Patrick, without fear of offending any camera crew. Unfortunately this game did not reach the echelons of *Match of the Day* and I doubt it even made it to the pages of the *Oldham Chronicle*.

Whereas at the Baseball Ground I had my own room to relax in, here I spent much of the pre-match outside in the bitter cold of Boundary Park. An open terrace behind the goal to my right, which I now knew was my right, exposed a handful of Derby supporters who had made the same journey from the East Midlands, whereas elsewhere a spattering of Oldham fans occupied the rest of the New Year's Day attendance of 7,085, mostly in the imposing Broadway Stand opposite. Biding time, I was asked if I wanted to run around the pitch before the game, which I did, much to the joy of those travelling supporters at the Derby end.

When I ran past they surged down the terrace, all 12 of them, thrusting their arms out through the perimeter fence to shake my hand. I felt like Archie Gemmill, but after that I couldn't continue around the pitch for fear of abuse if I wandered in front of the home supporters and so instead I headed back to the dugout.

My Dad had given me a football to run out with and insisted that I get it signed before the match, so I walked into the away team's changing room only to be confronted by a stark-naked Archie Gemmill. Traumatised, I managed to compose myself enough to pass the ball around as a memento that stayed in my bedroom for years.

Elsewhere in the changing room the Derby manager, Peter Taylor, stood, fully clothed. He had been one half of the dynamic pairing, alongside Brian Clough, in making Derby one of the greatest teams of the 1970s. Both him and Clough had left Derby in 1973 and managed Brighton & Hove Albion, although Clough left the south coast in 1974 for an inglorious 44 day spell at Leeds United. It was only after Taylor was reunited with Clough at Nottingham Forest in 1976 that the pair went on to achieve the pinnacle of their success. Peter Taylor retired from football and Nottingham Forest in May 1982 but had since returned to manage Derby in November the same year.

As a pairing, Peter Taylor and Brian Clough achieved great things with unfashionable clubs but alone they were less successful. Taylor could not revive Derby's fortunes and although Forest were a good first division side well into the late 90s, with several appearances at Wembley, they were never close to reaching the heights of European dominance that they had done when both Clough and Taylor were at the helm.

Leading the team out at Boundary Park was more difficult for me than running out at the Baseball Ground had been. Shallow concrete steps led down from inside the stand and by this time, rather than trainers, I had proper football boots with studs. Trying to get a grip on the hard surface proved difficult but by the time my feet hit the turf I was fine, looking back first to make sure our captain, Archie Gemmill, had made it safe and had put his shorts on, and then sprinting out towards those fans who had given me such a great welcome earlier.

I spent the warm-up taking shots at goalkeeper Steve Cherry, much to the delight of all but one of the dozen Derby fans who applauded enthusiastically behind the goal. The other stood with her hands clasped firmly around a cup of Bovril, which steamed into the Lancashire afternoon like it belonged on a Lowry painting, probably wishing she had pulled someone else at the previous night's New Year's Eve party.

Me, my Dad, Uncle Paul and Ian all had tickets for the seats in the Main Stand and so after being introduced to the referee and the opposing club captain I left the pitch, met Dad and got changed before going up to sit with the others. Ian was moaning about the cold, much as he had been moaning about the clouds and the long journey since we had left Long Eaton, but I was left feeling warm by the experience of leading my team out again.

By half-time the cold Oldham air was winning the battle against my fond memory and so Dad introduced Ian and I to our first football meat pies. For some reason I had expected Dad to return with it on a plate with potatoes and peas, but all I got was an individual pie in its foil case. Being too hot to eat straightaway I placed it on my lap and held my hands over it to warm them like a little furnace. The bitter weather was not abating though and by the end of the game I was watching the match through a tiny slit between my parker hood and scarf, which Dad had wrapped around my head several times.

The game resulted in a two-all draw, with goals from Dave Swindlehurst and Gemmill, with the few Derby fans celebrating each goal with a conga across their open terrace. It was reminiscent of our party the night before, but despite an urge to join in we had to keep quiet in among the Oldham fans around us.

After the game we drove back across the Peak District, which by then was in darkness and incredibly eerie. Our faces reflected off the windows and I could see the others in the car all in their own quiet reflection while the headlights picked out faint hills and mountains in the distance.

*****

A week after the trip to Oldham, fate placed Derby County against Nottingham Forest in the third round of the FA Cup. As well as pitching the two local teams against each other it was the first time that Peter Taylor had had to contest a game against his old partner, Brian Clough.

Clough and Taylor were no longer on speaking terms, as Clough felt betrayed that after announcing his retirement when leaving the City Ground, Taylor had gone back to Derby. The feud continued until Taylor's death in 1990, and although he had enjoyed the last word when Derby ran out winners in this, their last encounter, neither men had had the last laugh.

Derby's reward for knocking their neighbours out of the trophy was a fourth round tie at home to Chelsea. Again the Rams were victorious and then went on to win every League match in February. Unfortunately there were only two, sitting either side of a fifth round Cup tie against Manchester United, attended by over 33,000 fans at the Baseball Ground.

A single goal was enough to give Manchester United victory and gloomy times descended upon the Baseball Ground and our home once again. There is a mentality to supporting a football club though which makes you believe that better times are just around the corner.

Even when clubs are relegated supporters continue to attend, like people standing in a park on 6 November waiting for fireworks. Me and my Dad were among those who stayed firm and carried on attending matches, and I have many fond memories of running through the Normanton streets on cold afternoons trying to avoid the puddles. That April, with the season petering out to a damp and disappointing end, the arrival of a football legend at the Baseball Ground provided a glimmer of consolation for us both.

Derby County 2 Newcastle United 1

Monday 4 April 1983

I could never sleep the night before a match and would often lie in bed thinking about what the result would be and how the goals would come. Would we have to come from behind like we did against Watford, or would we emerge as easy winners, scoring four, five or even six goals like they did in Roy of the Rovers? Someday I dreamed we might even score seven and the BBC would have to spell it out as if nobody would believe the number alone; Nottingham Forest 0 Derby County 7 (SEVEN).

Insomnia was bearable if Dad was decorating, papering the walls at night while listening to the soundtrack of Duran Duran, Haircut 100 and Bonnie Tyler on the radio. When he wasn't though the silence enveloped the upstairs of our home like the American Soccer Allstars quilt that covered my bed. More often than not I'd lie there trying to keep my brother awake and occasionally be told sharply by either Mum or Dad that it was time to get to sleep.

The night of Sunday 3 April was no different, as the following day Dad was taking me to see Kevin Keegan play at the Baseball Ground.

Keegan had helped Liverpool win three Division One titles, two UEFA Cups, one FA Cup and the European Cup and had played for England 63 times, scoring 21 goals in the process. He had then moved to the German side, Hamburg, and received the European Footballer of the Year in both 1978 and 1979.

Despite these honours I had a nagging doubt that Kevin Keegan wasn't that special. After all, it was his side that were beaten in the European Cup Final by Forest in 1979, and Dad always used to say that, 'Only idiots and dustbins lose to Forest!'

Since playing in Germany, Keegan had moved to second division Newcastle United, via Southampton, and was now coming to play at Derby. When Dad told me we were going to Derby to see Kevin Keegan I assumed that he had signed for the Rams, and despite me thinking he was either an idiot or a dustbin I was ecstatic. I was still smarting over losing Alan Biley to Everton, the sale of which I had eventually come to realise in much the same way as when my goldfish found its new home. One afternoon, long after his departure, I looked quizzically at the pitch as Dave Swindlehurst ran towards us in the Normanton End, before turning to my Dad and asking quizzically, 'That's not Alan Biley!'

Keegan ran out in the black and white of Newcastle though, and while I was disappointed, Dad's enthusiasm was always contagious. Whenever he was excited about something it was impossible for me not to feel the same way.

The match attracted 19,779, a crowd more than 2,000 higher than Derby's biggest League attendance so far that season. The club were ill-prepared though and me and my Dad had to join the back of a huge queue waiting for seat tickets at the office on Shaftsbury Crescent. There were several booths open, each 20 deep with men trying to buy tickets and as usual the excitement was building within me. My small hands, wrapped in my Dad's, soon became clammy.

There were still seven or eight people between us and the office when a sudden and almighty roar erupted like that which greeted a goal. The mass of people started legging it down the road towards the Normanton End of the ground, engulfing those who had just bought their tickets like a tidal wave consuming a beach. Dad grabbed my hand and we started running with them, but I was slowing him down and we were being passed by what must have been hundreds of men, none of whom were afflicted by their children.

Without explanation Dad kept dragging me along with the rest of the crowd, some of whom were shouting while others were laughing, each one eager to get as far from where they had been and get ahead of the next man. When we eventually stopped running I was out of breath and my tiny lungs gasped desperately for air as I looked up, scared to see my Dad in fear or anguish, but instead I was met by his familiar grin. By now we were in another queue, with the same people between us and the ground, and I looked at him bewildered.

'They sold out of seat tickets Craigy, I think we're gonna have to stand. But don't worry, I can see if we can get some seats at half-time', he finally explained.

Once through the turnstiles I didn't care about seat tickets. I was just pleased to be in the ground and glad that I hadn't stopped my Dad from being able to watch the match. These games seemed to be as important to him as they were to me and when we scored we would cheer as loud as each other.

On Saturday evenings, if we hadn't been to the match, Dad would be in the kitchen listening to the local radio station as he made the tea. The score would be read out and if it was a loss then he would momentarily stop chopping and sigh, prompting me to return to the living room and give the grave news. If we had won though, then we would dance around the kitchen, remembering to put the knife down first, and sing as if we were on the terraces.

The emotions of supporting Derby County didn't stop at me and my Dad but permeated the rest of the house. On our arrival home after defeat Mum would know just by looking at us how the result had gone and reciprocate our despondency. She would join in with the silence, sympathetic of our mood that would infiltrate the early evening.

With the higher attendance and Kevin Keegan in the opposition line-up, that particular afternoon seemed to take on an extra element of occasion and along with the rest of the crowd I was shouting my own encouragement, copying phrases like, 'Good ball!' and 'Come on Derby!', off my Dad and the rest of the supporters around us. The game progressed and we were holding our own.

Half-time arrived and Dad headed towards the back of the terrace where he motioned for me to follow. I assumed we were going to the toilet, but we didn't join the rest of the supporters heading beneath the stand and instead went down a few concrete steps to a quieter area where a couple of boys about twice my age were hanging around. On the other side of a fence I could see some of the people who had been well ahead of us in the queue for the seat tickets and realised that this was the area where those in the seats got their half-time teas and pies.

'Do you want to get in the seats?' Dad asked the boys, to which they eagerly agreed. I then watched in total disbelief as he helped them all over the fence that separated those who had seats from those of us who were standing.

I was stunned. My Mum and Dad had always instilled in me the importance of being well-behaved and this was not the sort of behaviour they had come to expect from me and certainly not what I would have expected from either of them.

After he had helped the other lads over the fence, Dad turned to me.

'Right, I'll lift you onto the top of the fence, then jump over myself, and then I'll grab you from the bottom.'

I had no choice but to follow his instructions, and as I climbed the fence a knot of anxiety crept into my stomach. Once at the top I hung on gingerly as he athletically scaled the fence and landed on the other side, but when he looked up at me and motioned for me to let go, I just looked at him.

'No Dad...it's wrong.' I said.

My Dad's face was a mixture of concern, pride and hilarity as he pleaded with me to jump down.

'Just let go and grab on to me.' he begged, but still I wasn't moving.

'No Dad...it's wrong.' I continued.

This went on for a few minutes, with Dad becoming increasingly frustrated that he had instilled such good behaviour in his child, but after eventually convincing me that he knew that it was wrong, that we would never do anything like this again and that he wouldn't tell Mum, I jumped down from the fence and we headed into the seating area of the stand.

After drying my tears we sat down to occupy two seats, which Dad convinced me were used by season ticket holders who could not get to the game that day.

Despite having to face the legendary Kevin Keegan Derby won the game 2–1, with goals from Paul Hooks and Kevin Wilson. The next five matches saw us unbeaten, but two losses away at Blackburn Rovers and Crystal Palace tainted the season's finale.

On the last day of the season Fulham came to the Baseball Ground needing a win to achieve promotion. In front of a crowd of 21,124, Bobby Davison opened the scoring but the match had to be abandoned before full-time due to rioting Derby fans. Despite later protests from the London club the Football Association deemed that the result should remain, which allowed one of Derby County's other local rivals, Leicester City, to secure the final promotion place instead.

A final League position of 13th for us was no great achievement but it was better than the 16th we had achieved the previous season. It was a glimmer of hope for me and my Dad, which in the history of watching Derby County, forever seemed to be burning brightest right before being extinguished.

English Second Division 1982–83

Pos		Pl	W	D	L	F	A	GD	Pts
1	Queens Park Rangers	42	26	7	9	77	36	41	85
2	Wolverhampton W	42	20	15	7	68	44	24	75
3	Leicester City	42	20	10	12	72	44	28	70
11	Blackburn Rovers	42	15	12	15	58	58	0	57
12	Cambridge United	42	13	12	17	42	60	-18	51
13	**Derby County**	**42**	**10**	**19**	**13**	**49**	**58**	**-9**	**49**
14	Carlisle United	42	12	12	18	68	70	-2	48
15	Crystal Palace	42	12	12	18	43	52	-9	48
20	Rotherham United	42	10	15	17	45	68	-23	45
21	Burnley	42	12	8	22	56	66	-10	44
22	Bolton Wanderers	42	11	11	20	42	81	-19	44

1983–84

For Mark Archer, Frankie Middleton and I, the Derby crest had become a badge of honour among the other kids in the playground, with the three of us continuing our loyal supporters' group up to the Junior school. Now other kids were getting into football but they seemed to be attracted to the big clubs like Manchester United, Liverpool or even Forest, who would finish the 1983–84 season in third place in Division One.

Those who followed clubs from cities 90 and 70 miles from Derby, and even the kids who revelled in the glory of supporting Nottingham Forest, could never call themselves real fans though. Only those who travelled to Oldham, through the clouds of the Peak District, listening to their brother being sick in the seat beside them while being so blindly guided by faith that Joe bloody Royle of all people had to show them the way, could say 'I truly support my club!' At least that's what we said to ourselves on a Monday morning after another weekend defeat to either Carlisle, Huddersfield or Grimsby.

By February, Derby had only won twice in the first 12 matches, against Swansea who would be relegated at the end of the season, and at Crystal Palace who would finish in a lowly 18th in the final table. It was not just on the pitch that the team had problems either. After years of financial mismanagement chasing the successes of the 1970s, Derby faced winding-up orders from both the Inland Revenue and Customs and Excise, the latter of which I misheard as 'costumes and exercise' and thought it related to our kit and the training methods. When we were drawn at home against non-League Telford United in the FA Cup, the club couldn't even afford to pay the visitors their share of the gate receipts.

Derby County 3 Telford United 2
Wednesday 1 February 1984

As fourth round draws in the FA Cup go it could not have been any kinder. Dad and I had a quick tea at home before heading out to the game, which Dad still took me to even though it was a night match. We finished off the snack with a United chocolate bar, which I was not going to eat as it had our opponent's name on it.

'Don't you think it will be like us crushing them to bits?' asked Dad. And I guess it did, as I soon rammed it whole into my mouth and almost choked on the biscuit.

Until 1969 Telford had been known as Wellington Town, but changed their name with the inauguration of the new town, which was built from among the conurbations of Wellington, Oakengates, Madeley and Dawley. The planners decided against naming the new settlement WOMaD and instead recognised the contribution of civil engineer, Thomas Telford, which was lucky for the organisers of the World of Music, Arts and Dance Festival.

At only nine years old I already had my own identity, wearing the orange shirt I had adorned at Oldham for every match, and the scarf that my Dad had given me before the Watford game.

I'd walk to the ground with great purpose, banging on the boarded up windows of the houses on Douglas Street and Dairy House Road, surrounded by the safety of the crowd and my Dad to look out for me, meanwhile my ears would strain to pick up the first rumblings of any chant, eager to join in but being careful first to make sure it wasn't one that contained foul language before I started to sing.

I enjoyed the night matches the most, when the floodlights of the Baseball Ground, usually hidden among the tight streets, illuminated the ground and you could see the glow for miles. Supporters would stream towards it like moths while the headlights of the surrounding cars and buses swarmed in the air like fireflies.

Although me and my Dad had already had tea we stopped off at Satty's Baseball Fish Bar on the corner of Cambridge Street and Reeves Road for chips. Pies were piled high in the warming cabinets while pickled gherkins and eggs sat in huge jars of brine like freak-show exhibits on the shelves beneath the menu. I could barely see over the counter and so Dad put the salt and vinegar on my chips before passing them gently down to me. Such was my impatience that I burnt my fingers raising the chips to my mouth and then burnt my tongue eating them.

I was so eager to get to the ground that Dad had to shout me back as I exited the chip shop, walking on autopilot to get to our place inside the stadium. I knew the way instinctively and while Dad was collecting his change my feet were already in the grooves of the gutter and heading to the Normanton End. I sped ahead like the Scalextric cars that Mum and Dad had given Ian and I that Christmas, but his shout stopped my feet in their tracks, waiting for him to catch up as a chip hung midway between the white polystyrene tray and my mouth.

I was stationary until his presence beside me ignited me once more, walking together along Shaftsbury Crescent with the glow of the floodlights high above spilling out of the stadium and onto the fans outside. Our shadows were cast long onto the wet tarmac while the steam from our supper illuminated ahead of us as if we were guided by ghosts. Finally, as I reached to push the turnstiles, the grease and vinegar glistened on my fingers as I seemed to leave the outside world behind.

Supporting Derby was becoming a habit to me. I knew the rituals on the way to the ground and I knew the complex mechanisms of the gates. Our place on the terraces was secure and I no longer had to ask Dad who the players were or what the fans were chanting.

The result of the match was closer than it should have been and Derby emerged victorious, courtesy of a hat-trick by Bobby Davison. One of Peter Taylor's strengths was his ability to spot a good player, and Davison, his first signing for Derby, went on to be the club's top scorer for five consecutive seasons. In response though, Telford scored twice themselves to offer a nervy end for the 21,488 inside the ground that night.

Our reward was a fifth round tie against Division One side Norwich City, again at home. 25,793 supporters came to watch when only 13,020 fans had attended the previous League match to see us draw against Blackburn Rovers. Again the Rams were victorious and progressed to the quarter-finals where we drew third division Plymouth Argyle out of the Football Association's velvet bag. Dad and I were already cheering our foregone place in the semi-final.

Derby County 0 Plymouth Argyle 1
Wednesday 14 March 1984

Plymouth Argyle became a professional club in 1903 but in their 81 year history had never played in the top-flight. Formed in the Borough Arms Coffee Tavern, which is probably now a Starbucks, the club's founders, F. Howard Grose and W. Pethybridge, wanted a name to reflect the style of the Argyll and Sutherland Highlanders army regiment based in the city, and so chose the unique moniker.

A staggering 34,365 fans turned up to watch the first game at Home Park, Plymouth, with the resulting 0–0 draw meaning a replay at Derby the following Wednesday. As far as we were concerned the tie was over, as everybody knows in football the underdogs don't get two opportunities to win an FA Cup tie. Derby were by no means setting the second division alight but Plymouth were struggling too and would end their season in 19th position in Division Three, avoiding relegation to the basement League by just five points.

Another night match meant more chips on the way to the ground, which didn't impress Mum, but as I was well behaved and good at schoolwork Dad convinced her that this was a one-off.

'Just like the Telford match?' she asked good-naturedly, to which Dad shot her a winning smile, which I tried to mimic.

'Don't you flipping-well start!' she said to me, and suitably chastised I ran after my Dad who was already at the top of the driveway where Uncle Paul was waiting for us in his car.

Victory that night would see us play in the semi-finals, which meant a trip to a neutral ground where the stadium would be split between both sets of supporters. It sounded enchanting and Dad was already looking at the possible venues.

'If we get Everton we'll probably play at Hillsborough, but if we get Watford then it'll be Villa Park.'

Mum made sure I was wrapped in layers of jumpers and my scarf, sealing me in with the huge zip on my parker that buzzed as she drew it up towards my chin.

The evening was still light when we left home but all too soon it was invaded by the night as we parked up in one of the Normanton side streets and made our way expectantly to the stadium. Supporters trickled towards the ground from the train station, bus stops and car parks, gathering pace as they merged with one another like streams towards a lake. By the time we were at the ground we were positively running and once inside me, my Dad and Uncle Paul took our place on the Pop-Side terrace.

I waited patiently on the cold concrete, which I could still feel permeating into my feet despite the three pairs of socks that Dad insisted I wear.

'Once you've got cold feet, Craigy,' he used to say, 'you've had it'. Rather like some British General addressing troops on the Somme.

The darkness was no match for the candid glare of the floodlights and in front of the eyes of almost 27,000 others I looked up at my Dad.

That December at our New Year's Eve party I'd overheard him talking with one of my aunties.

'I don't really have the passion anymore,' he said about our club, 'Craigy loves it but I've lost interest to be honest.'

Hearing him say those words was like feeling him, a man who had never once laid a finger on any of his boys in anger, punch me square in the stomach. It was a million times worse than what the kids at school used to dish out to me, Mark and Frankie in the playground and a thousand times worse than listening to Ian's constant gloating at night in our shared bedroom.

But who could blame him? Ian was right, Derby were rubbish, and the fact that we had spent most of the previous decade as one of the finest teams in the land only added to the insult. How could my Dad continue watching us being beaten in front of paltry crowds after tasting the glory of success?

In the 1970s he had seen players parade around the ground with trophies, whereas the 80s had offered nothing more than former greats like Kevin Hector, Archie Gemmill and Steve Powell bowing out empty-handed on the memories of applause.

That night against Plymouth was different though. The atmosphere was incredible and I felt that I could almost reach out, take a chunk and put it in my pocket alongside my Texan bar that Dad had bought me as a half-time treat.

Standing at one of the crush barriers, with Dad's arms either side of me, he held the swaying crowd off as they surged forward and back to get a better view of the action. The singing was louder than ever and I had to shout so that I could be heard, which only added to the noise. Even the floodlights seemed to burn brighter in recognition of the occasion.

The glory days were back, with almost 30,000 crammed into the old ground and a place in the FA Cup semi-final just around the corner. Thoughts of Dad's increasing apathy were put to one side and as we sang together from the terraces a calm assuredness filled me with warmth to combat the cold. That was until Plymouth won a corner. And lofted the ball into the box. Which squirmed under our goalkeeper. And into the goal.

A small pocket of fans erupted while the rest of us stood stationary and stunned. After the volume of our own voices the cheers that came to us along the breeze from the Plymouth supporters sounded muted while our own silence crept over us like a mist, invading our mouths so that none of us could speak. It was like witnessing the death of something in front of our eyes which we thought we could command, only to realise that we had no control over it whatsoever.

It was only a one goal lead but we found it insurmountable. The ground became a time-machine as it sped us towards the final whistle, while for the Plymouth fans it must have dragged like decades. Shots went agonisingly wide while stray passes felt like daggers to the stomach. The ghosts of those great teams such as Benfica and Real Madrid who had been defeated in the Baseball Ground mud seemed to rise up from the dead in revenge and grab the heels of the living to stop us from equalising.

Usually after matches the spectators spill out of the exits and head home. Some supporters hang around to cheer the team off the pitch if they've done well, but most of the time there is a mass exodus into the night and back to whichever transport brought us to the ground. On Wednesday 14 March 1984 nobody left. Instead we stood rooted to the terraces as if we were all waiting for someone to walk out of the tunnel, tell us they didn't mean it and start the match again.

Just two days prior to the match the club had faced its winding-up petition in the High Court. The FA Cup run had taken all of our minds off both our dismal League position and the financial crisis, but now it was over the realisation sped towards us like a train. It was apparent why Dad had lost interest and I wondered then whether we would stop coming completely. I stood there on the terrace feeling like I'd been taken to the Headmaster's office but not done anything wrong, or had food poisoning when I hadn't even eaten. It felt like being bullied but I didn't have my Dad to help me out because he was being bullied too.

Having been left suspended at the ground we arrived home later than usual. Nobody had spoken on the way back to the car and nobody had spoken as we drove back home either. As ever I was watching to see how the grown men around me reacted, learning through mimicry the way children do.

I was glad of the silence as I didn't feel like talking either. I didn't feel like doing anything. Instead I stared solemnly out of the window, occasionally meeting the eyes of some other passenger who looked out from their own car as sadly as me, when, after a moment's recognition passed between us, we moved off at different speeds.

Uncle Paul didn't come in for a cup of tea as he usually did when dropping us off. He left with barely a hint of recognition on either side and with neither my Dad nor Uncle Paul committing to future matches my concern that our relationship with Derby County was over was too difficult to ignore.

Ian was still downstairs when we walked into the living room as he and Mum watched a horse jumping competition on BBC2. Ian liked horse jumping a lot and often we would spend hours building a course like Hickstead in the back garden from bikes, pieces of wood and anything Dad had hanging around in either of the two sheds that stood in the back garden. Then we'd spend more hours jumping over them pretending to be Harvey Smith.

If our two teams had been in the same division then there may have been more tension between us, but since my first match in November of 1979 the teams had been in different divisions and so didn't play each other, apart from when we had drawn them in the FA Cup. I could argue that Derby County were the better team as we had beaten Forest on the last two occasions, but Ian said that Nottingham Forest were the better team as they were in a higher division. Mum said that we should stop arguing otherwise she would bang our heads together.

From her position on the settee Mum looked up, and she seemed to be joining in the game of not talking. She had the same expression as when I had lost control of my bike and ridden into a pile of nettles. Ian was celebrating a clear round in the competition and Dad took one look at him and then turned back to my Mum.

'Why is he still up?' he demanded.

'Craigy's still up!' was her terse response.

They seemed a completely different couple than the one who had parted earlier in the evening.

I could count on one hand how many arguments I had witnessed between my Mum and Dad and although this was not really an argument, it shocked me nonetheless. There was always a cordial air to our home, filled with love and support which I assumed all families enjoyed. This was naïve, but I was only nine years old and had yet to encounter any other family on which to draw any comparison.

For the first time ever Dad went to bed before me. I didn't know what to do so stood idly in the front room before Mum announced to everyone that it was time for bed. I wandered up the stairs, cleaned my teeth, put my pyjamas on and got under the quilt, wanting the day to be over but there was still its end to endure.

In the darkness of the bedroom Ian started whispering taunts about how rubbish Derby were and how we had been beaten by a team from the third division. My tactic of ignoring him was not working but I had no other choice. I didn't want to add to the tension in the home and so had to lie there and listen to my brother's taunts. Lying on my back, staring blankly at the ceiling all I could do was vow that the next time I built a horse jump for Ian on the back garden, it would be bloody massive.

*****

Peter Taylor left the following month to be replaced by Roy McFarland, who had been a towering centre-back in the great sides of the 1970s. He could not avoid the inevitable relegation though, which not only affects the club but drags the supporters and the city down too.

By the end of the 1983–84 season Derby were reaching rock bottom, and a century after the football club was founded as an offshoot of Derbyshire County Cricket Club, the Rams suffered their second relegation in five years. Despite winning their last four home matches their away form was wretched. During that season I was not the only one who suffered from travel-sickness, as the team failed to win away from the Baseball Ground after Bonfire Night.

Crowds were hovering around 10,000 in an arena that had once hosted 41,826 supporters against Tottenham Hotspur when the good times had started to come in 1969. The club was going downhill faster than a small child who has been told not to roll down a huge grass bank because he will get wet and be too cold to run and catch a bus after a game.

Canon Second Division 1983–84

Pos		Pl	W	D	L	F	A	GD	Pts
1	Chelsea	42	25	13	4	90	40	50	88
2	Sheffield Wednesday	42	26	10	6	72	34	38	88
3	Newcastle United	42	24	8	10	85	53	32	80
18	Crystal Palace	42	12	11	19	42	52	-10	47
19	Oldham Athletic	42	13	8	21	47	73	-26	47
20	**Derby County**	**42**	**11**	**9**	**22**	**36**	**72**	**-36**	**42**
21	Swansea City	42	7	8	27	36	85	-49	29
22	Cambridge United	42	4	12	26	28	77	-49	24

1984–85

At the start of the 1984–85 season Derby County found themselves in the third tier of English football. It was the first time since Ray Straw's 37 goals had dragged us out of the Division Three North 28 years before that our club had seen such lows.

Despite four wins out of nine at the end of the 1983–84 season, Roy McFarland had been replaced as manager in the close season by Arthur Cox, the manager who had brought Kevin Keegan to Newcastle and had just celebrated promotion with the Magpies from Division Two. McFarland stayed as Cox's assistant but an inauspicious start saw us beaten at Bournemouth, which is never a good indication as to how a season will progress. The pair saw a steady improvement turn into a white Christmas though as the Rams lost only one game in eight between 10 November and 1 January.

Another disastrous defeat away from home at fourth division Hartlepool in November had already seen us exit the FA Cup, even though we'd beaten them 6–1 on aggregate in the League Cup earlier that same year. Meanwhile in the League we were getting twice the number of supporters than others in the same division. The only supporter that mattered to me though was my Dad.

It would be romantic to say that me and my Dad continued to go, but with fixtures at York City and Cambridge United, who were destined to be relegated out of the Football League in 2004 and 2005 respectively, and Newport County who went out of business altogether in 1989, the appeal was no longer there.

The season peaked when over 14,000 supporters witnessed an uninspiring 0–0 draw against Bradford City who would finish as champions, but for me and my Dad the party seemed to be over. A promising end to the 1984–85 season saw the Rams only lose twice in the last 15 games, with Bobby Davison scoring 24 goals. We finished in seventh position but a massive 17 points behind the final promotion placed Hull City.

Instead of being on the terraces or in the stands to witness our result I was becoming more reliant on James Alexander Gordon to read the scores on Radio 5. Instead my entertainment came at the cinema, but while the films were good I felt no connection with Micheal J. Fox and his attempts to get back to the future, and when Mum told us we were going to see *The Goonies* I thought she meant Dad had got seats in the executive boxes at Forest again.

At Derby the thrill of moving uncontrollably towards an outcome that had yet to be written was immense, success meant everything whereas defeat signalled despair, and while I had no control over what happened at either the cinema or the football ground at least at Derby I thought my support was helping out.

More often than not that season the outcome went against us and Dad would continue to tell me that winning wasn't important. But while Dad was worried that another loss was distancing us from the teams at the top of the League, I worried that each distanced us further from the prospect of going to any more games together.

Canon Third Division 1984–85

Pos		Pl	W	D	L	F	A	GD	Pts
1	Bradford City	46	28	10	8	77	45	32	94
2	Millwall	46	26	12	8	73	42	31	90
3	Hull City	46	25	12	9	78	49	29	87
4	Gillingham	46	25	8	13	80	62	18	83
5	Bristol City	46	24	9	13	74	47	27	81
6	Bristol Rovers	46	21	12	13	66	48	18	75
7	**Derby County**	**46**	**19**	**13**	**14**	**65**	**54**	**11**	**70**
8	York City	46	20	9	17	70	57	13	69
9	Reading	46	19	12	15	68	62	6	69

1985–86

In 1986 I was in my final year at Junior school. Secondary school awaited in September and I felt like I was walking out into a world that was bigger yet far more accessible. A-ha, Berlin and Europe were bringing their brand of European music to the UK charts while a panini was an album of football stickers that gave us a deeper insight and knowledge into our beautiful game, rather than a posh cob from Pret A Manger. Not only could we recite the names of our own players on the playground, but we were also well-versed in teams like Coventry City, Ipswich Town and West Ham United.

Further afield the Cold War was at a peak so high even Primary school kids knew something about global politics, and when a reactor blew up at the Chernobyl nuclear power plant on 26 April, near to the Ukrainian town of Pripyat, a radioactive plume spread across most of Europe, which according to the WHO (the World Health Organisation, not the band that my Dad liked) could potentially result in 4,000 deaths. Greenpeace thought that figure might reach 200,000. The accident was beamed via television news into our living rooms, teaching us even more about the nuclear threat and of Ukraine, although back then it was still classed as the USSR. Unable to grab the enormity of the disaster at school though, me and my mates would run up to each other and say jokes like, 'Why don't you leave your trouser zip open in a Russian nuclear power station? Because Chernobyl fall out.'

Sheffield United 0 Derby County 1

Saturday 25 January 1986

It was on this backdrop of opening horizons that Dad took me to only my second away match, an FA Cup fixture at Bramall Lane, the home of Sheffield United. We had already laid to rest the last two ghosts of Plymouth Argyle and Hartlepool by beating Crewe Alexandra, Telford United again, and Gillingham in the preceding rounds. Having started the season in Division Three though Derby County had entered the Cup in round one, and so despite those victories we were still only at the fourth round stage. This time we were the underdogs from Division Three, with the home team in the division above.

Me and my Dad caught the train up to Sheffield, which seemed a long way from home, and also took my younger brother, Daniel. He had been born in the August of 1981 and by now Dad had learnt that the best way to transfuse black and white blood, or blue and white as it was then, into the veins of his offspring was to start them at the age of four. Mum must have been tearing her hair out.

As it was an away game Dad said that it would be wise not to wear either my Derby shirt or my scarf, but it was January and as we were travelling north Mum insisted I have something round my neck. She pulled out an old yellow, black and red scarf, which smelled like a wet dog but I supposed it was as close as you could get to being neutral, unless you supported Watford.

Derby had started the season well and by the time we arrived in Sheffield we had only lost three matches, having not been beaten since October. Crowds were returning to the Baseball Ground, creeping steadily up from 10,000 to 14,000 supporters, and culminating in an attendance of 16,140 fans when we played Reading at the end of November.

As we entered Bramall Lane the click of the turnstiles sounded the same but the acoustics of the ground were different. While the steep-sided Baseball Ground poured her noise back onto you, Bramall Lane, probably due to its roots as a cricket ground, was expansive. From the huge kop at the opposite end to our own stand the chants seemed to hang in the air as if too polite to leave.

The Baseball Ground had tiers and was a homely blue whereas the stands here were simple banks of garish red seats and as uncompromising as a Yorkshireman announcing, ''ere's your football, bloody watch it!'

Estimates suggest that almost 10,000 Derby fans took the trip up to Sheffield that Saturday afternoon, filling the away terrace and the seats above. Me and my Dad were unable to stop smiling as we eagerly tried to grab any view of the pitch while Daniel wandered through the legs of the supporters around us.

All of the songs that I had learnt over the last seven years were sung, with us all believing in the voice of thousands of others who were straining to be heard on foreign soil.

At your own ground complacency often takes hold and monotony reduces the spirit, but when you're at a different stadium there is an urgency to make a noise and show the opposition that you are there. On this occasion, not only were we from another city, but the fact that we were from another division urged us to sing louder, which in turn urged the team to better themselves.

We went to the game hoping for a draw and a chance to bring the Blades back to the Baseball Ground but our captain, Rob Hindmarch, and the rest of the team thought otherwise.

Arthur Cox had signed Hindmarch in the close-season on a free transfer from Sunderland and he went on to play 133 times for the Rams. As captain he was instrumental in the years that followed before moving to Wolves in 1990. While the most we could hope for was a replay back at Derby, his single goal on that cold afternoon in Sheffield was enough to win the tie outright.

After the final whistle all 10,000 of us stood rooted to the spot. It was like Plymouth Argyle, where the world around us was advancing but we remained, caught in the moment that we all wanted to continue, but this time for a different reason. The chant that rose up from the travelling support was nothing intricate like *Take My Breath Away*, and if we were clever we could have adapted A-ha's current Number 1 to *The Sun Always Shines on Derby*, but instead we simply stood and sang out of our hearts and lungs.

'We love you Derby, we do, we love you Derby, we do, we love you Derby, we do, oh Derby we love you.'

It was a chant that lasted a millions years, so much so that Arthur Cox stopped the players walking down the tunnel and led them back to the stand behind the goal where we all stood.

In the post-match interview Cox, a man heralding from the footballing hotbed of the North East went on to say that this club, our club, had gotten under his skin, and it was not difficult to see why. The last 10 years had seen a huge decline in Derby County, with players moving on, managers moving on and chairmen moving on, but supporters don't get to make that decision. Supporters have to stick with the teams that they started to watch ever since their Dad's had taken them when they were four years old.

Mum had been right, it was freezing that afternoon but on the concrete terrace beneath the imposing shadow of the Bramall Lane stand, under that slate-grey Sheffield sky in January, I looked up at my Dad. He was singing with as much heart and desire as me and I felt foolish for ever thinking that he would give up on our team.

*****

Our reward for beating Sheffield United was a fifth round tie against the other League team from Sheffield, Sheffield Wednesday. Wednesday were in Division One and although we were showing promise and had punched above our weight in the previous round we were still a team from Division Three. Derby were at home though and we felt that we could get a result against any team that came to visit, and as Billy Ocean was singing at the time, 'When the going gets tough, the tough get going'.

The Baseball Ground was originally built in the 1880s by industrialist, Sir Francis Ley, as a recreational area for his employees. After witnessing the game of baseball on a trip to the United States Ley was smitten and wanted to promote the sport in Great Britain.

Derby's first match as owners of the Baseball Ground was against Sunderland on 14 September 1895. The club had already played there before when horseracing at the city's County Ground, where the club originally played, had forced them to relocate. 10,000 people turned up at that first match, many of whom worked for Sir Francis Ley and lived close-by in the surrounding streets, allaying fears that a move across the city would result in a lowering of attendances. Output at Ley's foundry that Saturday afternoon meanwhile hit an all-time low.

On 4 September 1926 a new stand was built named 'B' Pavillion, which ran along the length of Shaftsbury Crescent. By the time Sheffield Wednesday were drawn out of the hat in 1986 this had become known as the A, B and C Stand and still housed the changing rooms and offices that were built almost 60 years before.

The imposing stand at the Osmaston End of the ground was built in 1933, with an almost identical one built opposite at the Normanton End in 1935. These steep-sided stands created an intimidating arena for visitors and not just because they could make a 20,000 strong crowd sound like 40,000. As the Normanton End was not built parallel to the pitch it gave the illusion when running towards it that it was looming faster than it actually was, while the terraces were just inches from the touchline. I was once able to say a cheery, 'Hello!' to Gary Micklewhite as he came over to take a throw-in while we were sitting at the front paddock of the A-Stand.

There were 22,781 supporters in attendance at the Baseball Ground to see whether Billy Ocean was right, and admirably we held the visitors, who that year would finish fifth in Division One, to a 1–1 draw. Again the team took the trip up to Sheffield where 29,077 people, the second largest crowd to see a Derby County team play since being relegated from the top-flight in the 1979–80 season, were there, but me and my Dad were absent.

Sheffield Wednesday 2 Derby County 0

Wednesday 5 March 1986

Our family had just moved to a larger house on a new housing estate in Long Eaton, which meant I no longer had to share my room with Ian and therefore could avoid the nocturnal taunts whenever Derby lost. The estate had been built by the side of the new bypass that ran through farmland from the town's railway station to Main Street, with the contractors sympathetically maintaining the rural theme by naming the strip of tarmac, Fields Farm Road. In hindsight a better name would probably have been New Houses, Industrial Estate and Factory Outlet Boulevard.

I can't recall where we were that evening but I know I came into the house late and headed straight upstairs to my bedroom. I had a pocket radio that used to belong to my Dad, which he had given me when he had bought a new one for when he was decorating or in the garden. Naturally it was preset to Radio Derby and I immediately heard the familiar voices of commentators, Graham Richards and Colin Gibson, when I turned it on.

Those first few moments listening to the game were agony as I tried to gauge the score. Occasionally there is the clichéd, 'And if you've just come in from work, the score is…' or in my case, 'And if you've just got back after having been dragged out somewhere with your parents, and by the way you had better have taken your shoes off before you went upstairs as these are new carpets, the score is…' but occasionally radio commentators will add the score at various intervals, 'And Derby, who are 17 goals to the good here at the City Ground, Nottingham, have another corner.'

When Graham Richards finally got round to confirming the score I wanted to return to that previous agony of ignorance. Derby were 2–0 down and with Sheffield Wednesday being at home they were in full control of the match. Richards, a commentator who most Derby fans loved to listen to because of his lively and partisan style, was livid at the negative tactics being employed by the home side who understandably were keeping the ball in defence. That they were not attempting to attack was infuriating the commentator and his annoyance soon transferred to me, which to be fair was not difficult.

Upstairs in our new home I was kicking every ball, reacting to the commentary and the crowd noise coming from the radio while every now and again a call would come from downstairs ordering me to stop banging around. I was caught in some awful disease though and felt anguish each time we lost the ball, as it resulted in long periods of Sheffield Wednesday possession as the clocked ticked relentlessly towards full-time.

In the end we were no match for our opposition and were out of the Cup again. Dad tried to console me with sage words but I was blinded by my loyalty to my club, to the point where I could not see past the statistic of losing and that sometimes you came up against better opposition. More importantly though I still had the vision of being on the Pop-Side terrace not two years before after being knocked out of the same competition, and my Dad's reaction when we'd been beaten by Plymouth Argyle.

Since then our visits to the Baseball Ground had seen a dramatic decline, which was understandable when playing teams from cities better known for their Vikings, universities and transporter bridges. It was impossible for me to see a return to the glory days which, I thought, would see me and Dad wander to matches as regularly as he took Daniel to Grandma's house so she could look after him while he and my Mum were at work.

Derby's financial crisis of 1984 had been averted and we were winning matches again, but as Ian kept on informing me despite us now having our separate rooms, we were still in the third division. The belief that we could maybe scrape through a fourth round match against second division opposition had been enough to see Dad take me to Sheffield United, but I guessed that missing tonight's game meant that that was the limit of his expectation. From a man who had seen us win the Division One Championship twice there was only so long that commitment to this pale imitation of Derby County could continue.

Maybe the time called for a mature passionate plea to my Dad to tell him that, win, lose or draw, it was simply going to the matches that counted, or maybe I should have trusted in my club and waited patiently for better days to arrive. Instead though I was so incensed that I got a piece of paper and a thick biro and scrawled, 'SHEFFIELD WEDNESDAY ARE RUBBISH AND WASTE TIME WHEN THEY ARE WINNING!' before screwing it up and kicking the radio.

*****

Supporting a football club is a roller coaster ride. Even those devotees at Old Trafford, Anfield and those who have moved from Highbury to the Emirates Stadium have their bad days. The only consistency in being a football supporter is that, sooner or later, depression or euphoria is going to be replaced by euphoria or depression.

Three days after losing at Hillsborough we had an away fixture at Meadow Lane, the home of Nottingham's other club, Notts County.

Among Derby supporters there has never been the level of rivalry with Notts County that there is with Nottingham Forest, even though the former is marginally closer to our city. More bizarre is that the supporters of Nottingham Forest have more cause to celebrate when Derby do poorly than their own close neighbours. To supporters of Forest, Notts County are seen as the annoying cousin rather than the hated sibling, while Derby will forever be the black sheep at the other end of Brian Clough Way.

Derby beat Notts County with two goals from Bobby Davison and one from Gary Micklewhite in front of 13,086 supporters. We went on to lose just one of the next eight matches and continued towards the end of the season with wins and draws, punctuated by only four losses.

On a rain-soaked night against Rotherham, Derby clinched promotion back to the second division courtesy of a Trevor Christie penalty in front of 21,036 fans.

The only other time in the club's history that Derby had plummeted to the depths of the third tier of English football had been after relegation at the end of the 1954–55 season. It had taken manager, Harry Storer, two seasons to get the club back into Division Two and relative respectability. Arthur Cox had done the same and even defeat away at Darlington on the last day in front of just 3,585 diehard fans could not dampen our spirits.

Canon Third Division 1985–86

Pos		Pl	W	D	L	F	A	GD	Pts
1	Reading	46	29	7	10	67	51	16	94
2	Plymouth Argyle	46	26	9	11	88	53	35	87
3	**Derby County**	**46**	**23**	**15**	**8**	**80**	**41**	**39**	**84**
4	Wigan Athletic	46	23	14	9	82	48	34	83

SUMMER — 1986

Liverpool 3 Everton 1
Saturday 10 May 1986

Each year the Long Eaton Sunday League is allocated a small number of tickets for the FA Cup Final. These are always hard to come by for the supporters of each club and they bemoan the allocation for FA officials and sponsors, however, my Dad gave up a great deal of his time on a voluntary basis, as do others, to ensure non-League football and the associations that govern them run efficiently.

My Dad didn't take advantage of the offer very often and there were plenty more people working for the Sunday League than there were tickets. He had always promised to take me to see Derby play at Wembley Stadium in the FA Cup Final though and by the time I was 11 this looked like it was never going to happen.

The Cup Final always reminds me of the first beer I drank with my Dad. I was about six years old and sat on the floor of our living room with my back against the settee. The sound of the Coldstream Guards blew into the room as they left the Wembley Stadium field and I was worried in case Dad missed the teams walking out onto the pitch. He soon caught my attention though as his figure appeared through the door from the living room.

Dad's face was aglow with the green light coming from the square wooden television set that occupied one corner of our living room like Mr Strong. I was assuming Dad was going to bring in orange squash or maybe fizzy pop as it was a special occasion, but despite my tender years he bought in two 330ml cans of Watney's Pale Ale, and further infuriated the health and safety police of the 21st century by bringing peanuts for us as well. He opened both cans, poured the peanuts into a cereal bowl, sat down next to me and told me not to drink it all at once.

I felt like a grown-up and that somehow Dad was also my mate, like Mark Archer and Frankie Middleton, and that here in front of BBC1 we had our own little supporters club sat watching the Cup Final in our own world.

I took my first sip of beer and as with everyone's first taste immediately wondered what on earth the fuss was about. It tasted like stagnant pond water and so I looked up towards my Dad to ask for cherryade instead. Dad was drinking his beer though and so I decided to persevere, wanting to be just like him, and after a few of the salted peanuts my mouth was sufficiently thirsty to try again. Slowly I drank my way through the can during the 90 minutes.

By 1986 Dad had decided to take me to the Cup Final regardless of the opposition. During Derby's glory years back in the seventies my Dad had assumed that the good times were going to last forever, even missing the 1975 Charity Shield, which we won courtesy of a 2–0 victory over West Ham United, because he assumed that he would soon get the chance to go again. The next time Derby would get to play at the famous arena though was in 1992, against Cremonese in the Anglo-Italian Cup.

The day before that 1986 FA Cup Final I had a contented grin on my face at school, prompting my maths teacher to ask why I was smiling so much. After I told her Dad had got me a ticket for the Cup Final she said, 'I know people who would cut your arm off for that.' Having never heard the expression before I took her remark at face value and spent the entire afternoon with my arms beneath my school jumper, feeling like the guy in the Sword of Damocles, which our Head teacher had read us in assembly that morning.

Regardless of my concern about my upper limbs the comment had still filled me with enormous pride. Dad had made me the kid at school who was going to the Cup Final, the one that everyone wanted to speak to and the one that everyone wanted to be.

Driving down to London was just like travelling to Oldham, kind of, with me and my Dad as passengers while Uncle Paul drove. Meanwhile back at home Ian was on his Casio keyboard pretending to be Falco (the one who sang Rock Me Amadeus, not the Spurs player who had just signed for Watford).

Just travelling on the motorway was exciting enough, racing along at what I imagined to be great speed, with all the vehicles on the carriageway travelling in the same direction adding to the excitement. It was as if we were all in one giant race together to get to the end of the road.

Once at the end of the M1 we drove around in unfamiliar surroundings, with wide, tree-lined streets offering plenty of room to park. It was a far cry from the tight terraced streets of Normanton and felt more like a summer afternoon out in the park rather than being enclosed in a huge city.

Whereas I was expecting thousands of supporters to be making their way in huge queues to the stadium, instead we took a gentle stroll under the sun as birds swooped from beneath the eaves of the houses and onto the telegraph wires above. As we got nearer though at last it started to resemble what I had expected. The clamour and excitement started to build as people edged closer to the turnstiles and as we approached the noise increased in an excited chatter that reminded me of Ken Dodd and Jimmy Tarbuck.

As usual Dad was pulling me along, guiding me through the crowds that seemed to part before him, easing my own passage through, and after climbing what seemed an immense stairway we were faced with the entrance to the famous stadium.

The turnstiles were a lot bigger than the ones we had at the Baseball Ground and stood formidably in our way. Those at Derby were at waist height and seemed to concede that we could always get in if we really wanted to. The stadium itself represented a castle and with everyone eager to get inside I felt like a mediaeval knight in battle.

After queuing for 20 minutes it was our time to enter, with Dad holding the tickets in his pocket until the last moment lest one errant supporter grab the precious paper out of his hand. With my Dad there was never any danger of this happening though and as the creek of the huge turnstile signalled our arrival, the excited noise of the outside was enhanced as it bounced off the heavy concrete of the concourse.

The three of us made our way onto the terrace at the back of the goal where the players would later emerge and claimed our place among both sets of fans who shared the stands that day. This was the first time both teams from Liverpool had met in the Final and unlike most rivalries across football the two sets of fans could actually stand side-by-side and be courteous in either defeat or victory.

To get some kind of parity with the grown men and women with whom I shared the Pop-Side terrace with at the Baseball Ground, I had started taking a foldable camping chair along to matches along with a wooden plank. This was the time when young kids could be seen walking to the games clutching milk crates, clipping the backs of adult legs as they ran alongside their striding dads, but it was not uncommon for my own Dad to always try and go one further to get us that extra advantage.

I set up my chair, placed the plank of wood on top and held my arms out wide for my Dad to lift me on. I then started to wave the Everton flag that Dad had bought me outside the ground, choosing them to adopt because their blue shirts had a white panel at the top, which I thought was different. Dad validated the decision when he turned to Uncle Paul and said, 'We're not going to support the Reds are we?'

Having never had cause to fly any flags at Derby matches I was rather exuberant in my waving until being warned to stop if anyone complained. Soon the whole terrace was a sea of scarves and banners though, both blue and red, and I felt justified in displaying my own small rectangle of material with as much vigour as one of the Hitler Youth circa 1939.

All around supporters were hemmed in tightly, squashing each other in the crowd and for the first time ever I was starting to feel glad about my chair, which I never really appreciated at the time. I thought I looked like an idiot walking along to the showpiece football match of the year with a camping chair and a slab of two by four but I didn't have to worry for too long.

After 27 minutes Everton's new signing, Gary Lineker, scored the opening goal and the place erupted like I had never seen before. Me, my Dad, Uncle Paul, 40,000 others, my camping chair and the plank of wood spun wildly around in the melee, lurching forward to the front of the terrace before receding back like small children running to the sea only to change their mind. Despite only being my adopted team that had scored it still felt like joyous fun, surging with the crowd as it ebbed and flowed as I was overtaken by the euphoria of all those around me.

The cheering lasted far longer than any goal I had ever seen but eventually my Dad managed to rescue my flag, although my chair and plank were long gone, thrown wildly around in the crowd surge that greeted the important goals of the day. It was probably 10 minutes later when Uncle Paul pointed out a grown man about two feet taller than anyone else on the terrace.

'Hey, Craigy,' he said, 'I think that bloke's got your chair.'

In the second half Ian Rush equalised before Craig Johnston put Liverpool ahead. With almost half-an-hour still to play the tie could have gone either way but Rush sealed a 3–1 victory with seven minutes to go.

We didn't stay to see Liverpool lift the trophy but headed straight back to the car to beat the traffic. Unencumbered by any camping equipment I managed to keep up with Dad and Uncle Paul as we walked swiftly back to the car before returning to the excitement of the motorway and home with a big smile. Although it wasn't Derby, it was still my Dad.

Ark Royal 4 Sandiacre Livingston 2

Between 1982 and 1986 I was a cub scout at a local cub pack, attending every Tuesday evening at a small hut by the banks of the Erewash Canal. My Mum had joined as a leader when Ian had enrolled a few years before, which gave us our own weekly ritual in much the same way as me and my Dad went to watch Derby.

In 1987 the scout group somehow inherited the hut used in *Auf Wiedersehen Pet*, the ITV comedy drama about a group of British migrants working on a German building site, but whereas in the programme the hut burnt down, the one seen on fire was actually a prop, otherwise the gift from Central Television would have been a bit crap.

Each cub pack in the district had a football team and by the time I came to my final year we were one of the best sides in the district. We had just missed out on winning the League though owing to the fact that when we played eventual champions, Sandiacre Livingston, most of our players were on holiday. We ended up losing 5–2 but as a consolation had progressed through to the Cup Final and by the time it arrived we were back to full strength.

Being a good team at that level meant you had a goalkeeper who didn't wear glasses and a central defender who could kick a ball. It helped to have a striker who knew where the goal was while midfield did not exist. Having said that our goalkeeper could actually make saves and one of our strikers went on to play for Borrowash Victoria, who although only a non-League team still charge for entry. Our centre-backs could not only kick the ball but could kick it half the length of the pitch. And in the right direction. Most of the time.

I was the other centre-forward and could be relied upon to grab a few goals. I remember playing what was often referred to as 'a blinder' in one match, scoring a late goal and coming off the pitch rather pleased with myself. When Dad said to me afterwards, 'You didn't have to score in that match, you played fantastic.' I was beaming even more.

Dad also taught me that the only way to improve at anything was to play someone better than yourself, and the importance of the game rather than the win. After tennis matches me and Dad played against each other he'd remark on how I wouldn't want to leave the court until I'd beaten him, whereas having a good game was enough for him. During those tennis matches he would always make allowances for my poor serves.

We sometimes played snooker as well on the six-foot table that we erected in the garage. Just like allowing for my poor serves at tennis Dad would let me off my foul shots but his generosity only went so far. Once when we were playing for a 10 pence bet I beat him, only to be told that he couldn't give me the money as the bet was invalid as we had made up our own rules.

After travelling to see the Final of the FA Cup a few weeks before I felt inspired on the day that the team I played for would contest a trophy. The rest of the cub pack were gripped by Cup fever too and Akela even went out and bought new green shorts and socks for everyone to go along with the gold jerseys we'd be wearing.

The team started well and my strike-partner scored a great goal from the edge of the box, which for a 10-year-old was classed as a 'belter' and it seemed that as soon as it left his foot the scouts from Borrowash Victoria were scribbling away in their notebooks.

At one-nil up and in full control it looked like we would get revenge for the humiliating League defeat earlier on in the season. Meanwhile I wasn't in the game, with the occasion getting to my nerves and stunting my ability.

Effectively we were playing with 10 men and Sandiacre inevitably equalised, cancelling our own fine effort with the type of goal usually seen at such a standard. The ball reached our penalty area, causing panic among the defence and allowing the opposition striker to score off the post. It was a bad goal to concede and Sandiacre ran back to their own end almost too embarrassed to cheer.

Their second was even worse.

The ball found its way deep into our half, close to the corner flag, but with no attacking player near our right-back we felt safe. Our goalkeeper ran to the edge of the box to plead for a pass, thinking he could kick the ball further than the defender, but instead the defender committed the schoolboy error of passing the ball across the face of the goal, which was understandable seeing as though he was a schoolboy. Luckily the ball went straight to another of our defenders who could kick it half the length of the pitch. And in the right direction. Most of the time.

The defender decided to pass the ball back to the 'keeper, not knowing that he had already ran out to retrieve the ball himself. It was paralysing in its inevitability and with nobody in front of the goal the ball went unhindered into the back of the net while we all looked on in disbelief.

If scoring an own goal in the Cup Final is about as bad as it gets as a kid then you've had a pretty good upbringing, considering what some children have to endure, but our own nightmares are what haunt us. On that pitch James England had to face his worst fear. The nearest teammate must have been less than 10 yards away but on that football field he looked a forlorn figure a million miles from anyone else.

I didn't know what to do, the team didn't know what to do, and neither did our manager. I think even the referee was considering disallowing the goal out of pity for the boy. But then my Dad sprinted onto the field, a lone pitch invader breaking all the rules but knowing that what really mattered at that time was for someone to go up and speak to that heartbroken lad. It was the same man who knew that to jump over a gate at the Baseball Ground and get into the seats was wrong, but what was more important was getting a good view of Kevin Keegan for his son. It was the same man who taught me that it wasn't necessarily the rules that were right, but what was important was always right.

At half-time we went off for orange juice trailing by those two goals to one. There was talk of bringing me off, such was my inept performance but Dad looked at the manager calmly.

'The only way you will win this match is to keep our Craigy on.' he said, demonstrating that it's often not the loudest you can shout which makes you the most persuasive. He spoke with a calmness that was backed by a self-assured certainty, which was enough to convince our manager of the right thing to do.

Our team went back after the break, including me, and eventually I found my feet. I ran after a long kick forward by James, who was taking his frustration of scoring an own-goal out on the ball and kicking it 10 metres further than he usually did. While the Sandiacre centre-back seemed to have it covered, experience at this level had taught me that there was no such thing.

His poor header landed five yards in front of him and stopped dead in the mud right before me. Without breaking my stride I scooped the ball out of the ploughed pitch like a hockey player taking a penalty and ran past the stricken defender. Clear on goal I took one touch, and another, and just kicked the ball as hard as I could.

As hard as I could was hard enough and the ball glided along the small islands of turf and into the goal. As it hit the back of the net the parents who had come to watch cheered on the sidelines while I was swamped by yellow jerseys. As a team we headed back to our own end for the kick-off but along the way I still managed to look up and see Dad and give him a 'thumbs-up'. I think he was as relieved as I was.

After that I was like a different player, or rather like my old self, and scored again to put us ahead in the match. Leading by three goals to two we just needed to hang on to lift the trophy but further drama was to come.

With a minute left the ball was crossed low from the right hand side of the pitch. The Sandiacre goalkeeper came out for the ball but I just beat him to it. We both ended up on the floor, mud staining my brand new shorts, and watched the ball roll gingerly towards the back of the net for another goal. A hat-trick in the Cup Final was the thing dreams were made of and so when one of our central midfielders ran towards me I thought I was in for another mobbing. Instead the little shit ran past me and the stricken 'keeper, and toe-poked my goal from just a yard out.

It didn't matter. We had won the match, but what was more important to me was that my Dad had told the manager to keep me on and I had repaid his faith in me.

Many years later I asked James what my Dad had said to him that day. He told me that after running onto the pitch, Dad had rubbed his back, looked directly at him, smiled and said, 'James, you're playing a blinder, but if you do that again I'll break your bloody legs!'

1986–87

Derby County 0 Portsmouth 0

Wednesday 4 March 1987

Since 41,826 supporters crammed into the Baseball Ground in 1969 the club's attendances, along with its League position, had dwindled. The capacity at the old ground also fell, with seats replacing many of the standing areas while other seats were removed to widen gangways.

The segregation of fans in the light of increased hooliganism meant that huge areas of terrace had to be left unoccupied while the disaster at Bradford City's Valley Parade in May 1985, which claimed the lives of 56 people, led fire chiefs to further reduce the number of people who were allowed into the grounds, especially those made from old timber that was decades old.

When Portsmouth came to the Baseball Ground on the night of Wednesday 4 March in 1987 both teams were competing for the Championship at the top of Division Two. Derby County were hoping for their second promotion in as many seasons.

These were very exciting times. The last time I had seen Derby in the first division was almost eight years before, at that match against Nottingham Forest that had set me on the course for the many memorable afternoons and evenings out with my Dad. We had boarded the roller coaster together and nearly became derailed at that low point in 1984 but we had hung on grimly, much as I had done on the Big Dipper at Great Yarmouth fairground where we had been the previous summer while what can only be described as vocally shitting myself.

Derby were on the up but I desperately wanted them to continue rising, to keep going all the way into Division One. I wanted big teams and big crowds back at the Baseball Ground, banishing those memories I had of the silence after Plymouth Argyle and that overheard conversation of lost interest from my Dad. A win tonight would see us one step further to achieving that dream.

After leaving the chip shop me and my Dad turned the corner onto Shaftsbury Crescent but instead of hitting our groove and coasting into the ground we stopped. The queue for the Pop-Side terrace ran the length of Vulcan Street at the back of the Normanton End and all along Shaftsbury Crescent.

I was dismayed. All seat tickets had been sold out well before the game and with the Normanton End now an exclusive family area for members the Pop-Side was the only place to watch the game.

That was unless you went to football matches with my Dad.

Now at Secondary school, Mark Archer told me the next day that people were queuing right outside the stadium and as far as Dairy House Road that night. How many people we could have got into the stadium that night had it been 17 years before can only be estimated.

I joined the back of the queue, which with 45 minutes to kick-off was already level with the ticket office close to the Osmaston End of the ground while Dad went to see whether it was moving fast enough to get us in before half-past seven. After about 15 minutes though he still had not returned and the queue had moved only a fraction.

Ben E. King's *Stand By Me* was Number One at the time and a few laughs were raised when someone a few yards back launched into their own version. Ian was the record collector in our house though and had made Mum laugh earlier that month after listening to his *Good Morning Vietnam* soundtrack and naively asking her, 'Have you heard of that cool new band, 'Martha Reeves and the Vandellas?''

'Yes Ian,' she replied, 'back in 1963!'

I could hear the crowd already inside the ground and the chants rising on the darkness over the stand and towards me. Usually it gave me great comfort and the feeling I belonged to something huge but tonight it was against me, telling me to stay outside and that the welcome was not for me. Opposite the ground was the club car park and I was still only in line with Gordon Guthrie's pale blue Vauxhall Viva, the trainer's vehicle which was always parked halfway along the car park across from the main entrance at the centre of the A, B and C Stand.

Gordon Guthrie initially represented the Rams at reserve team level but an injury to his knee ended his playing days. Instead of giving up on a career in football he turned his attention to physiotherapy, with Brian Clough making Guthrie second-team trainer at the club in 1968. He had been among the staff ever since.

Eventually Dad returned and pulled me out of the queue. Even though I had been expecting it I was devastated that we would miss the match and was also annoyed that Dad had given up so soon.

We headed back along Shaftsbury Crescent but instead of turning the corner onto Cambridge Street we stopped and went to stand at the gate that me and my Dad had walked through when I had been mascot in 1981. It was here that Dad introduced me to a policeman who he knew through his work with the Long Eaton Sunday League.

The policeman ushered us both through the gate and into the ground where we walked through the warren of corridors beneath the stand and out by the pitch. At this time the terrace at the front of the Osmaston End of the Baseball Ground was given over to away supporters and was split into three sections, which were open or closed depending on how many away supporters were expected. Regardless of their position at the top of the League a midweek 290 mile round trip to Derby was what you would term, 'a bit of an ask' and credit should be given to the Portsmouth fans as they filled the middle section. However this left the two areas either side for segregation and the chance for a policeman to do a favour to a guy he knew through football.

The people we passed all looked suspiciously towards us, this man with his son being led by a policeman out of the underbelly of the stadium, but I was too excited to notice. We continued to the terrace behind the goal where the policeman opened a gate for us and let us onto the vast expanse that was solely for me and my Dad. As he closed the gate the officer smiled at me.

'Just don't cheer too loud when we score!' he said, and winked.

The policeman didn't have to worry. Portsmouth knew that a draw would be a great result against a team who had not been beaten at home since a first day defeat by Oldham Athletic. Pompey stifled the game resulting in a poor, infuriating goalless draw and the 21,385 supporters who managed to get in, especially those from the south coast, deserved better. I felt as aggrieved as I had after listening to our FA Cup defeat at Sheffield Wednesday on the radio the year before.

Dad always instilled within us the ideals of sportsmanship, often in the aftermath of the many family games that remained unfinished as when faced with inevitable defeat I would always opt for an inglorious retreat to my room, accompanied by stamping feet and slamming doors. At 12 years old fairness ranked about as highly as introspection and self awareness and I would never put my losses down to me simply not being good enough. I once went so far to claim that the joystick of our Acorn Electron home computer could read my fingerprints, ensuring my games of Scramble and Repton were made harder just for me.

That this unfairness could ascend into professional sport, especially football, was of intense irritation to me but I was blinkered and Derby's success was just as important to me as my own. When we lost it was always at the hands of a biased referee or a linesman's poor decision, or that the opposition's goals were always offside. Dad meanwhile remained unpartisan.

'Craigy, sometimes you need to admit that the opposition are better.'

To me though these wise words were tantamount to treason.

The benefit of Dad's level-headedness was that when he joined me in my siege mentality it elevated it to sensible and made it right. He was angry at Portsmouth's tactics too and our discussion was animated as we dodged our way through the crowds and back to the railway station after the game. The conversation continued as the train eased its way past the foreboding shadow of the Courtaulds factory, still bellowing out smoke and steam into the Spondon sky, and through the dark fields of Draycott and Breaston on our way home.

Sheffield United 0 Derby County 1
Saturday 25 April 1987

At the end of April 1987 we visited Bramall Lane again and this time, even though we were the visiting team, we were not the underdogs. We had only lost twice away from home since January and a second successive promotion under Arthur Cox was looking more certain. Meanwhile Sheffield United would finish the season in ninth.

Like the previous season when we had played there in the FA Cup the away end at Bramall Lane was full of fans who had made the short journey up from the south.

Instead of travelling by train, me and my Dad got a lift with one of his colleagues from work and rather than being on the terrace below we were sat in the seats, without having to revert to any half-time gate-crashing.

I hadn't realised that the huge seated section had been above us the previous year and knowing that there was just as many Derby fans below us cheering on the team added to the sense of belonging. And as it was a group that both me and my Dad were a part of it somehow brought us closer together.

Just like on our previous visit we won the match by a goal to nil. The ball was played up to midfielder Nigel Callaghan in the centre of the pitch, who flicked it neatly between two defenders for Phil Gee to run onto. Gee, who cost just £5,000 from non-League Gresley Rovers, was soon two yards clear and running towards the goal behind which almost 10,000 of us stood urging him forward.

It seemed to take the striker a decade to reach us but I guess it couldn't have done because the defenders didn't catch him. Instead he slid the ball past the advancing goalkeeper to send us all into rampant ecstasy behind the goal.

Things were looking up for Derby and even the chants were getting better. As the players celebrated in front of us the chant rose up from our own section and those standing below. To the tune of 'Let It Be', we all sang,
'Phillip Gee, Phillip Gee, Phillip Gee, Phillip Gee, scoring goals for Derby, Phillip Gee, Phillip Gee.'

*****

A week later a home victory against Leeds United was enough to see us promoted to Division One. Dad didn't want to take me though, fearing the reputation of the two sets of supporters and the occasion could combine to create an atmosphere not conducive for a man and his son. Instead we stayed away and learned of the result via the radio.

Derby won the match 2–1 and the big times were returning to the Baseball Ground. Phil Gee scored again, as did that year's top-scorer, Bobby Davison, whose name fitted in perfectly with the tune of Chicory Tip's 1972 Number One single, *Son of My Father*.

That season we had played Brighton, Grimsby, Shrewsbury and Huddersfield. Next season we'd be playing Manchester United, Liverpool, Arsenal and Nottingham Forest. Eight years after relegation from Division One Derby were back, and this time I was going with them.

Derby County 4 Plymouth Argyle 2

Saturday 9 May 1987

Before the season closed there was still the Championship to resolve. We went into our last game against Plymouth Argyle on 81 points with Portsmouth in second on 78. A win for Pompey and our own downfall would hand the title to them.

20,798 supporters turned up to the game that Saturday afternoon, which was amazing considering most of the people who attended that FA Cup game in 1984 had vowed that they would never watch Plymouth Argyle play again if it was the last thing they'd do.

1986–87 was the first season that the Play-offs were introduced and in their formative years the teams who finished from third to fifth place, plus that which finished fourth from bottom in Division One, fought for the right to play in the top-flight the following year. As Plymouth Argyle were still in with a chance to finish in fifth they had no intention of letting us enjoy the party.

We arrived at the ground an hour earlier than usual for a Saturday match, earning the proprietor of our favourite chip shop extra trade and Dad also bought me a 'Derby County Promotion 1986–87' flag from a stall on Cambridge Street, hoping that today we could go one better and become champions. Four years had passed since I had been the mascot at Boundary Park in Oldham but I was still wearing my orange away shirt to games. Either it had been very large or I had yet to put on a growth-spurt.

A loss in our previous match at Elm Park, Reading, had set up a tantalising finale and getting to the ground early had meant me and my Dad had a perfect viewpoint, wedged against one of the crowd barriers on the Pop-Side. Again he stood with his arms either side of me to protect me from the swaying crowd.

All eyes were focussed on the Baseball Ground pitch but many people had brought pocket radios with them to keep up to date with the score between Portsmouth and Sheffield United. Dad had his with him too and although reception was poor beneath the concrete roof of the Ley Stand above us we could just make out the distinctive voice of Graham Richards through the hiss of static and the noise of the fans around us.

Derby were awful that afternoon, leaving me drawing comparisons with my own performance in the Cup Final I had played with the cub scouts the summer before. The expectancy seemed to envelope them and coming at the end of a draining season, both physically and mentally, the team had little with which to respond.

Plymouth went ahead and we were set to settle with merely promotion, which was not a bad consolation prize when considering that the previous season we had been plying our trade in the third division. But it was under this mood of acceptance that Dad heard over the radio that while we could not help ourselves in securing the title Sheffield United were doing it for us. The Blades had scored against Portsmouth and Dad immediately yelled out the news to me and everyone around us.

The words, 'Sheffield are winning!' spread through the stadium like a tide, washing over everyone before continuing into the rest of the valley. 'Sheffield are winning!', starting with my Dad and then filtering into the Ley Stand above and then down the length of the Pop-Side. 'Sheffield are winning!', out of our area and into the Normanton End to see it ignite the stand.

Plymouth supporters in the Osmaston End failed to pass on the message and so those opposite us in the C Stand had to wait for the news to travel through to them like some cartoon telegraph. The crowd's sudden change from despondency to joy should have been enough for those opposite us but with so much at stake they needed to be sure. Only when the news reached them in voice could we all celebrate together.

As the ball trundled aimlessly out for a Plymouth throw-in about 10 yards from the halfway line the Baseball Ground crowd sprung to life as the fans started cheering a phantom goal. Here we all were, chanting for Sheffield United barely a fortnight after urging Phil Gee and his surge towards their goal.

It wasn't the news of the score that excited me though. The joy that had spread across Dad's face mirrored my own. The enthusiasm with which he had told those around him could have been me telling my classmates that Derby had won. Victory for the team meant victory for us and from a dark landscape of failure, looking at the new horizon of Division One, I knew then that me, my Dad and Derby County had made it through.

With the crowd around them in a rapture of excitement the players were left in no doubt as to the situation. The pressure was off and suddenly they were able to play to their full potential, eventually winning by four goals to two. Meanwhile Sheffield United beat Portsmouth, leaving us champions by six points.

Me and my Dad stood on the Pop-Side terrace cheering the team as they made their way around the pitch after the game. Scarves were thrown on for the players to wear along with daft hats and other souvenirs. The chanting went on long into the evening but I didn't mind the fact that we'd be late for tea or miss *Strike It Lucky*.

Eventually both me and my Dad walked back to the train station, looking forward to getting home and celebrating a great day and a great future. Starship's *Nothing's Gonna Stop Us Now* was aptly at the top of the charts as we finished top of the League.

The train pulled into Long Eaton and me and my Dad walked the mile down Fields Farm Road. Occasionally one of the passing cars would sound their horn in support, urging me to wave my flag in response and I was still waving my flag as we listened to the reports on Dad's radio, getting a lot better reception than we had in the ground. Rob Hindmarch was being interviewed and questioned about the reasons why the team had put in such a poor early performance. Our captain's reply was to simple state:

'We were nervous and that had an impact on the way we played, but then the fans told us that Sheffield were winning which took the pressure off and allowed us to win.'

I couldn't believe it. Here was the captain of Derby County admitting live on radio that my Dad had been solely responsible for Derby winning the Championship.

Today Second Division 1986–87

Pos		Pl	W	D	L	F	A	GD	Pts
1	**Derby County**	42	25	9	8	64	38	26	84
2	Portsmouth	42	23	9	10	53	28	25	78
3	Oldham Athletic	42	22	9	11	65	44	21	75
4	Leeds United	42	19	11	12	58	44	14	68
5	Ipswich Town	42	17	13	12	59	43	16	64
6	Crystal Palace	42	19	5	18	51	53	-2	62
7	Plymouth Argyle	42	16	13	13	62	57	5	61

1987–88

The euphoria of being promoted to Division One lasted the whole of the summer, despite many supporters wondering how Derby would fair in the top-flight. Nine of the players who started the match against Plymouth Argyle on the last day of the previous season had been regulars among the team who had played in the third division but the club soon signalled their intention by signing England goalkeeper, Peter Shilton, from Southampton in July of 1987 and then added one of the country's centre-backs, Mark Wright, in August for £760,000.

Derby started the season with a confidence boosting 1–0 win over Luton Town with the visitors reduced to 10 men after just four minutes when Mick Harford was sent off for a foul on defender Mel Sage, but the next home game saw us brought back down to earth with a 0–1 reverse against unfashionable Wimbledon.

Results were inconsistent and attendances were low. When Oxford United arrived on 26 September the average was just under 16,000 spectators, which was well below the 20,000 that Chairman, Robert Maxwell, was hoping for. By November 1987, seemingly bored of Derby County, he approached Elton John to see if the megastar would be interested in selling Watford. It was a sad, sad situation, and was getting more and more absurd.

After a 1–1 draw with Maxwell's coveted Watford on 5 December we sat comfortably in ninth position in the League while the Hornets were left in 19th, leading many fans to the conclusion that Maxwell was welcome to pursue his interests at Vicarage Road. Meanwhile at the top of the table Liverpool were running away with the League title having won 12 of their opening 16 games. Despite Ian Rush finally moving to Italian giants Juventus, having been sold the season before yet remaining at Anfield on loan, players of the quality of John Barnes and new star striker, John Aldridge, meant that the absence was hardly felt.

Derby County 1 Tottenham Hotspur 2

Sunday 20 December 1987

The best teams in the land were now coming to the Baseball Ground with better players gracing the hallowed turf. A further benefit of being in Division One meant that we didn't have to wait so long for James Alexander Gordon to get to our result and if Arsenal, Charlton, Chelsea and Coventry were all playing away that season we were the first team to be read out.

Greater media coverage was a further perk and the prospect of matches played live on ITV had many Derby fans flocking to Rumbelows for the latest 42 inch Mitsubishi Projection television. *The Big Match* beamed football straight from the grounds to our armchairs, which for our family gave Dad an opportunity to enjoy football with his other sons. Meanwhile Mum would look up from her ironing and reminisce about how she and Dad travelled the country to watch Derby before we were born while in the midst of all this I could be found dying from embarrassment as adolescents my age stood waving inappropriate banners and body parts live into our living room.

Derby's turn on television came one Sunday afternoon in December when we hosted Tottenham Hotspur in a game that cynics said was only picked in the hope that there would be a repeat of scenes in 1983, when fans at the Baseball Ground used seats as missiles in a show of hooliganism that was blighting the sport at the time. What mattered to me though was that this represented the chance for everyone who had stared sympathetically at me whenever I told them that my weekend had involved going to watch Derby County play and for them to see that now we were one of the best teams in the country.

Tottenham had been beaten in the FA Cup Final the previous summer by Coventry City, which at that time was the greatest shock in the competition since Stan Mortenson woke the morning after scoring a hat-trick for Blackpool in 1953, only to discover the match had been named after Stanley bloody Matthews.

At first me and my Dad weren't going to go and I was going to have to settle for an afternoon with Brian Moore and Ian St John, the patron saint of ambulances, rather than the fans on the Pop-Side. That was until Uncle Paul called to say that the son of a chap at his work supported Spurs and wanted to go.

Initially I was a bit dubious as Paul worked as a physical training instructor at a prison, so, 'a chap at his work' could easily have been a murderer or something, but instead it turned out to be a fellow warden and my initial fears were eased.

At the time Derby County weren't the only football club in my life. I was representing a junior football team on Sunday mornings, which coincided with a disastrous period in the club's history and ended with us being bottom-of-the-league, avoiding relegation by the fact that we were already in the lowest division.

Dad didn't have a very high opinion of organised football for that age and didn't like me playing for the side. Uncle Paul had been an aspiring young player but the extent of games that he had been asked to play had injured his growing limbs. By the time he was old enough to think of a professional career his knees were unable to carry his ambitions, and my Dad saw history repeating itself for his son.

That Sunday in December, before Derby took to the Baseball Ground, my other team had a match on the playing fields of a local school. My earlier success at cub football had been knocked out of me when I joined Secondary school and, bored with playing the forward's role I went into defence for a change. This wasn't the smartest move and I spent many a cold morning stood idly on the sidelines waiting for my chance to get onto the pitch. In the dressing room before the match that morning I was preparing myself for the usual substitute's jersey but instead I was handed the number eight shirt and told by our manager that he had run out of ideas. I'd be playing left-wing.

Relieved of being in the usual position in the defence, which consisted of taking it in turns with the rest of the back four to pick the ball out of the back of our own net I took to the position with much enthusiasm.

A third of the way through the second half and already five goals down, our centre-forward made a break through the centre. I ran ahead of him and out towards the wing, trying to drag a defender with me to create space but instead the attacker passed the ball forward for me to run on to and I found myself clean through. With only the goalkeeper to beat and with the ball at my feet I suddenly went blind, in a similar way to when I'd fallen over on ice in the Junior school playground and got concussion a couple of winters before. All I had to guide me was a small pinprick of light in the centre of my blurred vision and the shouts of my teammates and the manager behind me.

I just kept running and from five yards out, with the goalkeeper still trying to make up ground from the centre of the goal, I kicked the ball as hard as I could and hit the post, but luckily it hit the right side of the post and ricocheted in.

Cheers erupted, lifting my blurred vision and I turned to run back to our own half of the pitch not knowing if you were allowed to celebrate a goal when you were five-nil down. My question was soon answered though by the sight of my manic teammates and their attempts at performing cartwheels in the mud.

I was on cloud nine when I got home and had barely gotten into the bath when Uncle Paul arrived. Mum called me from downstairs and so I quickly swept the remnants of mud off my knees and ran back into my room to get changed. Once there though I stood paralysed with horror as I looked on my bed to see that, despite being 12 years old, Mum had already laid out some clothes for me to wear.

The pile resembled the fake Watford scarf I had been given those many years before at Sheffield United, a smorgasbord of blacks, yellows and reds but this time split among jeans, socks and a t-shirt. Before I could think about changing though the shout came again from downstairs for me to hurry up and so I dived into the clothes and ran straight into the car.

Once inside the vehicle brief introductions were made, with me being none too committal to our visitor partly because I was too young to appreciate a conversation with a rival fan and also because I didn't want to be recognised should I meet him on future occasions as the clown who had turned up to a match looking like the lollipop of a school crossing patrol.

As the game was being televised the attendance was even lower than usual and so it was easy to find space on the Pop-Side with many people preferring to watch at home instead of having to brave a cold December afternoon in Derby. When the option was to watch it in front of the fire it was difficult to see why would anyone choose to attend but there is something about actually being there and taking part which overrides any sane and rational thought about comfort, cost and ease of transport.

Inside the Baseball Ground supporters were more interested in where the cameras were, with rogue pieces of scaffold rising from the steps of the Pop-Side upon which television pictures were beamed across the country.

The game kicked off as normal but the crowd's reaction was different, almost theatrical as we all reacted in blind panic whenever the ball came our way, sensing that Andy Warhol had been right and that this really was our 15 minutes of fame. Supporters in the A-Stand, which could make a morgue look like an after-show party at a Primal Scream gig erupted madly whenever the ball left the field in front of them while chants directed straight at rival teams were bellowed into the microphones that stood to attention along the pitch side.

Despite John Gregory scoring a stunning goal, which had commentators purring, 'If a Brazilian had've scored that, they would be showing it around the world!' to those avid fans watching in Glossop, we lost 2–1, and as we trudged disappointed out of the ground I expected to see closing titles burnt onto the clouds of the darkening skies above us.

My earlier optimism had again been overridden by despair. We had been defeated live on television and I knew that the other lads in class who were starting to jump on the football bandwagon that me, Mark Archer and Frankie Middleton had been riding since infant school would be waiting by the school gates the next day, or at least between the rusted poles where the gates used to have been, to roundly take the piss.

*****

The defeat against Tottenham saw us down in 13th and it would take another nine games for Derby to win again. We were making a habit of losing by two goals to one, which saw us slump to 18th and just one point above the automatic relegation places. A draw at Oxford United on 20 February arrested the slide though and ignited a run of six matches without defeat, including a 1—1 draw at home to runaway leaders, Liverpool.

The overly ambitious behaviour of Robert Maxwell was far from finished and in April 1988 the owner made an audacious bid to tempt Dutch legend Johan Cruyff to the Baseball Ground as Technical Director. Manager Arthur Cox, a down-to-earth Geordie who probably thought Holland's Total Football was total bollocks remained nonplussed. Cruyff turned his back on the Rams, undoubtedly with a little trademark pirouette, and went to Barcelona instead.

The season ended with us securing our Division One status in 15th place in the table although we gained just one more point than Chelsea who were relegated. Despite finishing fourth from bottom the London club went down after losing to Middlesbrough in the Play-offs.

Results elsewhere didn't matter to me though. Derby had remained in the top-flight and could enjoy the likes of Liverpool and Manchester United returning to the Baseball Ground the following season. Despite losing twice to Nottingham Forest I could hold my head up high at home as we retained our status after being away for so long.

With another season over I was a teenager, eager to be an adult yet so far from being grown up. Like Tom Hanks racing to become a grown-up in the film *Big* I couldn't help but want to age and take myself to the Baseball Ground. After years waiting for Derby to excel, believing that success would be the catalyst to me and my Dad going to many more games, I was as disappointed with Dad's attendance at the Baseball Ground as Robert Maxwell was with the rest of us.

With the blinkers of a teenage boy I failed to see that my Dad had two other sons and a wife with which to spend time with and spent most of the time juggling between his job as an engineer at Rolls-Royce, our family, and the work he still did voluntarily for the Long Eaton Sunday League. He had also started running half marathons, which added to the pressure on his time. To him, Derby County had to take a back seat, while I wanted to be driving.

Barclays First Division 1987–88

Pos		Pl	W	D	L	F	A	GD	Pts
1	Liverpool	40	26	12	2	87	24	63	90
2	Manchester United	40	23	12	5	71	38	33	81
3	Nottingham Forest	40	20	13	7	67	39	28	73
13	Tottenham Hotspur	40	12	11	17	38	48	-10	47
14	Norwich City	40	12	9	19	40	52	-12	45
15	**Derby County**	**40**	**10**	**13**	**17**	**35**	**45**	**–10**	**43**
16	West Ham United	40	9	15	16	40	52	-12	42
17	Charlton Athletic	40	9	15	16	38	52	-14	42
18	Chelsea	40	9	15	16	50	68	-18	42
19	Portsmouth	40	7	14	19	36	66	-30	35
20	Watford	40	7	11	22	27	51	-24	32
21	Oxford United	40	6	13	21	44	80	-36	31

1988–89

In 1988 I made the step up from being a casual supporter and became a season ticket holder. Despite it only being August, Mum and Dad bought me the cherished gift as an early Christmas present even before Argos had put their in-store decorations up.

The only negative aspect was that the ticket was for the Key Club family enclosure, which in Mum and Dad's eyes would keep me away from the Columbo end of the Pop-Side terrace located nearest to the away following. If trouble was ever to happen the Columbo end was the place it would be but this was also the area containing the most vocal support and I wanted to sing my heart out.

Songs in the Key Club were sparse and predictable and while the foul language of the Pop-Side rarely entered the family enclosure, neither did the humour. The previous season I had been in stitches when Everton came to the Baseball Ground and halfway through the second half, with the visitors on the attack, their goalkeeper, Neville Southall was crouched down on the edge of his area.

The chant went up,

'Southall, have a shit, Southall, Southall have a shit…'

Feeling slightly embarrassed by the attention of a few thousand raucous supporters the Welsh Number One immediately stood up, after which a new chant went up,

'Southall, wipe your arse, Southall, Southall wipe your arse!'

Our opening match of the 1988–89 season was against Middlesbrough and I took my place behind the goal at the Normanton End of the ground, finding it easy to stake my claim on the new terrace largely because I arrived stupidly early. The excitement used to grip me as soon as I woke on those Saturday mornings and I couldn't wait to set off on my way to the ground.

We won that first match by a single goal but then travelled to newly promoted Millwall and lost by the same scoreline. A home game against Newcastle United followed, when a stunning strike by summer signing, Trevor Hebberd, resulted in a 2–0 win and the season was well underway.

Often Dad would have a shift on Saturday mornings at Rolls-Royce and then meet me at the ground, wandering in at five minutes to three and taking a position next to me and right behind the goal. Meanwhile I'd have read the programme from cover to cover, digesting the news, working out where we would rise to in the table if we won and eagerly looking at who we would be playing in the next fixture.

When Dad didn't come along I was content watching the matches alone, shouting out the odd encouraging phrase that I had learnt from him over the course of the previous nine years. Despite my young age I seemed to have a deeper understanding of the game than most, which I had no doubt adopted from the wise head which had accompanied me until now.

After matches that Dad had not attended I'd leap out of the gates at the back of the Normanton End, skirt the ground and run up the lengthy rise of Douglas Street before coasting along the shallow fall back to the train station, eager to get back home with my match report. With the attendance, scorers, and anything else that had made the match memorable I'd burst in through the back door and into the kitchen like Elton Welsby on Red Bull. Finally I'd finish off with how many places we could climb the next game if we won and who we were playing, leaving the sentence hanging in the hope that Dad would say he was coming along.

Nottingham Forest 1 Derby County 1
Saturday 17 September 1988
By 1988 Dad had decided to learn how to drive and having bought an old Mark 1 Ford Escort estate car new opportunities for travel were presented. This was often not as liberating as first imagined though especially for the big games when traffic built up long before kick-off in the streets and roads leading up to the grounds.

So it was when we played away at Nottingham Forest in September 1988, when our progress stumbled to a crawl as soon as we turned off University Boulevard in Nottingham and onto the A52.

England was still clinging to summer and we had driven with the windows down for most of the journey. At first the gentle warming scent of popcorn emanating from the multiplex cinema on our right was pleasant but unfortunately on the other side of the road was Pork Farms sausage-roll factory and so the windows soon had to come up.

Finally we managed to park on Victoria Embankment, which sits beside the River Trent in the vicinity of the City Ground as well as Trent Bridge Cricket Ground and Meadow Lane, the home of Notts County.

With the fixture against our local rivals neither me or my Dad were showing any signs of being from Derby and we slipped inconspicuously among the Forest fans making their way eagerly to the ground who were all hoping for a repeat of last season's two victories against us. These results had urged Ian to start singing, 'Thank you very much for the six points Derby!' to the tune of the advert for Rose's chocolates, which unfortunately for him I had translated as, 'Hey Craig, would you like to kick me in the bollocks?'

Me and my Dad's nerves were soon tested when, ahead, we saw a huge group of supporters milling around and we expected a fight to have begun. This simply turned out to be the Avery pub though, which by this time was a heaving mass of beer-fuelled excitement with chants emanating from the crowd even before they had reached the stadium.

We walked across Trent Bridge, which offered a perfect view of the City Ground to our left and with the huge Executive Stand dwarfing the other smaller stands it seemed that it could quite easily become unbalanced and slip into the river.

As our terrace was on the other side of the stadium we walked along Radcliffe Road and along the back of the cricket ground to get there. More fans congregated outside the Trent Bridge Inn while newsagents sat with their front doors open, full to the brim inside with men buying programmes and special editions of the Nottingham Evening Post. Meanwhile plumes of steam escaped from fryers in the many chip shops and out into the sky through open doors.

In spite of being wary to talk, me and my Dad still managed to hold an excited conversation as we neared the back of the stands, careful not to give our allegiance away but animated in having the other to talk to. At 13 there aren't a great many things you can talk to on a similar level with adults but football was one of those subjects that we could share an opinion, as well as disagreeing on, without me appearing childish.

As we approached the back of the West Bridgford Stand, an open bank of terrace, behind the goal at the opposite end of the ground to the river, split between the two sets of supporters, so we had to break our cover and veered away from the pack that we had been walking with. A few supporters glanced our way, recognising our illicit behaviour, but by that time we were out of earshot to hear the words that were mouthed our way.

Once on the terrace we could feel the hatred spill from the stands around. Venomous chants were carried out of the small, shed-like Trent End opposite and upon the breeze coming off the river as if that body of water itself wanted us to turn back and return home.

The police presence was huge but rather than feeling protected this only added to the sense of foreboding, leaving us thinking that if they needed this many members of the force then we must truly be despised.

It should have been an enjoyable occasion but it soon seemed to turn sour as the atmosphere went beyond hostile. Things weren't any better on the pitch as Derby favourite, Ted McMinn, was singled out by the opposition and systematically fouled. Forest's Stuart Pearce, who had earned the nickname 'Psycho' from the home fans because of his reputation as a tough tackler, furthered his reputation that afternoon. McMinn was accused of diving to earn free kicks when in effect he was just diving out of the way.

Forest scored the opening goal and all around went jubilantly ecstatic. A juggernaut of sound came our way and despite there being a sizeable crowd in the Derby end the sense of loneliness was everywhere.

I was devastated and envisaged Ian's reaction when he got home from his paper round that evening and saw me for the first time. Then I looked up and caught my Dad's glance.

'I'm gutted Craigy!' he said, 'We've been robbed.'

With those words the air of defeat lifted and I no longer felt the burden of having conceded that goal. Dad was always the first person to recognise and applaud the better team and so when it came to him speaking highly of our own I knew to trust his word. Derby weren't second best after all. And we weren't finished either.

With time in the match running out the ball came to the edge of the area from the right hand side of the pitch, falling kindly to Trevor Hebberd who had scored that magnificent goal a week earlier. He brought the ball down to his feet, took one look at the goal and buried it into the back of the net before the goalkeeper even saw it.

This was our time to shout jubilantly and our own terrace jumped around like a box-load of power-balls falling down stairs. It was enough to earn us a point and furthermore restore one more piece of pride in a team and its supporters who had been through such ignominy in recent times.

After the final whistle we were hemmed into the ground for the usual 15 minutes, which the police insisted was to allow home supporters to disperse but which actually gave them more time to set up traps. The time didn't matter though as we directed our songs back towards the ground, its exiting supporters and towards the river that had never wanted us in the first place.

*****

In October 1988 Derby signed their first £1 million player, Dean Saunders, from Oxford United. Oxford were 12th in Division Two at the time and saw Saunders as the foil that would see them promoted to the top-flight but with Oxford's chairman being Kevin Maxwell, Robert Maxwell's son, a deal was done regardless to take the Welshman away from the Manor Ground. The Oxford manager, Mark Lawrenson, was far from impressed and was later sacked after airing his grievances in public. He would later get his own back on Derby by constantly slating the team as a pundit on Match of the Day.

Saunders' success was as instant as Kenco, scoring twice in his first game, a 4–1 rout of Wimbledon, and scoring a further 15 in 30 games that season. He excited the crowd with electric place and his permed hair, which was reminiscent of football legend Kevin Keegan on a good day but singing legend Cher on a bad one. His goals were to turn Derby County from a team making up the numbers in the top-flight to one that was to become a real force in the first division.

In the League we were flying although in the FA Cup we were knocked out in the second round by Watford, who were now back down in Division Two. We subsequently missed out on the bizarre sight on the terraces that year when people started taking inflatable objects to football matches.

The craze had started at Manchester City the season before when a fan decided to take a five foot inflatable banana along to a match for a laugh. This behaviour soon spread to other supporters, especially in the FA Cup, and that season's *Match of the Day* was as entertaining for what was going on in the stands as it was for the football on the pitch. Grimsby had inflatable fish and West Ham inflatable hammers, while there was a rumour at the time that it was Derby who had actually started the craze at their last FA Cup Final appearance in 1946, but in fact those inflatables had been Zeppelins.

The world seemed to be turning on its head. In 1989 the Berlin Wall separating East and West Germany was demolished, signifying a thawing of the Cold War and forcing Pink Floyd to find something else to sing about. Meanwhile Derby finished the 1988–89 season in fifth place, beating eventual champions Arsenal both home and away en route to the club's highest finish since they ended the 1975–76 season in fourth. We were now among the country's elite and even though the television concentrated their coverage of the 'Big Five' of Arsenal, Liverpool, Tottenham, Everton and Manchester United, who finished first, second, sixth, eighth and eleventh, I now had every right to hold my head high at school.

At this time though English clubs had an indefinite ban from competing in European competitions after the rioting among supporters of Liverpool and Juventus before the 1985 European Cup Final. Therefore we missed out on a place in the UEFA Cup that could have heightened the club's profile across the continent and maybe seen potential investors buy the club from Chairman Robert Maxwell, who had obviously lost interest in Derby County.

Despite the lack of further investment though these were good times to be supporting the club. My own experiences were matching those of the past and great players were now coming to the Baseball Ground on merit along with the best teams in the world. Meanwhile on the Baseball Ground pitch we had our own great players to support and had at long last drew parity with Ian's Nottingham Forest. All I needed now was to see my Derby County reach the same level as that which my Dad had been privileged to support.

Barclays First Division 1988–89

Pos		Pl	W	D	L	F	A	GD	Pts
1	Arsenal	38	22	10	6	73	28	37	76
2	Liverpool	38	22	10	6	65	28	37	76
3	Nottingham Forest	38	17	13	8	64	43	21	64
4	Norwich City	38	17	11	10	48	45	3	62
5	**Derby County**	**38**	**17**	**7**	**14**	**40**	**38**	**2**	**58**
6	Tottenham Hotspur	38	15	12	11	60	46	14	57
7	Coventry City	38	14	13	11	47	42	5	55

1989–90

By the time the 1989–90 season kicked-off football was still coming to terms with the events at Sheffield Wednesday's Hillsborough football stadium the previous April. Ninety-Six Liverpool fans had lost their lives during the semi-final of the FA Cup against Nottingham Forest when overcrowding on the terraces had turned into tragedy.

Over the following seasons the football experience would be significantly altered although the progress would be slow. Fences surrounding the pitches at most grounds came down almost overnight, or the following day for those clubs who couldn't afford to pay overtime, and despite the Taylor Report which was published in 1990 in the wake of the tragedy stating that standing areas were not intrinsically unsafe, the Government still decreed that stadia in the top two divisions would have to be all-seated arenas by the start of the 1994–95 season.

Clubs began to change their grounds in earnest with the most notable being the redevelopment of Arsenal's Highbury Stadium. The North Bank was demolished at the end of the 1991–92 season and while under construction a huge mural of a stand full of supporters was put in place to detract players and fans from the void. The club were criticised when it turned out that none of the people painted were of an ethnic minority background while further inconsistencies were that crowd noise was piped from speakers from the end which was notoriously quiet.

That season I took my place on the terrace behind the Normanton End goal of the Baseball Ground once again, assuring Mum that the Key Club was a safe place to be and that nothing was going to happen to me. Dad was still meeting me at the ground for occasional games but mostly I found that I was now going with friends from school.

I knew James England, the lad who had scored the own goal in the cub's Cup Final, through cubs and then scouts and got to know him better when I moved up to Secondary school. Another lad who started coming along, David Scarsdale, was in most of my lessons at school due to the fact that our surnames were close on the register. Mark Archer and I had remained friends right from Infant school but Frankie and his bogey now seemed to move in different circles.

In 1989 other topics soon began invading our lives apart from football. Tanks rolled into Tienenman Square in China to silence protesting students, and when *John's Not Mad*, a documentary which first highlighted Tourettes Syndrome was shown on television, nobody at school talked about anything other than the boy who constantly swore and spat fish pie at his mum.

At the cinema a new film about an old hero, *Batman*, was released and with it came a new rating of Certificate 12. Elsewhere Robin Williams starred in *Dead Poets' Society* and Daniel Day-Lewis's left foot became what would be Ireland's most recognisable limb until Thierry Henry's left hand usurped it in a World Cup Qualifying match 20 years later, using it to keep the ball in play before setting up Wiliam Gallas to score and ensure France went to the Finals and not the Irish.

Football was increasingly taking a backseat in our home as well. After surprising myself by finishing fourth in a recent cross-country organised by the scouts I had started taking part in fun-runs that accompanied the half-marathon races that Dad was running on Sunday mornings. When Mum started running too the car adopted the look of the storeroom at Mayfield Sports as an array of shorts, vests, tracksters and various training shoes littered the boot as we trundled off in the small hours.

Whereas it used to be just me and Dad who went to the Baseball Ground on Saturday afternoons, Mum, Ian and Daniel crammed into our Ford Escort like some modern-day equivalent of the Waltons, spending Sunday mornings at random towns and cities across the country that were dictated to us by the running events calendar. In the past me and my Dad had been impelled to travel to places like Oldham and Sheffield at the whim of the football fixtures whereas now we found ourselves in Lincoln, Bolsover and Worksop, hurtling through the streets by foot while the rest of the country woke up from their Saturday night slumber.

Dad was easy to spot among the hoards of other runners as they headed away from the start, en masse, to scare the living bejeezus out of early morning dog-walkers who were out for a relaxing morning stroll and late-night revellers who were taking the walk of shame. Having joined a local running club, who met at nearby Sandiacre, he wore their colours of bright yellow with black and red stripes.

If it is possible to be haunted by a colour combination then that yellow, black and red ensemble was certainly mine. Compared to the running club jumper at the time that me, Ian and Daniel all received as a Christmas present one year, the faux-Watford scarf I had been given to wear on that memorable afternoon in Sheffield almost four years before was the height of fashion. Since then I had endured the ignominy of having my Mum dress me as such against Tottenham Hotspur live on television and then spend repeated Sunday mornings dashing the length of some dormant High Street with my two brothers like a small busload of misplaced German tourists.

Derby County 6 Manchester City 0

Saturday 11 November 1989

Derby had started the 1989–90 season poorly and had only won three of their 12 League games by the time Manchester City came to the Baseball Ground on 11 November. A 1–0 defeat at Luton the previous week saw us in 17th position, with the same points as Wimbledon who sat uncomfortably inside the relegation zone along with Queen's Park Rangers and Sheffield Wednesday.

As usual that day I walked to the ground alone, nipping in to the newsagent opposite the train station in Long Eaton first to get some herbal sweets, with it nearly being winter, before boarding the usual train to Derby. Once out of the station I fed discreetly in among the few other fans heading to the ground who were also either too eager to leave it any later or arriving from towns and villages with nothing much to do on a Saturday morning.

By catching the train there was always the possibility of running into rival gangs of football supporters although by arriving so early I often avoided fans from both sides. There were a few regular faces on the platform at Long Eaton though, all with their own rituals and ways of walking to the ground but mostly it was a solitary stroll as I led the way for all to follow on my Saturday afternoons.

Alone and in the silence I could fully immerse myself in the prospects of the match to come and as I walked my imagination ran away from me, forming premonitions of the team taking to the field, asking myself who would represent us that day and the odds of a win. In my own world my feet would retrace the steps that me and my Dad had taken so many times before, never veering from the pilgrimage we had made for a decade. I crossed the roads in the same places, passed the same buildings and felt the same sense of awe when turning the corner from Douglas Street onto Cambridge Street and seeing the stadium in front of me.

Despite our lowly position that afternoon I still felt excited walking along the rear of the A, B and C Stand to access the turnstiles. The scarcity of a crowd on the roads leading to the Baseball Ground soon changed once I reached the stadium, where there was always a flurry of activity with programme sellers setting out their pitches, chip shops stoking their fryers and early birds bursting through the pub doors of the Baseball Hotel, the pub which used to stand proudly on the corner of Shaftsbury Crescent and Vulcan Street opposite where the A, B and C Stand met the Normanton End.

In addition to the programme sellers that day was a woman selling a new Derby County fanzine. These magazines were already popular among most clubs and, written by the supporters, they represented an alternative view of the team that was given in the official programme. They were often photocopied badly, probably at the expense of whichever local business the editor worked at and stapled by hand. What they lacked in style was certainly made up for in substance though and it was largely accepted that they would print anything that was sent in, which was often better than, 'Housewife from Duffield dyes her hair blue and white!', which was on offer in the Ram Magazine.

As well as entertaining, the fanzines were written as a backlash against the way football supporters were being viewed in the wake of Hillsborough and Heysel, allowing the more educated and creative fans to demonstrate that they didn't all fit the mould portrayed by the Daily Mail. And because these alternative magazines were often produced in protest at the way clubs were being run and also had the possibility of diverting supporters' money away from the traditional programme, they were largely frowned upon by the clubs but this only added to their appeal.

Ian had often returned from the City Ground with a copy of *The Tricky Tree*, half of which was made up of articles about Forest and the other 50 percent making derogatory remarks about Derby. Our own fanzine, *The Sheep*, cost 50 pence and started with the front page headline, 'Maxwell, we'd rather have Max Wall!'

The Sheep offered something else for me to read in the hour's build up to the match as I stood soaking up the atmosphere in the stadium while the crowd slowly grew around me. At half-past two the silence was punctuated by a ripple of applause greeting the emergence of the odd player running out to warm-up but really that was all. There was no reason for me to be there that early but I was happy to guarantee my spot right behind the goal and halfway back along the terrace, the bottom of which was about four feet below the playing surface.

Manchester City had not had their best start to a season and were just two points and three places ahead of the Rams. The closeness in the table pointed to a draw or slender victory at most but in the end we ran out winners by six goals to nil. Our low League position had suggested we were a poor team but that season we just seemed to be waiting to get started and with this catalyst the supporters left the ground assured that this was exactly what the team had needed to get them going.

We were proven right as this result sparked a run of six wins, conceding just one goal and by December we were up into sixth position. Relative disaster soon struck though as influential players, Ted McMinn and Gary Micklewhite, suffered serious injuries leaving us short in a squad lacking in depth due to Maxwell's underinvestment. The crisis deepened when striker Paul Goddard, who had developed a fantastic partnership up front with Dean Saunders, was sold to Millwall for £800,000 in December. Goddard had always maintained a desire to play in

London and when the Lions came in with what was considered an acceptable offer, manager Arthur Cox felt obliged not to stand in the player's way.

A run of seven matches without a win, starting in March, turned our attention from the top half of the table towards the bottom and alarmingly we finished in 16th position, ending the 1989–90 season just three points from safety.

Barclays First Division 1989–90

Pos		Pl	W	D	L	F	A	GD	Pts
1	Liverpool	38	23	10	5	78	37	41	79
2	Aston Villa	38	21	7	10	57	38	19	70
3	Tottenham Hotspur	38	19	6	13	59	47	12	63
13	Manchester United	38	13	9	16	46	47	-1	48
14	Manchester City	38	12	12	14	43	52	-9	48
15	Crystal Palace	38	13	9	16	42	66	-24	48
16	**Derby County**	**38**	**13**	**7**	**18**	**43**	**40**	**3**	**46**
17	Luton Town	38	10	13	15	43	57	-14	43
18	Sheffield Wednesday	38	11	10	17	35	51	-16	43
19	Charlton Athletic	38	7	9	22	31	57	-26	30
20	Millwall	38	5	11	22	39	65	-26	26

1990–91

By the time the 1990–91 season dawned my parents had upgraded me from the Key Club to a season ticket for the Pop-Side. Being out of the strictly members area meant that I could start going along to matches with James, Mark and David, as well as a few girls from school. At 15 years old I had long-since forgotten the sight of that quivering woman at Boundary Park and had yet to discover how to show the ladies a good time.

After years of scaring the media and local folk who lived around the stadia, football in England was enjoying a renaissance, which has largely remained ever since. The widespread redevelopment of grounds to replace the terraces in light of the Taylor Report was finally getting underway and new stands meant improved facilities in place of the crumbling structures that supporters had called home since before World War Two.

In the past new facilities would have been to the detriment of the playing squad but the hugely inflated royalties from the new television deals meant that clubs could make improvements both on and off the pitch.

Despite the television income the gradual change from standing areas to seating meant that prices still rose for most fans. One consolation though was that the hooligans who had blighted the sport for decades were priced out and instead they started taking ecstasy in clubs and chilled-out a bit. It would be many seasons before the devaluing of the Football League Cup made clubs reduce ticket prices to about £10 for games, therefore allowing the hooligans back inside the grounds to re-enact the battles of yesteryear.

On the international stage the England football team enjoyed a successful World Cup in the summer of 1990, reaching the semi-finals only to be knocked out of the competition on penalties, which is often considered to be 'the cruellest way' by those who have never witnessed Phil Babb's attempt to defend a goal-bound shot on a wet Anfield pitch.

Terry Butcher had already ignited the passions of England's male population by emerging from the qualifying game against Sweden with blood oozing from a wound to his head. Despite being stitched and bandaged Butcher continued to head the ball throughout the match resulting in a hero's performance that the common supporter dreams about, although manager Bobby Robson had to concede that he was exaggerating when he'd told the media that the defender deserved a Victoria Cross for his contribution.

By the end of the tournament we were also treated to the softer side of the game as Paul Gascoigne's tears flowed as easily as the yellow card from referee, José Roberto White's pocket. Gazza's second booking of the tournament meant that he would be banned from playing in the Final although misses by both Stuart Pearce and Chris Waddle in the penalty shoot-out meant that the rest of us would too. The tragedy was heartbreaking but from out of that wonderful misfortune came happiness at what was the Beautiful Game's extreme makeover.

Despite Derby finishing in 16th place the season before both Peter Shilton and Mark Wright maintained their places in the England side and catapulted Derby County as a global brand and a fashionable team to support. We were riding on English football's new found popularity and suddenly going to a match was no longer a dirty pastime.

Unfortunately the bug failed to grip my Dad and he was coming to fewer games than he had done before. Maybe he didn't think I'd want him along if my mates were there but the truth was that I would have been more than happy for him to come with us. The matches that he did attend were all the better for his presence as he offered a sensible opinion instead of the blinkered partisan nonsense that me and my friends gave. Most of the time there was a core group of about six of us though who stood either side of me on the terraces where I always used to stand with my Dad.

Derby County 1 Sheffield United 1
Wednesday 29 August 1990

Our first home match of the 1990–91 season was a midweek game against Sheffield United. Despite spending the last two seasons at the Normanton End I found it easy to become immersed back into the tide that seemed to sweep me all the way from Long Eaton and straight onto the Pop-Side.

It was summer but still the cold of the concrete seeped into our feet as we waited for the teams to emerge from the tunnel opposite, just as it had done on so many occasions before. I had the same view as when me, my Dad and Uncle Paul had stood to watch that FA Cup semi-final place slip away so ingloriously against Plymouth Argyle years before.

Derby opened well and as full-time beckoned we were ahead. Things were looking bright beneath the Baseball Ground floodlights but someone had not read the script. United gained a late equaliser and the evening was ruined.

Three days later we were back, at a different time but at the same location having chosen our spot, although in reality I think I had arrived there more out of instinct than from any conscious decision. Like birds flying south or migrating salmon I wandered without thought and ended up rooted to those steps. The fact that Derby were failing on the pitch meant that it was easy for us to maintain our place on the terrace. On 1 September only 12,469 supporters turned up to our second home match against Wimbledon. We had yet to win and the opposition were far from attractive, and as Robert Maxwell had put the club up for sale in the summer people were reluctant to see their cash bypassing their club and going straight into his pockets.

Over the coming season we would regularly see the same faces of people who we knew but only by association with the club. Their customs were as repetitive as our own and it soon became a game of ours to predict what they would do.

Close to us a father regularly attended with his son, who was probably the same age as me, and at half-time they would immediately sit down on the terrace only to stand up when the crowd applauded to announce the re-emergence of the team. On one occasion we all looked at each other and just knew what we were going to do. With still five minutes of half-time remaining the six of us turned towards the pitch and applauded enthusiastically. Sure enough the guy and his lad stood up for what they thought was the second half and looked around bewildered when it wasn't.

Maybe that was what my Dad wanted to avoid. Maybe he thought that dads with 15-year-old kids no longer went to the match with them, or maybe this was the time when I should have been asking him whether he wanted to go to the match rather than waiting for him to fill me with excitement by telling me he wanted to go along.

It was either that or the fact that Dad wasn't as blinkered as I was. I had spent so long wanting Derby to return to the top division that I hadn't envisaged what a cruel place it could be. That season we had to wait until 27 October to see our team's first win, which came 139 miles away at Southampton.

November was a better month with defeat over Luton Town and sweet victory against Nottingham Forest, combined with holding Manchester United to a goalless draw that had us believing that a corner had been turned, but then on Saturday 15 December Chelsea turned up at the Baseball Ground.

The game looked all but over at half-time with the Rams 3–1 down but we fought back to take a 4–3 lead with only 12 minutes to go. Chelsea weren't finished though and the match ended in a crushing 4–6 reverse, denting the confidence of an already fragile Derby team and their supporters.

Sheffield United 1 Derby County 0

Saturday 26 January 1991

Some away matches are special but others are obligatory. Sheffield United at Bramall Lane falls into the latter category and so when Derby travelled north in January of 1991 so did we. James, Mark, David and I met at Long Eaton train station early on Saturday 26 January, bought our tickets and then waited for the train like the cast of *Stand by Me*.

My impatience must have been contagious as we arrived into the city of Sheffield for the three o'clock kick-off at about half past 11. With the stadium within walking distance we headed out of the station and stopped off at a greasy café where they drowned our chip butties with ketchup.

By half-past 12 we arrived at the ground but the turnstiles had yet to open. Still too young for pubs we wandered around a roundabout and brought chocolate and Lucozade from a petrol station, for want of anything better to do, and by one o'clock assumed that the gates would be open and so headed back to Bramall Lane.

Inside we were the only ones on the terraces and so took a place directly behind the goal. It was like being back on the playground at Infant school, wondering whether we were first there or whether we were late and everyone else had gone inside.

Memories came flooding back of my previous visits with Dad, standing side by side beneath the floodlights at the edge of the terrace, rejoicing after that FA Cup win which seemed to signal our rise from the ashes and that victory in the League a year later which seemed to cement our return to the Big Time.

I remembered how concerned I was after Plymouth Argyle had unceremoniously knocked us out of the FA Cup at the quarter-final stage and how I thought that days coming to watch Derby County with my Dad would come to an end. And I thought of the victory against that very same club which meant we were better than anyone else in Division Two and could maybe become a force in Division One, which quashed those earlier fears.

I wondered what had happened to me and my Dad but the answer was right in front of me. It wasn't what was on the pitch that mattered but what we did off it.

I had always questioned how Dad could watch his team, our team, play out of the top-flight after he had seen us champions of it twice, wondering how teams from Leyton could ever compare to teams from Liverpool. What I'd failed to recognise was that we shared a love for the club and that it didn't matter who we played or who ran out onto the turf in that famous white shirt, it was still Derby County. The only thing that had stopped him coming was that somewhere along the line the relationship between father and son had changed.

Adolescence is a terrible time for both those children desperate to grow up and for their parents who don't know whether to treat their kids as children or behave as if they are young adults. As the other three lads kicked an empty bottle of pop among themselves I tried to imagine what Dad would get out of coming to watch Derby with me now. He always seemed to be so busy running from one job to the next whereas I was happy to spend hours wandering around city centres waiting for the turnstiles to open.

Football grounds are magnificent places when full but when nobody is there then the emptiness echoes aggressively. I looked around at the empty Bramall Lane stands and the isolation choked me. All of a sudden I no longer wanted to be there, wandering around with nothing to do but eat chocolate, circumnavigate roundabouts and lick tomato ketchup off my fingers. I wanted a conversation about the match, and one that went further than people agreeing with me that the referee was biased and that the linesman was crap. I had no option though and so walked gingerly to the others instead and sat down for the next two hours.

After a few minutes the public address system kicked into life so at least, we thought, we would have some music to take us through until kick-off. Mark Archer was heavily into the Manchester bands like the Happy Mondays and the Farm, while me and James England had just discovered Depeche Mode. David Scarsdale preferred the Beautiful South, which prompted us to go up to him endless times and aggressively shout, 'You know your problem?' before patting him on the back and adding, 'you keep it all in.' Our hearts sank, however, when the stadium announcer proceeded to tell us that Sheffield United always had a featured artist and for that day's game it was the legendary Roy Orbison.

Roy Orbison has a few catchy numbers in his discography but not what you would fill over 100 minutes with and so we sat through the best of, and possibly the worst of, the singer's collection that afternoon. In spite of this and my earlier despondency, our excitement slowly built towards kick-off and with half an hour to go we stood up again to see our perfect view directly behind the goal. Only people who arrived at games as early as we had could secure such great positions, I thought, but with 10 minutes to go a familiar voice came from directly behind me.

'Hi Craigy!' It was my Dad, with my Uncle Paul.

'I didn't know you were coming?' I asked, unable to hide my pleasure at seeing him there.

'Paul turned up at about two o'clock and asked me if I wanted to come.' Dad explained, before tapping James on the shoulder and adding, 'Score any own-goals lately?'

Two o'clock was about the time we were being subjected to *Only the Lonely* but all that was lost in my happiness that my Dad was there. I should have told him that I was pleased to see him but 15-year-olds don't say stuff like that to their fathers.

Dad said he was sure that there were a million worse singers than Roy Orbison, he just couldn't name one, which made us and most of those around us collapse into fits of laughter. The match had yet to kick-off but already it was becoming folklore, what with the subjection of our ears to Roy Orbison and my Dad and Uncle Paul turning up with 10 minutes to go. It was one of those games that we would trade like Top Trumps cards whenever we recalled our Derby County experiences on many a later date.

*****

The ban on English teams playing in European competitions was eventually lifted in 1990 but by the end of the 1990–91 season, with the club still not yet sold, Derby County had slumped. A token protest against Tottenham Hotspur in January in front of the television cameras was seen and heard but not reacted to and afterwards banners like the one which read, 'Fat cheques, not fat Czechs' littered the Baseball Ground pitch but simply blew away with the rest of the litter.

In March 1991 we had a German exchange visit at school and so I took my pen-friend to see Derby play Liverpool at the Baseball Ground. The Reds annihilated us by seven goals to one, after which Matthias asked, 'What has happened to Derby, Craig, I thought they were good?'

What with Germany beating England at the semi-final stage of the World Cup the previous summer that boy was walking a fine line.

Derby were relegated that season on Saturday 20 April at Maine Road. Manchester City forward, Niall Quinn, opened the scoring but Derby were then given a lifeline when the Rams were given a penalty, with City goalkeeper, Tony Coton, sent off in the process. City's scorer, Niall Quinn, replaced the absent keeper and in a scenario that even the writers of Roy of the Rovers had yet to come up with the Irishman subsequently saved the penalty.

After our initial excitement built up from the previous summer of football it was a dreadful season in which Derby went from 1 December until 4 May without winning a single League game. At one stage supporters actually chanted, 'Let's pretend we've scored a goal.' before breaking out into mock celebration. This despite scoring 25 goals at the Baseball Ground, which was only one shy of Everton's total at Goodison Park who finished the season in ninth place.

A return to Division Two saw the team break up in a similar manner to how the countries of the old USSR were jumping ship. England defender, Mark Wright, went to Liverpool for £2.3 million, swiftly followed by striker Dean Saunders for £2.9 million, which was a domestic transfer record at the time. The chances of the club benefitting with these sales with Maxwell holding the purse-strings though was negligible and instead the club had to use the money to buy him out.

It was easy to be infuriated by Maxwell's antics and I would often give angry outbursts about the man's actions. Dad was always on hand to calm me down though citing the fact that when Stuart Web brought Maxwell into the club in 1984 nobody else was interested and that he'd actually saved the club from those winding up orders from the Inland Revenue and Customs and Excise. As ever, Dad was a sobering voice to my mad adolescent rants.

Barclays First Division 1990–91

Pos		Pl	W	D	L	F	A	GD	Pts
1	Arsenal*	38	24	13	1	74	18	56	83
2	Liverpool	38	23	7	8	77	40	37	76
3	Crystal Palace	38	20	9	9	50	41	9	69
18	Luton Town	38	10	7	21	42	61	-19	37
19	Sunderland	38	8	10	20	38	60	-22	34
20	**Derby County**	**38**	**5**	**9**	**24**	**37**	**75**	**-38**	**24**

two points deducted

1991–92

The fixture computer was kind to us on our opening game back in Division Two and drew Derby to play Sunderland at Roker Park. It wasn't that Sunderland were crap, despite them being one of only two teams we beat on our travels the previous season, but more like by replicating the top-flight at least we could dream we were still in Division One.

We drew the match 1–1 and followed this up with a 2–0 win at home against Middlesbrough with things suddenly not seeming so bad. I had called Radio Derby's phone-in programme, which quickly became known among supporters as the Monday Night Moan-In, towards the end of the previous season to express my view that I would rather see Derby in the second division and winning as opposed to losing in Division One. The show's presenter, Colin Gibson, replied that Division One was on the world stage though and we should strive to be there but my response was that all the world was seeing was Derby County losing week after week.

Derby County 1 Southend United 2
Saturday 24 August 1991

On Saturday 24 August we were brought back down to earth when Southend United visited the Baseball Ground. The previous season had given the Pop-Side a dark sense of humour that had failed to lighten and as the Shrimpers were sponsored by Hi-Tec we spent most of the second-half chanting, 'Cheap and nasty trainers', to the tune of the *Conga*. In return they beat us 2–1.

Derby were still too easy to play against and by Christmas we had already lost five games at home. It was not the sort of form that would see an immediate return to the top-flight even though we had vehemently declared from the terraces the previous year that we would be back in '92.

It wasn't just Derby County who were in unfamiliar surroundings. After five years attending the town's Secondary school I decided to move away from its sixth form and instead travelled to a local college in Heanor to study my A-Levels. In doing so I lost touch with a great number of friends, although watching Derby meant that at least I remained in touch with those who I went to matches with.

Educationally I was just going through the motions to get me to university, neither trying particularly hard nor slacking and the resulting three grade Es were evidence of this apathy. While Derby County remained of paramount importance my own wellbeing concerned me very little.

Robert Maxwell had been bought out of the club in time for the start of the new campaign and as supporters we could approach the future with some kind of hope. By November that hope was being transformed into expectation as local businessman, Lionel Pickering, became the majority shareholder at the club. Pickering soon went to work on developing the team, which had seen such little improvement over the preceding few years.

Burnley 2 Derby County 2

Saturday 4 January 1992

The third round of the FA Cup always offered a change from the monotony of a humdrum season in the League and so, four days into Queen Elizabeth II's annus horribilis, Derby were awarded a trip to fourth division Burnley.

I was ecstatic when the draw was made and Dad asked if I wanted to go. I didn't know where Burnley was and as Dad's response when asked was, 'I don't know, somewhere near Oldham,' suddenly visions of travel-sickness and driving through clouds shrouded the prospect. Still, away games were always appealing and so me and my Dad travelled to the North West, along with my younger brother, Daniel, who was now 10 years old, and James England.

We arrived in Lancashire at around quarter to three and having managed to find a space to park the car at the bottom of a side-street we raced towards the ground. Despite the importance of the game and the fact that it was the FA Cup the streets were relatively empty and it was easy for us to get to the entrance at the back of the stand.

Burnley had spent the last seven seasons in the fourth division and had almost gone out of the League completely in 1987, having to rely on a win against Orient on the last game of the season to survive. Most of their history had seen them entertaining teams in the top two flights though and along with Derby County they had been founder members of the Football League. They remained one of only three teams to have won the title of all four domestic divisions.

The Derby fans were housed on a massive terrace that ran along one side of Turf Moor pitch which, based on the fact that we had an allocation of 4,000 people and only filled a third of it, must have held 12,000 supporters. The Burnley faithful, plus those who had only come because it was Derby, watched from their own end at the other edge of the terrace with as much of a gap in between for segregation.

Having arrived late we entered the terrace to be met by a wall of people, which was probably why we had found nobody outside the ground. There was no room to wander through and no gaps in the terrace to walk anywhere else and so all we could do was merge into the crowd and gradually find a place to stand and get a glimpse of the game. Dad had his own idea though and wanting to get Daniel a better view set off to find somewhere else. I didn't want to go with him, thinking there'd be no way he'd get anywhere better than where we were and so he told James and I that he'd see us back at the car.

I was forgetting that this was the man who had gotten me and him into the seats to see Kevin Keegan when the Baseball Ground had sold-out and the man who had made me mascot for the second time on my birthday at an away fixture in Oldham. This was also the man who had ensured we saw a top-of-the-table clash against Portsmouth when outside the queue had stretched back from the stadium and into the streets of Derby.

After about 20 minutes the match entered a particularly slow passage of play when James loudly lamented, 'I don't fuckin' believe it!' Thinking we were about to make an unwarranted substitution or that a star player was limping I looked at him with curiosity. He just pointed right the way to the bottom of the terrace, over the heads of 4,000 Derby fans crammed onto that terrace and to the perimeter fencing that, at Turf Moor, had yet to be taken down. There, clinging to the fence with a perfect view of the game was the unmistakable little silhouette of our Daniel.

The match finished in a two-all draw and so we didn't hang around to applaud the team from the field. Instead James and I headed back to the car while trying to avoid the few skirmishes outside. It was like we'd taken a 10-year step back into the early 80s and after one Derby fan had his hat stolen I instinctively held tighter onto the scarf that Dad had given me almost a decade before.

When Dad and Daniel arrived back at the car, via a chip shop where they served hot porkpies, Daniel was beaming after getting so close to the action. Dad's excitement was infectious and it seemed to have seeped into Daniel as much as it had into me. For some reason though it failed to stick with my younger brother and he later turned his attention to supporting Liverpool. He still retained a soft spot for Derby though, adopted in no small part to that afternoon stuck on the fence at Burnley.

The following replay at the Baseball Ground saw Derby take a comfortable lead and we looked like we were heading into the fourth round. During the second half though thick fog rolled in over the stands like dry-ice at a Shakespeare's Sister concert and made the game unplayable. The match was abandoned and eventually replayed on Saturday 25 January, when 18,374 fans were there, including the many Burnley fans who had made the journey and took the whole three tiers of the Osmaston End with the top tier usually reserved for home supporters.

Derby ran out 2–0 winners but the match will be remembered for the constant backing by the claret and blue army who sang constantly for the entire second half. The catalyst came when the visiting goalkeeper went to retrieve the ball from behind the goal and, looking up at the fans who had made the journey south once again, he motioned with his hand to raise the volume. In return they responded as if Bono himself had stuck a microphone in their direction for a chorus of *With or Without You* and no Derby fan at the Baseball Ground that afternoon could begrudge them when they ended the season at the top of the fourth division.

*****

An incredible fourth round match at home to top-flight Aston Villa ended with the visitors winning by four goals to three, despite one of the best goals ever seen at the Baseball Ground by Derby's Paul Williams. The prospect of welcoming Division One opposition was daunting after the previous year but we had learned lessons from those travelling Burnley fans and the atmosphere in the stands exploded onto the pitch.

A couple of defeats after the Villa game threatened to put us into a rut although the two losses didn't affect our League position. We remained in 11th but we were losing ground on those teams in the Play-offs. The season then ignited with four wins and a draw in the next five games, catapulting us up to fourth. Three losses out of the next four saw us drop back to eighth but with eight games remaining we were unbeaten in the next six.

The reason for the change in form was obvious. At this time Derby were the big spenders in the division and trying to claw our way back into the top-flight. Money was always important in football but with the advent of the Premier League and its realisation that it could be a real bargaining tool with television companies the rewards for achievement were not just glorious but financial.

Lionel Pickering's cash may now seem minimal but at the time Derby County were grabbing all the column inches across the footballing world. Marco Gabbiadini had come from Crystal Palace in a Lamborghini, according to one of the chants on the Pop-Side, for £1 million in January while February saw Paul

Simpson arrive at a bargain £500,000 from Oxford United. In March we welcomed Tommy Johnson from Notts County for £1.375 million, as well as Paul Kitson from Leicester City in return for Ian Ormondroyd, Phil Gee and £800,000. Despite Kitson being dubbed 'the New Gary Lineker' though he was just one of the players who failed to live up to the hype and never went on to play for England nor advertise crisps on the television.

Bristol City 1 Derby County 2

Saturday 25 April 1992

With two matches of the season left Derby were in third position in the League, although we had played at least one game more than everyone else around us. We were just two points behind Leicester City in the second automatic promotion spot but only five points ahead of Charlton Athletic in seventh who had two games in hand over us.

The away match at Bristol City on 25 April was one of those games that calls to all supporters and invokes images of volunteers in tiny fishing villages running to the lifeboats to support stricken vessels. In Derby, men, women and children dropped what they were doing that day and all headed to Bristol.

Dad may have been keeping his distance from the Baseball Ground but away matches always proved a great attraction. Two weeks before Derby had played Oxford at home and I was beaming when he'd asked me if I could stay behind and get tickets for the trip to the South West.

We drew the Oxford match 2–2, which were to be the only points dropped in the last seven games and I walked away from the Pop-Side in the direction of the ticket office. My mates didn't stay with me but I was only too happy to wait on my own in the queue on Shaftsbury Crescent. It was the same spot where me and my Dad had queued for seat tickets to watch Kevin Keegan play and I was almost living the memory.

As the crowds disappeared into the evening all that remained was that slim slither of people waiting patiently to enter the tiny ticket office, while around us it was just the essence of the club that hung in the heavy spring air.

I looked up at the brick exterior of the Baseball Ground, which stood majestically waiting for the crowd to return. In truth it was an ugly building but the club's history leant it a beauty that was all too appealing. Despite its patchwork of additions it remained the backdrop of many famous photographs and its tiers contained the hope and excitement of countless victories and the despair of many defeats. As those final, fleeting supporters drifted around the corner and away they seemed to take the memories of the match with them but also left a little behind for the old stadium to keep for herself.

Unlike when Kevin Keegan had entertained us the club hadn't ran out of tickets by the time I reached the counter. I placed them in my pocket and then kept my hand on them all the way back to the train station as I wandered back alone.

Without the usual crowds the streets took on a desolate, empty feel. Their normality cried out for something more, like an aged supermodel after one last contract, as if they knew their place in history and how they imprinted their image onto those who travelled here to watch their football. Children peered out of the windows of the terraced houses, checking that the crowds had gone while shopkeepers pulled their advertising boards inside and red traffic lights signalled for nobody to stop.

As I walked along those empty streets I felt like the last one at the party. The person left hanging around after the music has stopped. The streets were heaving a sigh of relief and I hadn't realised until that moment the effect that we, the supporters, had on this community.

The Normanton streets were never a community to me, just an atlas of roads that took me to the Baseball Ground. I didn't know there were schools and a library and that the pubs opened throughout the week and not just on Saturday afternoons or Wednesday nights. The only times I had been there I had been too busy wandering blind to it all just waiting for the slightest roar of the crowd or that faint glow of the floodlights above the terraced houses to signal my proximity to the ground.

The train back to Long Eaton was relatively deserted compared to all the other journeys I had taken and again it struck me how supporters come like a rampaging army only to disappear to our own lands once the battle has been fought. We return to our normal lives and let the city return to its.

When I arrived home I was still holding onto the tickets in my pocket. Dad was in the kitchen making tea while Mum and Daniel were settled in front of the television watching *Noel's House Party*. Ian had a job at the local Asda superstore in Long Eaton and wouldn't be home until later. As soon as I walked through the door I pulled the tickets out of my pocket and I could tell Dad was excited, which conjured up more excitement in me.

'It's gonna be a belter!' he said.

I took my coat upstairs and put it in my room, along with my shoes and joined Mum and Daniel in the living room just in time to see some hapless celebrity receive a 'Gotcha!'.

Two weeks later me and my Dad embarked on the 260 mile round trip. Rather than being a deterrent the distance acted as encouragement and the Derby contingent travelled as if it was a trip along the A52 to Nottingham.

As me and my Dad were travelling from Long Eaton we drove down the M42 to pick up the M5 just south of Birmingham whereas most other supporters travelled out of Derby along the A38. The first half of the journey passed by without note, with me and my Dad compromising on listening to the radio as our music tastes had yet to converge.

When we joined the M5 it was like merging with a carnival of fellow supporters as streams of fans raced by as we gallantly made our way along the inside lane. Almost every other car seemed to have black and white scarves out of the windows and flags draped across the parcel shelves. Occasionally we too would be the ones overtaking when it came to passing camper vans or coaches and when these contained more Derby fans the waving passengers inside made it feel like a guard of honour.

It was only when we got as far as the Michaelwood Service Station, just past junction 13, that me and my Dad realised that that day was going to be very special. Thousands of Rams fans were already there stocking up on Ginsters pasties and Mars bars and looking around excitedly at the size of the crowd.

Uncharacteristically for Dad we arrived in Bristol at around one o'clock and parked up beneath the beautiful April sunshine of the South West. Not knowing what the weather was going to be like we'd packed the usual wardrobe of thick coats, jumpers and cagoules to see us through any outcome and as it was an estate car there was plenty of room in the back and we could afford to be prepared.

The sunshine convinced us to leave it all behind and we headed towards Ashton Gate in just our t-shirts. Despite our early arrival many supporters were already milling around the entrance to our terrace behind the goal and with the gates yet to be opened we passed the time conversing with other supporters about the journey down, which way they'd come and had they stopped off at Michaelwood Services for Ginsters and Mars bars.

Despite its size the city of Bristol has never enjoyed much success in terms of football. City's highest position had been runners-up in Division One in 1907 but since then the team had largely been consigned to the lower Leagues. In the 1980s they suffered three successive relegations, plummeting from the top-flight to the fourth division quicker than you can say, 'That's gert lush, that!'

Eventually we were allowed inside the ground and took our place a few steps up the open terrace directly behind the goal. Together we combined to make one of those typical end-of-season images where the stands are full and spectators mostly clad in short-sleeved replica shirts bask in the early summer sunshine.

By the time the teams emerged the atmosphere was building excitedly and the two sections of the terrace allocated to away fans were full to capacity. The early scenes at the service station were replicated as thousands of Derby fans filled onto the concrete steps to cheer our team on to promotion, while to our left the large Dolman Stand cast a formidable shadow. It was encouraging to see that several Derby supporters had infiltrated this area of the ground as well.

Bristol City were in 17th position and in no danger of relegation but it was their last home game of the season and they would want to end on a high. They were also still within reach of their local rivals, Bristol Rovers, and so any idea that they would roll over and allow us to win was quickly banished.

The home team also had Andy Cole in the side, who had recently signed from Arsenal after making just one League appearance for the Gunners. He had spent most of his time at Fulham though who were then in the third tier of English football. After playing in Bristol, Cole later moved to Newcastle United, helping them win promotion to the Premier League before moving to Manchester United and claiming five Premier League titles, two FA Cup medals, two Charity Shield medals, the Champions League title and a partridge in a pear tree.

Despite the opposition's prolific forward the Rams won the match by two goals to one but not before Andy Comyn, the Derby centre-back who had left Manchester United to study a degree in physics, expertly judged the speed, direction and flight of the spherical gamepiece to head it off the line and secure the victory. And it wasn't before the heavens opened up over Bristol and our open terrace to throw a torrential storm over the travelling fans, who all seemed to have left their winter clothes in the car.

The rain merely spurred us on to chant and jump around even more though with the atmosphere taking on a comical element. Even after the final whistle, when, in spite of the rain we were still kept in the ground for quarter of an hour to allow the home fans to get home and put on some dry clothes, we remained upbeat.

Derby stood in third place in the table just two points behind Leicester in second but six behind Ipswich Town who had already been promoted. Middlesbrough in fourth, and Charlton in sixth, still had two games left to play. Meanwhile we could still miss out on a Play-off position altogether with seventh-placed Blackburn Rovers also having two games left to play and only being five points behind us.

Saturday 25 April 1992 – 17:00
Barclays Second Division 1991–92

Pos		Pl	W	D	L	F	A	GD	Pts
1	Ipswich Town	45	23	12	10	67	49	18	81
2	Leicester City	45	23	8	14	61	53	8	77
3	**Derby County**	**45**	**22**	**9**	**14**	**67**	**50**	**17**	**75**
4	Middlesbrough	44	21	11	12	54	40	14	74
5	Cambridge United	45	19	16	10	63	45	18	73
6	Charlton Athletic	44	20	11	13	54	46	8	71
7	Blackburn Rovers	44	20	10	14	65	50	15	70
8	Swindon Town	44	18	14	12	68	53	15	68
9	Portsmouth	44	18	12	14	62	49	13	66

In the week between our victory at Bristol City and the final League match of the season Middlesbrough beat Grimsby Town, which put them up into second, ahead of Leicester on goal difference. Meanwhile Blackburn drew with Sunderland while Charlton lost at home to Tranmere Rovers, moving Blackburn into the final Play-off position on goal difference.

The results secured Derby a Play-off position but we all wanted to go one better. If Derby won their final match against Swindon, who themselves could get into the Play-offs with a win at the Baseball Ground, we would be promoted if both Middlesbrough and Leicester failed to secure all three points.

Saturday 2 May 1992 – 15:00
Barclays Second Division 1991–92

Pos		Pl	W	D	L	F	A	GD	Pts
1	Ipswich Town	45	23	12	10	67	49	18	81
2	Middlesbrough	45	22	11	12	55	40	16	77
3	Leicester City	45	23	8	14	61	53	8	77
4	**Derby County**	**45**	**22**	**9**	**14**	**67**	**50**	**17**	**75**
5	Cambridge United	45	19	16	10	63	45	18	73
6	Charlton Athletic	45	20	11	14	54	47	7	71
7	Swindon Town	45	18	15	12	68	53	15	69

At half-time in that final home match Derby led, whereas Middlesbrough were only drawing at Wolverhampton Wanderers. Had the scores remained the same at full-time Derby would have been promoted at the first time of asking. It was not to be though as Middlesbrough went on to win their match 2–1 and assigned Derby to the Play-offs.

Blackburn Rovers had finished four points behind Derby but had beaten us home and away that season. The first leg saw Derby take the lead at Ewood Park but then the team collapsed and came away trailing by four goals to two.

Again the Baseball Ground was shifting on its axis for the second leg as the supporters clamoured for success. The roar just before the team kicked-off enveloped the stadium as if Sir Frank Whittle himself was doing a fly past in his jet-plane. Despite winning the game though the 2–1 scoreline was not enough to overcome the deficit from the first leg.

As the top-flight prepared for its rebrand and the unveiling of the Premier League Derby would find themselves in Division One, although this was only because it was the new name for the second tier of English football.

Saturday 2 May 1992 – 17:00
Barclays Second Division 1991–92

Pos		Pl	W	D	L	F	A	GD	Pts
1	Ipswich Town	46	24	12	10	70	50	20	84
2	Middlesbrough	46	23	11	12	58	41	17	80
3	**Derby County**	**46**	**23**	**9**	**14**	**69**	**51**	**18**	**78**
4	Leicester City	46	23	8	15	62	55	7	77
5	Cambridge United	46	19	17	10	65	47	18	74
6	Blackburn Rovers	46	21	11	14	70	53	17	74
7	Charlton Athletic	46	20	11	15	54	48	6	71
8	Swindon Town	46	18	15	13	69	55	69	14

1992–93

Derby's plundering in the transfer market that had started the previous season had continued into the summer. In June came the capture of Welshman, Mark Pembridge, from Luton Town for £1.25 million and the thought of us having all of our expensive signings from the start of the season gave everyone an immense sense of anticipation as time rolled towards the opening match on 15 August.

Me and most of my mates bought season tickets for the Pop-Side again and it almost became irrelevant who we were playing. Sometimes even the score didn't matter. At 17 years old watching football was more about having something to do, somewhere to go and people to be with.

Peterborough United 1 Derby County 0
Saturday 15 August 1992

The first match of the 1992–93 season saw us travel to Peterborough and with the host of big-money signings James England and I were in good spirits. Although we had both learned to drive our parents had convinced us that travelling on the club's organised transport, the Roadrider, would be safer and so we boarded the coach at the old Derby Bus Station at 12 o'clock and waited for that season's journey to begin.

We were used to travelling either north or south along the M1 but instead the coach trundled along the A roads east like something out of *Last of the Summer Wine*. After two hours the coach still had not made the 75 miles to Peterborough but the anticipation of the first game of the season was enough to make the journey spectacular.

We were just passed Stamford on the A1 when James dipped into the bacon and egg sandwiches that his Mum had made him for the journey. I declined the offer and instead let my gaze drift across the Lincolnshire countryside.

Travelling to an away game was as good a reason as any to leave the house and get out of our hometown. The looming second year of A-Levels was making me realise how much I needed to start improving at college if I wanted to further my education and I still had visions of my history teacher at school telling me in the third year that if I didn't get a place at university he'd, 'kick my arse the entire length of the classroom.'

Things between me and my Dad had soured a little too. We seemed to argue all the time, mostly about college work and my younger brother, who I saw as getting all of the decisions his way. Looking back it was just Dad looking out for Daniel, a kid six years younger than me and behaving in the same protective way in which he used to look over me but being in the middle of the situation made it impossible for me to see it.

It wasn't as if I was completely blameless. When Daniel came up to me in the living room and stupidly told me to give him a pound coin lying on the arm of the chair I was sitting in, naturally I said no. When he reached for it I pretended that he'd punched me, resulting in him being banned from watching the *A-Team* for six months. I loved it when a plan came together.

Maybe this tension led to Dad's increasing absenteeism from matches or maybe he just wanted to spend more time at home. He was getting many hours of overtime at his job at Rolls-Royce and so I guess when he wasn't working he wanted to spend time at home with my Mum and the rest of the family. That and the Sunday morning running made Saturday afternoons too valuable to waste away in the stands at Derby County.

For me those afternoons represented a release though, a time that I could be away from all of the worries of the angst world of a 17-year-old. I didn't need to resort to self-harm or listening to The Cure when I could stand up in the open air on a Saturday afternoon and openly call someone a wanker at the top of my voice. And in a time when the make-up of my relationships with people were constantly challenged I could always rely on the Derby crowd to be standing in place at kick-off.

Less reliable were those 11 players who represented our club on the pitch. The amount of money spent on their transfers did not materialise into results and with most opposition seeing us as the team to beat it often created a situation that added pressure on the players who were already dealing with the millstones of being a big-money signing.

This was all hindsight though and so we piled onto the Moyes End terrace at London Road eager to see in the new season, as did the fans of Peterborough who had seen their own team promoted to English football's second tier for the first time in their history after beating Stockport County in that summer's Play-off Final.

The ground was an array of colour and even the seats in the Main Stand appeared to be different shades of blue, which they were, with the home side having to purchase 700 seats from Leicester's Filbert Street and 300 from The Den at Millwall in pre-season in order to increase seating capacity to that required by the League's standards.

The Posh, so called as the manager of Peterborough's original team, Fletton United, in 1921 asked for, 'posh players for a posh new team' to represent the club were the first to upset our flock of expensively assembled Rams that season. Ken Charlery scored the only goal of the game, leaving us as disappointed as a small child getting one of those crap plastic models in a Kinder Egg rather than a model kit that they could build.

On the way back to Derby the light seemed to prophetically dim all around the coach as we trundled home in silence. Meanwhile James started on his final bacon and egg sandwich that I had declined and which now looked like some bizarre attempt at origami. So much, I thought, for the release from trouble at home.

The route back skirted the edge of Long Eaton on our way home to Derby but the bus driver wouldn't stop to let us off. Instead we carried on along the A52 and over junction 25 of the M1, eventually being deposited at the bus station where we had left eight hours earlier. James' sandwich had left me feeling peckish and so I nipped to a newsagent on the way to the train station and bought two Marathons and the green *Derby Evening Telegraph*.

On the front of the paper the headline was unsympathetic to the team and to those thousands of fans who had travelled to Peterborough that afternoon. 'What a bunch of Charlerys' it exclaimed, heaping more pressure onto the team to perform. When I arrived home, without the usual match report for my Dad, I threw it down on the small table we had in the living room in disgust at both the paper for what I saw as its traitorous nature as well as disappointment in myself for being taken in by the hype surrounding our new team of superstars.

By the time Ian arrived home from his shift at Asda he was in good spirits. Forest were in the top-flight and entertaining Liverpool the following day in what was to be the first Premier League game televised live on Sky Sports. Meanwhile Derby had just lost to Peterborough. He took one look at the newspaper which I had stupidly left on the table, took a glance at me and suddenly turned all Rita Hayworth, woefully lamenting, 'What a bunch of Charlerys!'

It must have sounded good to him because he repeated again and again until I managed to make him stop, first with a polite request, then with a firm command and finally with violence. After I'd finished beating him with the newspaper it looked more like James' second bacon and egg sandwich than a periodical.

*****

Derby were suffering a hangover after going so near to promotion the previous season. In September we added defender Craig Short for £2.65 million, which for the next five years would be the highest amount paid in England for a player by a team outside of the top-flight. Like Tommy Johnson, Short came from Notts County and with the cash the Magpies were able to redevelop three sides of their ageing stadium.

Despite our poor start to the season it was never an option to stop going. Dad's vision was a little less clouded and mostly he stayed at home while me and my mates would travel to Derby and beyond to see the team underperform. Not just supporting the team but going out of our way to watch them was like that badge of honour we used to wear at Infant school, the one which stated your devotion to something that gave nothing in return.

There is a strange hook to supporting a football club that turns supporters into fanatics and it is often cited that they deserve more than what can be achieved on the pitch. But football is a product without assurances and therefore offers no money-back guarantee. The option is there for us never to be duped again, to never fall for the romance of an away fixture at Middlesbrough where more often than not we end up conceding six goals but we never take it. That season we carried on going, home and away, with each victory having us believe it was the start of something new and with each defeat convincing us that things had to change.

In some ways the team mirrored my own attempts at passing my A-Levels, with neither of us putting in the true amount of effort needed but thinking that everything was going to be alright in the end. To me the football was more important than my own education though and throughout the week all I could think about was who we were playing on Saturday, how many positions we could climb if we won and whether, if it was an away game, I could afford to go.

Craig Short's arrival was the only source of brightness in a dark September as we didn't win a game until the back end of the month. This included a 4–3 reverse at the hands of Bristol City in which Paul Simpson scored a hat-trick but still ended up on the losing side. October was little better and saw manager, Arthur Cox, leave the club after nine years at the helm, having apparently suffered from back trouble for some time. He soon turned up at Newcastle United as Kevin Keegan's right hand man, raising some suspicions with the Derby faithful when he was later seen celebrating goals at St James' Park in a way that would have put Lazarus to shame.

Roy McFarland, who had taken over the reins after Peter Taylor's departure in 1984 again took charge of the first team and there was immediate improvement, all be it against Southend United in the second leg of the League Cup first round. This was soon followed by a more convincing draw in the first leg of the second round against Arsenal, which reignited all of our interest. In the second leg we also held the Gunners to a 1–1 draw at Highbury only for them to win the tie in extra-time, eventually going on to win the trophy.

An encouraging run in the FA Cup saw us reach the sixth round, which drew us against Sheffield Wednesday. Wednesday would eventually finish the season in seventh place in the Premier League and contest both League and FA Cups against Arsenal in the Finals. A 3–3 draw at the Baseball Ground gave us a replay at Hillsborough but the Owls overcame us with a single goal. They had the lure of a semi-final match against Sheffield United to spur them on whereas our own nemesis, Forest, had been disposed of in the fifth round.

Derby had been knocked out of both Cup competitions by the eventual finalists in each but in the League it was like the team were scared of the Play-offs. Gingerly we'd get within touching distance and then run away from the flame, afraid of being burnt again. Going to the Baseball Ground was like watching Bill Murray in *Groundhog Day* with both me and the team going through the same motions until we got it right. But neither of us did. With four games to go we could give up completely when, 12 points behind sixth place, it became all but mathematically possible for us to reach the Play-off positions.

Barclays League Division One 1992–93

Pos		Pl	W	D	L	F	A	GD	Pts
1	Newcastle United	46	29	9	8	92	38	92	96
2	West Ham United	46	26	10	10	81	41	81	88
3	Portsmouth	46	26	10	10	80	46	80	88
4	Tranmere Rovers	46	23	10	13	72	56	72	79
5	Swindon Town	46	21	13	12	74	59	74	76
6	Leicester City	46	22	10	14	71	64	71	76
7	Millwall	46	18	16	12	65	53	65	70
8	**Derby County**	**46**	**19**	**9**	**18**	**68**	**57**	**68**	**66**
9	Grimsby Town	46	19	7	20	58	57	58	64

1993–94

1993 saw the end of an era, certainly in my time watching Derby County. While you couldn't go anywhere without hearing Dutch techno duo, 2Unlimited's, *No Limits* on the radio, university beckoned to some of us who had been rooted to the Baseball Ground and dispersed our group like shrapnel around the country. Others who I had shared those Saturday afternoons with the previous season were still in the sixth form in Long Eaton while Mark Archer and David Scarsdale had already drifted off at some point previously.

My friendships often were like flotsam and jetsam. Sometimes the tide would bring us back together but at other times the sea would take them away completely. Despite thinking at the time that Derby County would always keep us together things didn't often turn out the way I planned them when I was 18 years old.

James England went to study civil engineering, presumably hoping to follow in the footsteps of Thomas Telford and have a new town named after him, which would have actually been quite daft given his surname. Meanwhile I went to university in the North East and initially enrolled at what was labelled a university college, as if they couldn't make up their mind, which was a joint venture between the universities of Durham and Teesside.

By the time I graduated, Teesside had pulled out of the venture and it was officially a college of Durham University. So despite only achieving three grade Es at A-Level I secured a place on a degree course at one of the most prestigious universities in the country.

Naturally my mates and I tried to attend as many matches as we could before we departed to our new towns and cities. Derby didn't disappoint and on the opening day of the season the Baseball Ground hosted a comprehensive 5–0 win over Sunderland, which obviously saw us at the top of the League albeit after just one match. This still didn't stop the supporters chanting about the fact though.

A creditable draw away at Forest who had been relegated from the Premier League in its inaugural season added fuel to the fire of hope, as did home wins against Bristol City and last season's nemesis, Peterborough United. Heavy defeats away at Middlesbrough and Birmingham steadied our expectations but as we progressed toward the end of September we were ninth in the table and on level points with Wolverhampton Wanderers in sixth place.

Notts County 4 Derby County 1
Saturday 25 September 1993

Saturday 25 September was to be the last match James and I attended before heading north. We had already said our temporary farewells to the Baseball Ground earlier that month but living halfway between Derby and Nottingham, a match away at Notts County's Meadow Lane was as good as a home game anyway. We headed to Nottingham with the previous season's 2–0 win still in our memories and hoped for a similar result.

Formed in 1864, Notts County are regarded as the oldest professional club still in existence. They spent their early years playing friendly matches across the city and entering the FA Cup in 1877, reaching the semi-finals in 1883 and 1884. In 1903 the owner of Italian giants Juventus needed new kit but instead of nipping to the Turin branch of JD Sports he asked a member of the squad, Englishman John Savage, if he could source a replacement for the pink ensemble that they were wearing at the time. Savage brought the kit directly from the East Midlands and they have been the distinctive colours of the Italian side ever since.

We sat at the Kop end of Meadow Lane, which although less formidable than the one at Anfield still showed a shrewd investment with the money Notts County had received from the sales of Tommy Johnson and Craig Short. Like the previous season almost 8,000 fans had made their way from Derby but our voices were soon silenced as we were consistently torn apart down the right hand side of the field. I was getting increasingly frustrated and spent most of the afternoon out of my seat shouting at the inept defending and lamenting the ease with which we were being carved open. It was plain to see from up in my seat behind the goal and it should have been obvious on the pitch.

The original Magpies hadn't read our script and ran away with the game, winning by four goals to one. It was an embarrassing way for us to leave but as ever we dusted the result from ourselves and prepared for the next game, except on this occasion it felt like there would be no next game.

*****

I had been promised that the North East of England was a hotbed of football although the vehement passion of Newcastle and Sunderland had somehow failed to trickle down to Stockton-on-Tees. The nearest League club was Middlesbrough who had suffered similar financial trouble to Derby in the mid-80s.

In 1986 the club were just minutes away from failing to register for the Football League when Board member Steve Gibson brought together a consortium and raised the £350,000 needed to apply for a place in the competition. Without appearing too ungrateful, while these football club saviours may have a great deal of money they can certainly be found lacking in their time-management skills.

It was therefore understandable that the team were not the heart and soul of the region. In the year of Middlesbrough's answer to the Great Escape the club had called in provisional liquidators who padlocked the gates of their previous ground, Ayresome Park, in a similar way to how the area's factories and shipyards had been closed throughout the recession of that decade.

Fans of Middlesbrough saw the football club as just another example of how bad things were whereas elsewhere teams could be seen as a source of pride when everything else is falling down. At the time when Middlesbrough Football Club were going to the wall the city of Liverpool was gaining an ignominious reputation as an area of destitution. In 1981 riots broke out in the Toxteth area and resulted in police using tear-gas on civilians for the first time outside of Northern Ireland. Throughout the decade 12,000 people were leaving the conurbation each year and 15% of the land was disused. Meanwhile in the same decade the football club won the European Cup twice, the Division One Championship six times, the FA Cup twice, the League Cup four times and the Charity Shield four times, sharing it on another occasion in 1986 with Everton, who also come from Liverpool.

Dad drove me up to Stockton that first day, along with Mum and Daniel, with none of us knowing what to expect. Football matches had yet to bring us this far north and so it was new territory for all of us. Driving along the A1 as it skirted the North Yorkshire Moors drew pleasant approval with signs directing us to James Herriot country and beauty spots spread randomly along the road but as we approached Teesside the noise in the car silenced as we saw the horizon blanketed with chemical industry. This, I was later to learn, was the backdrop that had inspired film director, Ridley Scott, to produce post-apocalyptic worlds such as that of *Blade Runner*.

I was housed in a block of flats rented off the local hospital along with 16 other students who had been randomly split into groups of four absolute strangers to share their homes. One lad had arrived from Carlisle and was more of a cricketer than a football fan although he did have an affinity with his local team. As well as introducing me to local legend Eddie Stobbart he taught me how to slice an onion and ended his university days at the union bar in a Newcastle Brown t-shirt, Bermuda shorts and a pair of slippers. Another flatmate came from Whitby and supported Liverpool although this soon changed when he discovered that an attractive girl who shared our block was a fan of Newcastle United. The final lad to arrive into our block was not a fan of football at all, although this was understandable as he came from Shrewsbury.

Returning to Derby for matches was never an option, both because of the 270 mile round trip and money. Trips home by National Express cost around £20 but the journey took over five hours whereas train journeys were considerably quicker but a lot more expensive.

Instead I had to settle for listening to sporadic updates of our results if they were ever deemed significant enough for Radio 5 or wait for twenty-to-five when we'd descend on the only room in the halls that had a television. As the BBC1's videprinter scrolled into action we would wait for our team's results, using the time to educate the lad from Carlisle as to where teams like Port Vale, Aston Villa and Hibernian came from and that it was called an 'own goal' and not a 'home goal'.

Stoke City 2 Derby County 1
Saturday 1 January 1994

The Christmas break was a good time to catch up and re-establish the friendships that seemed to have been put on hold for the last few months while we had started new lives in our university towns. Living away from Long Eaton gave me the sense of a double-life and with the two being so far apart they would never cross. While the one I had in Stockton-on-Tees was full of opportunity and heralded the future my home life still anchored me to the past.

On 1 January we had an away fixture at Stoke City's Victoria Ground, the home which the club left for the Britannia Stadium in 1997. As ever with matches on New Year's Day, the bank holiday meant someone had to drive and the time of year ensured that the weather was hovering around freezing.

Me, my Dad, Uncle Paul and James England travelled to the match with Dad still driving the old red Ford Escort estate that had seen us reliably reach many destinations over the years. Instead of a sports shop the boot of the car now resembled a clearance sale at a Yeoman's Army and Navy Store, such was the amount of coats, cagoules, windcheaters and balaclavas contained within it. We also had a supply of turkey cobs, peanuts, crisps, porkpies, and even sausages on sticks, which had failed to tempt revellers at the Christmas parties that had been held over the festive period.

Stoke City supporters had a reputation as being unwelcoming and so we decided against trying to find a pub to drink in before the match. Instead we went straight onto the Boothen End terrace, which despite there being no public transport contained a healthy following of Rams fans that afternoon.

Our stand resembled the Osmaston or Normanton End at the Baseball Ground but without the top tier, with a terrace on the bottom level and seats in the tier just above where the home fans sat. As it slowly filled it became clear that the festive atmosphere had affected some supporters more than others, with one fan entering the ground with his woollen Derby County hat adorned with tinsel and bells.

'Take that stupid fuckin' hat off!' yelled a Stoke supporter sitting behind us.

'You take your stupid fuckin' head off!' the guy quickly retorted.

As the match approached we tried everything to avoid the infiltrating cold of the Potteries and the pre-match nerves. From among the hoard someone lamented, 'My wife's gonna kill me when I get home…I said I was only going out to buy a paper.'

After the match kicked off Dad soon started taking various items of Christmas fayre out of his pockets and handing them out. First he passed them to us but soon it was being distributed to any stranger who happened to have found themselves next to him on the terrace, such was Dad's ability to share his happiness with anyone. He'd bought everything we had from the car apart from, he said, the sausages on sticks as he thought the coppers would confiscate the sticks.

Stoke were in 10th position in the League, just one place behind us, which added to a tense affair. Derby were commanding the match though with midfielder Martin Kuhl running the show. Kuhl had more pedigree than an obese dog, having been signed from Portsmouth for £650,000 in September 1992 and had been in Pompey's second division team who took Liverpool to a replay and then a penalty shoot-out in the 1991–92 FA Cup semi-final.

City obviously recognised the midfielder's contribution and a crunching challenge in the centre of the pitch brought an early end to Kuhl's match. Without his presence Stoke soon exerted their own authority on the game and ended up winning by a single goal.

Despite the loss we wandered back to the car in high spirits, reciting victories of the past to dispel the defeat that we had just witnessed. I didn't think about the recent years when I had gone to the Baseball Ground with my mates though or the four years spent in Division One rubbing shoulders with the game's greats, beating Arsenal twice in their Championship winning year of 1988–89 and finishing as the fifth best team in the country. I didn't think about those Cup games against Sheffield Wednesday and Arsenal the previous season either when we had proved again that we could at least match the greatest teams in the land.

Instead I thought about Nottingham Forest in 1979. I thought about Orient in 1981 and Watford in 1982. I thought about Oldham, Newcastle and all the other matches that I'd gone to with my Dad. I even remembered the Plymouth match when I thought that it was all over, when just days after we were saved in the High Court I'd assumed the relationship between me, my Dad and Derby County would end as we slipped to that embarrassing defeat in 1984.

I thought back to that time at Bramall Lane when I had travelled with my mates only for my Dad to turn up with 10 minutes to spare. I remembered how lonely I had been on the terrace behind the goal, feeling the isolation that came like the train that had carried us that day roaring into me as I recognised that the bond between us had slipped.

Since leaving home though my relationship with my Dad had matured, as if in moving he could see me as more independent and make him realise that he needed to look out for me rather than look after me. Me being so far north had given him the opportunity to take a step back and see the young man that he, alongside my Mum, had made.

*****

Two wins in our next two League matches brought us back into the Play-off positions and softened the blow of a third round exit in the FA Cup at the hands of Premier League Oldham Athletic. Inconsistency remained within the team though and we were dipping in and out of the Play-offs like a child getting into a hot bath. Despite a run securing just five points from a possible 18 by mid-March we were still in sixth, as if the rest of the teams in the division were standing by politely and letting us through. A run of six matches without defeat then saw us climb up to fourth.

Forest spitefully put a stop to the run by beating us at the Baseball Ground and it was fortunate for both Ian and that Saturday's edition of the *Derby Evening Telegraph* that I was in Stockton-on-Tees that weekend. More fortunate was a 2–1 victory over Oxford United in the penultimate game of the season, which meant that only a Notts County victory by six goals or more would leave us without a Play-off spot. Even defeat at Southend United on the final day could not stop us finishing the season in sixth.

Endsleigh League Division One 1993–94

Pos		Pl	W	D	L	F	A	GD	Pts
1	Crystal Palace	46	27	9	10	73	46	73	90
2	Nottingham Forest	46	23	14	9	74	49	74	83
3	Millwall	46	19	17	10	58	49	58	74
4	Leicester City	46	19	16	11	72	59	72	73
5	Tranmere Rovers	46	21	9	16	69	53	69	72
6	**Derby County**	**46**	**20**	**11**	**15**	**73**	**68**	**73**	**71**
7	Notts County	46	20	8	18	65	69	65	68
8	Wolverhampton W	46	17	17	12	60	47	60	68

We approached the two legs of the Play-offs with optimism. Having never been close to automatic promotion, unlike having just missed out in the 1991–92 season, failure would feel like we had simply not gained something rather than had it taken from us. Still, by finishing only two points behind Millwall in the League and with both matches that season ending in 0–0 stalemates with the London club there was no reason why we could not go one better than two seasons before and get to the Play-off Final at Wembley Stadium.

We won the first leg comfortably by two goals to nil at the Baseball Ground and the question on the mind of the media was whether this could be maintained at the Den. What they failed to recognise was the fact that the Londoners had endured a wretched end to the season and not won a game by two clear goals since entertaining Crystal Palace at home on New Year's Day. Not only did Derby avoid defeat in the second leg but we went on to record a 3–1 victory to set up a mouthwatering Play-off Final against Leicester City.

Derby County 1 Leicester City 2

Monday 30 May 1994

The day of the Play-off Final was in the Whitsun holiday and Dad was helping out at a cub camp in Guernsey for the Ark Royal pack. As Daniel had started to attend Mum was a still a leader and so just as he had missed the Charity Shield in 1975, Dad again was not around to see Derby play at the famous stadium.

Despite my end of year exams starting the following Wednesday I travelled down to Long Eaton for the weekend in order to make the trip to London on the Bank Holiday Monday. My Grandma's brother, Uncle Alan, had organised a bus to travel down for the family and there was room available for my mates and I. In our house he was known as 'Derby County Uncle Alan', such was his affinity for the club, but he also shared that winning grin that I had seen on Dad so many times, especially when he was luring us into one of the gullible tales he always seemed to tell us.

It was somewhat of a reunion as me and my friends met each other in the car park at Long Eaton train station. The conversation was slightly stunted though as James and I tried to find common ground with those we had left behind but eventually we soon got back into the familiar banter that had seen us through many stressful encounters before.

As we travelled south it seemed that the whole of the M1 motorway had been given over to Derby fans on their trip to Wembley, with Leicester fans advised to travel down the A1 to avoid all 80,000 supporters using the same stretch of road. Every bus and car displayed black and white scarves out of windows and along the parcel shelves, proudly proclaiming the allegiance of those inside. All except for one bus full of schoolkids who were going to Wembley Arena to watch Gladiators.

I had felt a sense of antipathy towards the semi-finals, probably as a result of being removed from Derby but that soon lifted as the prize at stake came closer and the realisation of playing in the Premier League heightened the occasion. Unfortunately the feelings went further than simply wanting to win the match and the sheer importance made the whole experience of watching football an awful event, which I failed to enjoy.

Perhaps if we had won I would have felt differently but even after Tommy Johnson scored the opening goal to give us the lead I didn't feel elated. At the time the ball hit the back of the net I was screaming as loudly as James who was standing right next to me, with neither of us being able to hear a thing. This was soon replaced by stomach-wrenching anxiety though as the game restarted. Leicester eventually clawed their way back into the game and won by two goals to one.

After the match, when I was looking for someone to put some perspective onto the game and tell me that we would be stronger and maybe get automatic promotion the following year, my Dad wasn't around. Instead he was telling all of this to the inconsolable cub scouts who supported Derby instead.

Travelling back along the M1 and seeing the Leicester supporters celebrating on the bridges that spanned the carriageway not just poured salt into the wounds, it licked it out and rubbed it in again. They were having fun, laughing last and laughing loudest while I had nothing with which to console myself apart from the current D:Ream hit, *Things Can Only Get Better*. I was gutted.

I had planned to get the train back to Stockton-on-Tees that night but instead stayed out in the local pubs in Long Eaton. I travelled back to the North East the following morning and went on to fail those final year exams, which meant that I would not be allowed to return to university the following year. In her attempts to help my Grandma told me not to worry and that, 'as one door closes another one slams shut,' but I knew what she meant.

Poets would find some sort of bitter comparison in the way that my outcome and that of my team resembled one another. We had both tried to better ourselves, with me trying to gain a degree while Derby aimed for Premier League football, but unfortunately we had both failed and walked arm in arm through life's seemingly constant lows.

Sometimes when you're down your team can bring you round, like the great team of Liverpool in the 80s that gave the people of its city a sense of pride, but at others, like at Middlesbrough in 1986 it comes along as a companion and joins you in your despair.

For 15 years I had been in education and known exactly where I was going but the rug had been pulled from beneath my feet and I didn't have any ground to land on. Losing a football match, albeit one of the most important in my club's history suddenly became inconsequential.

1994–95

Barnsley 2 Derby County 1
Saturday 13 August 1994

After losing in the Play-off Final the season before Derby soon became known as the expensive flops of the division. We had allowed Leicester City to join Nottingham Forest in promotion to the Premier League and now both looked down from their lofty height as we continued to struggle against teams like Southend United and Luton Town.

Simon Goodhall, a lad from a nearby village who I knew from Secondary school and his brother, Ryan, had joined our fold while others had slipped silently away. The three of us approached our opening game away at Barnsley with the usual blind faith and travelled by train to stand on the old open terrace behind the goal at Oakwell.

Neither the money spent on players or the standard of the opposition could guarantee us a win and so we tried to kid everyone who questioned our loyalty that it was the cheap chip shop near the ground, which sold battered sausage and chips for less than a pound that drew our support.

As I travelled up that day though I was after something more than an away win and cheap chips. I was hoping for some kind of certainty in my life after everything else had gone awry. Fifteen years after starting my journey of education I had been derailed and prematurely so, and for the first time in my life I didn't know what the future held.

I was still serving up fries at the local theme park near Ilkeston, which was scheduled to come to an end when the schools went back in September and the trade dried up. With no second year at university to look forward to all I had was the prospect of unemployment.

Blessed certainty came in the form of predictable disappointment, which was largely what had been on offer to the supporters of Derby County since relegation from the first division back in 1992. So along with most other fans stood right at the back of the terrace that afternoon I turned round and watched the village cricket match taking place on the field behind the ground instead. After failing the first year of my degree course maybe this was indicative of me having to look at different avenues.

Barnsley Football Club had spent more time in the second division than any other club in history due in no small part to underhand dealings when the Football League was restarted after World War One in 1919. This year is not to be confused with the chorus of a 1985 Paul Hardcastle hit about war, which was actually highlighting that the average age of the combat soldier in Vietnam was 19.

With Division One increasing from 20 teams to 22, instead of the usual two down from the Division One and two promoted from the Division Two the idea was for one team to be relegated, Tottenham Hotspur, and three places made available from the second division. Derby and Preston North End were promoted as champions and runners-up, and having ended the season in third place, Barnsley assumed they would take their place in the top-flight as well. Instead the Football League held a ballot, which saw Woolwich Arsenal who had finished in fifth behind both Wolves and Barnsley secure promotion. Arsenal went on to win the Championship 13 times while Barnsley remained in the second division for the next 80 years.

It didn't take long to look through the dictionary to find a suitable adjective for Derby that day, who put in an abject performance to allow Barnsley to win the game 2–1. Further ignominy was reaped upon the Rams when Marco Gabbiadini, who had by now probably sold his Lamborghini, missed a late chance to equalise. The home fans had been waiting all afternoon to berate him with what was now becoming a common, 'What a waste of money!' chant. Our response was to point towards the 7,500 capacity East Stand built the season before and which was only a fifth full and chant the same.

After the final whistle, with our humorous chants and the scent of battered sausage dying in the wind, the three of us left the terrace along with the rest of our travelling support and joined the police procession back to the train station. It was like a parade of the afflicted with our affiliation given away by the depressed looks on our faces. Grown men laughed while their children pointed at us and mocked all the way through the streets of Barnsley until we arrived at the station where we were duly deposited in a cage to wait for our train back to Derby.

*****

Unable to continue at university I was back living at home, spending the latter quarter of 1994 scouring through the jobs pages of the *Derby Evening Telegraph* and the *Nottingham Evening Post*. Despite working voluntarily helping to transport the needy around supermarkets and day centres in the area my self esteem had plummeted and I was almost shying away from going out with the friends who had chosen to attend local universities in Nottingham and Loughborough and had therefore remained living at home.

It was this depression that prompted Dad to start going to more matches, taking me along and buying my ticket for me as I struggled to afford to go. It was like being five years old again but instead of taking the train my Dad would drive to matches and park up at the Sherwood Foresters pub near the ground where we could have a drink before the game.

The carpet and wallpapers of the pub peeled at the edges while the bar served Castlemaine XXXX on tap although what the four Xs stood for was the source of much conjecture. At one side of the bar a small vacant stage hung by the window begging to be used but all it had to do was catch the spilled beer of the men who talked animatedly about Kevin Hector and Brian Clough.

Often me and my Dad would talk about the matches we had gone to, displaying them to each other like kids playing Top Trumps with the winner being the person who had suffered the most.

'Notts County 4 Derby County 1, 25 September 1993.' I would offer.

Dad would look up from his deck of memories and beat me with, 'Derby County 1 Cardiff City 5, 1 September 1965.'

Sitting over a pint with my Dad and having a million other things to talk about somehow made choosing to talk about my predicament easier. For so long I had been opposed to Dad's requests at knowing why I acted the way I did, finding it intrusive as if he was setting me up to criticise me but here I could see that his queries were the genuine concerns of a worried parent.

It was here that he also spoke about the relationship that he'd had with his own father and it became clear why my Dad showed such concerns over me. My Granddad had always appeared largely disinterested and almost jealous of Dad, which was maybe understandable when looking at the two men's lives. While my Dad had grown up in the 1960s and enjoyed the liberation of a time of freedom and expanding horizons his Dad had spent his late teens and early 20s being shot at by the Führer.

We talked through my choices and while I was determined to retake my assignments and start the second year the following September Dad, rightly, was giving me all the options. Just like our Top Trumps of footballing history he always had more cards in his pack than I did.

The simple fact was that I didn't want to be a failure and it was then that Dad told me that the only way I could be a failure was to give up trying. The relief I felt then was incredible, as to know that he was behind me in my decision meant everything. All this time we had been supporting Derby County I hadn't appreciated that he was always supporting me, with the only difference being that when Dad was cheering me on, every day was a matchday, and every opportunity I had was a chance at goal. For my Dad and Mum, watching my desperate and fruitless attempts to succeed while they stood at the sidelines must have been as infuriating as how I got watching Derby County trying to beat Barnsley.

*****

We kept plugging away, me and Derby County, supported by my Dad and my Mum and in January I got a job at a company in town conducting building surveys and overseeing the removal of asbestos, which aptly demonstrated that sometimes life catches you just to jab you in the stomach and tell you not to settle for the cushion it has provided. The job meant an income and an injection of self-esteem though and 1995 was looking up.

Unfortunately Derby County were finding it harder to emerge from the gloom. The players who had ultimately underperformed were being sold off like spare parts with Paul Kitson having already been sold to Newcastle United in September of 1994 while in January 1995 Tommy Johnson moved to Aston Villa where he won a League Cup medal in 1996 and later went on to achieve success with Celtic in Scotland.

Despite two wins and a draw in January, as well as a narrow defeat in the third round of the FA Cup at Premier League Everton, we were still down in eighth. Buoyed by the fact that we were in a similar position the previous year and still managed to get to Wembley though the outlook was still fairly positive in the stands of the Baseball Ground.

Three losses followed dropping us alarmingly to 14th after which we won six and drew one of the next seven but this still only took us as high as seventh. Further difficulty came in the form of the League's reshuffle as the Premier League was being reduced from 22 clubs to 20 the following season. With ballots having gone out of fashion only the champions of the second division would be promoted, along with one other team through the Play-offs.

Derby only won two of their remaining nine matches although we were still in with an outside chance of the Play-offs with three games remaining. After a 0–0 draw away at West Bromwich Albion our fate was sealed for another season after which the team gave up and lost the last two matches, ending the season in ninth position and 10 points away from the Play-offs.

The only failure I experienced though was the failure to give up. Despite my resubmitted assignments still not being of the required standard, come July I enrolled on an alternative course at the same university and would start again that coming September. After a year on the sidelines and with the words of encouragement from my Dad and Mum in my ears, I was back in the game and more determined than ever to succeed.

Endsleigh League Division One 1994–95

Pos		Pl	W	D	L	F	A	GD	Pts
1	Middlesbrough	46	23	13	10	67	40	67	82
2	Reading	46	23	10	13	58	44	58	79
3	Bolton Wanderers	46	21	14	11	67	45	67	77
4	Wolverhampton W	46	21	13	12	77	61	77	76
5	Tranmere Rovers	46	22	10	14	67	58	67	76
6	Barnsley	46	20	12	14	63	52	63	72
7	Watford	46	19	13	14	52	46	52	70
8	Sheffield United	46	17	17	12	75	55	74	68
9	**Derby County**	**46**	**18**	**12**	**16**	**66**	**51**	**66**	**66**
10	Grimsby Town	46	17	14	15	62	56	62	65

1995–96

In the close season of 1995 the contract of manager Roy McFarland was not renewed. Just like my first degree course it was apparent that things weren't working and only a change would lead to any sort of progression. Some supporters saw this as harsh treatment after McFarland's main responsibility involved selling the expensive but unsuccessful team that Arthur Cox had assembled and further insult was added to McFarland's injury, in an industry not short on either, when he went to manage Bolton Wanderers only to find out at a press conference that he was actually joint manager alongside another former Ram's legend, Colin Todd.

One of Roy McFarland's last acts as Derby County manager was to sell Player of the Year, Craig Short, to Everton, bringing Gary Rowett to the Rams as part of the deal. It would not be the last time that the award proved to be the death knell of a Derby County career. Short later went on to help Blackburn gain promotion to the Premier League in 2000–01 and represented the club in the UEFA Cup. Mark Pembridge also left that close season to play at Sheffield Wednesday and despite being only five foot eight inches he later played for Portuguese giants, Benfica, and also Everton.

The Derby Board approached the Bald Eagle, Jim Smith, to be the new man in charge who at the time was working for the League Managers' Association. He took the opportunity with both claws and on joining the Rams he told reporters that the job at the Baseball Ground was the only one he would have left his former position for, which was widely disregarded by all but we were appreciative of the gesture all the same.

Smith did have experience in management and had most recently been at Fratton Park, Portsmouth, for four years. Derby's recent flirtations with success were nothing compared to a Pompey side who had reached the FA Cup semi-finals in 1991–92 and missed out on promotion to the Premier League by just one goal the following year.

Smith's arrival did not herald an instant change in form though and by the end of October we were in 14th position. Meanwhile I was back in Stockton-on-Tees, this time studying Human Sciences and re-establishing myself in university life having found a course that I was actually interested in. My first assignment was to write an essay on euthanasia and after standing on the terraces at Derby on many occasions hoping for a quick and painless death I found I was an expert in the subject.

Being once more marooned in the North East I didn't have access to local news and the Internet was yet to become widely available. Derby may have had a fleeting few lines in the national press but nothing with which I could keep track on how we were doing other than our results and our League standing. I did, however, receive sporadic editions of the green *Derby Evening Telegraph* that my Dad was posting to Stockton, but the arrival of Croatian, Igor Stimac, still almost passed me by. The rest of the division were soon to notice the introduction of the influential Croatian defender though.

On the afternoon of Saturday 4 November I was working in the student bar. As usual at around four o'clock students converged to enjoy their first pint of the evening, unless they had been in the pub on the High Street, which screened live Premier League football direct from Norway. There we'd sit like a church congregation and watch the videprinter scroll the news of our team's success or failure just like I had done two years before. Banter soon built up among the group who slowly started to take an interest in the results of Oxford United, Gillingham and Burnley, rather than the teams at the top of the Premier League who nobody supported.

That afternoon the cursor sprang into action and letter by letter spelled out our opponents, T-R-A-N-M-E-R-E, like Norman Collier choking on a boiled sweet. There followed a moment's hesitation, before…5.

My own cry of, 'Bollocks!' was drowned out by the derisive heckles of the rest of the bar and as all eyes turned to me I sloped off to get a fresh barrel of Worthington's from the store at the other end of the car park. I didn't even wait to see that Derby had scored one in return, with new boy Stimac getting his first goal on his debut.

Simon Goodhall was at university in Sheffield and so still had a season ticket at the Baseball Ground. He had gone to Prenton Park and assured me that the Rams had been unlucky, which presumably meant that Tranmere's fifth goal had been off-side. Naturally I thought this was just bravado but the result was a turning point for the season. With Stimac at the helm Derby won six and drew one out of the next seven matches and by the time leaders Sunderland came to the Baseball Ground at Christmas we were in second place and within one point of the Wearsiders.

Derby County 3 Sunderland 1

Saturday 23 December 1995
Dad could hardly be seen beneath the heavy woollen hat and thick scarf that he wore on that day. I was more exposed, having finally grown out of my orange away shirt and so put a few jumpers and my own thick jacket on to protect me from the winter cold. Mum thought that this was everyday attire for me as she pictured me freezing

close to death in the halls of residences up in the North East and eating cold beans straight from the can. Out on the driveway outside the house, breath escaped us both like an embarking steam train as we scraped ice off the car, which Dad had now upgraded to a Rover.

The inside of the car was like a freezer and it wasn't until we picked James England up from his home a good couple of miles away that the engine finally started blowing warm air through the ventilators. James joked that we wouldn't feel the benefit if we kept our coats on inside while I picked ice crystals off the inside of the window.

The trees and fields that cushion the gap between Old Sawley and the Derby suburbs stood stark against the white winter sky. Every car that came the opposite way seemed to be either black, white or grey and it was only the bright red of Dad's car that seemed to splash some colour on the afternoon.

We carried on along the A6, through Shardlow and past the road that leads down to Elvaston Castle at the opposite end to that which the bus travels on its way into Derby. Traffic started to build as we approached the Chellaston area of the city but to the background sound of the pre-match build up on Radio Derby Dad was eager to know how both James and I were getting on at university. His interest didn't stop with me though and one of the reasons for his popularity was that he took an interest in everyone.

The traffic was even slower on the ring road but eventually we arrived in the car park of the Sherwood Foresters and took shelter in the relative warmth of the building, which was far better than sitting on the freezing terraces listening to Roy Orbison. Still the carpets and wallpaper were peeling but at least the Gaffa tape which held them together had been changed since the summer.

The pub seemed to mimic the Baseball Ground, which itself seemed to be patched up and in need of a complete overhaul. In light of the Taylor Report seats had now been added to the Pop-Side terrace subsequently reducing the capacity to just over 18,000.

The previous year members of the Derby County Board had looked into a possible new development on the site of the disused Chaddesden railway sidings towards the east of the city. The area provided a huge expanse of land between the River Derwent and the railway lines, the potential of which excited some of those members, most of all Lionel Pickering who had expressed a keen interest in a new stadium.

As a city Derby had bid for that area to host the Millennium Exhibition at the turn of the new century, which would later become the Millenium Dome and later still the O2. It was in the centre of the country, 10 minute's drive from the M1 motorway and with an improved A50 soon to be running west it would provide access to the M6 in around 20 minutes. Unfortunately the decision was announced at the end of 1995 that the dome would be built in Greenwich, London, which pleased the creators of Eastenders as they could get some publicity by featuring the new building on their opening credits.

It was a bone of contention in the pub that afternoon as we sat hunched over the small table beneath a poster advertising the Rolling Clones tribute band. We all lamented that everything went to London, having the sort of conversation that Dad had probably been waiting for in the many years of us coming to matches. He was probably as eager as I was to be able to get into a pub before a game and have a decent discussion in the relative warmth rather than stand on the cold terraces for an hour with me while watching the warm-up and reading the programme.

Experience had removed our rose-tinted glasses and my mates and I could now see that sometimes we lost because the opposition were better than us or because we'd played poorly and not because the referee was biased or because the linesman constantly put his flag up.

'So, are you studying medicine at university?' Dad asked James, who looked confused so he repeated the question. 'Are you studying medicine at university?'

'No, civil engineering.' James responded, remembering that the talk in the car on the way to the ground had been about what he was studying.

'Oh,' said Dad, 'it's just that the way you're nursing your pint, I thought you were practising to be a doctor!'

I looked down at Dad's pint, which had about a quarter left in it. Mine was half full while James had barely touched his. He was suffering heavily from the night before and so, as kick-off was approaching, Dad helped himself to half of the available ale.

It was half past two but as the ground was now an all-seater stadium we had our tickets and there was no rush to be at the ground and get our place on the terraces. The fresh air was good for our health but as we walked past one of the burger vans that led to the ground James felt his stomach tense again and we wandered swiftly past as he dove into a small car park behind one of the factories on the not-so-famous Coronation Street.

Despite the introduction of seats the atmosphere inside the Pop-Side was still building intensely. The mix of the chance to go top of the League and the Christmas spirit combined to put people in a great mood that spilled out from the stands and onto the pitch. This was the chance for the players to prove themselves against the top team in the division and for once they weren't about to let anybody down.

Sunderland started the match kicking towards their own supporters at the Osmaston End of the ground. This was the end of the Pop-Side that the three of us had tickets for and the end that me and my Dad had stood to see us secure the Championship against Plymouth back in 1987. We found ourselves on the front row, almost touching the players as they ran down the wing, which felt like being in the dugout.

Early in the first half Derby were on the attack with me, my Dad and James all straining to see the other end of the pitch. Ultimately the move was unsuccessful and Sunderland broke away and started their own offense. The roar of the travelling Sunderland fans took off from when our own cheering had subsided as the visitors raced down the right hand side of the pitch. Sunderland winger, Steve Agnew, tried to push the ball past Igor Stimac, who had stayed back to defend and thankfully the Croatian managed to get a foot to the ball, which saw it spin out of touch and directly into the arms of my Dad.

Agnew didn't break his stride and continued running, looking at my Dad to throw the ball back to him. Suddenly from being merely a spectator Dad was catapulted into being part of the game, with the eyes of the players and the capacity crowd all looking at him to do something. I waited for him to throw the ball back but he just held onto it, seemingly paralysed in the glare as if time had stopped. The only thing moving was his mouth as the edges moved towards that familiar grin.

I looked out onto the pitch and saw that the defence had yet to retreat. Stimac was screaming for them to return while Steve Agnew was looking at Dad to give him the ball back so he could take a quick throw-in, using our own eagerness to attack to his advantage. Our defence didn't need to worry though as my Dad would have held on to that ball all afternoon waiting for the team to regroup. The players understood and even Steve Agnew stopped pleading for Dad to throw the ball back. Instead the Sunderland winger almost reciprocated in his grin as he realised what my Dad had done.

Derby won 3–1 and leapfrogged Sunderland to the top of the League. It was a glorious day and I couldn't wait to tell everyone how my Dad had helped Derby County to the top of the League, just like he had helped the team clinch the Championship from a similar position on the terraces seven and a half years before. I knew I'd get stick and that they'd all call me daft but sometimes I felt as proud of my Dad as a father is to his sons and I would stand by him in the face of taunts from anyone.

Derby County 2 Leeds United 4

Sunday 7 January 1996

Derby went on to win the next two matches while the cold weather intervened to stop Sunderland playing at all. I knew how cold it could be up there having experienced the North East winter standing on the open Fulwell End terrace behind the goal at Sunderland's Roker Park. Like the Baseball Ground it had seen gradual improvements over the course of its history and on 8 March 1933, despite only having a capacity of 60,000 people, a record 75,118 crammed into the stadium to see Derby County win a sixth round FA Cup replay courtesy of a single goal by Rams inside-forward Peter Ramage. Unfortunately our run ended in the semi-final when we were beaten 3–2 by Manchester City at Huddersfield's Leeds Road.

Those days had been good times for Derby, who finished as runners-up in Division One either side of that Cup run in 1929–30 and 1935–36. Sixty years later the supporters were all hoping for those good times to return. Derby were top of the League by seven points and awaiting Premier League Leeds United in the FA Cup.

Leeds had finished the previous season in fifth place in the top-flight and were entertaining sides like Monaco and PSV Eindhoven in the UEFA Cup. Meanwhile we had now won nine and drawn one of the last 10, deposing the leaders at the top of the League in the process and now stood as the best team outside the Premier League.

The match was screened live on television but as I was still home from university for the Christmas period I wanted to be at the match rather than watching at home or in the pub. I had my own reservations of televised football, having been subjected to Premier League action live on Sky Sports to the exclusion of all other Leagues and incensed by the way they spoke of history as if the sport didn't exist at all before the formation of the new League.

Meanwhile in the stands the increased revenue from television and sponsorship had relegated the supporter in their importance to their clubs and as we were no longer the chief source of income our needs soon fell down the pecking order at the clubs that we were devoted to. Kick-off times, which had traditionally been Saturday at three o'clock developed a mind of their own and whereas Sunday afternoons were uncommon they soon became the norm, with Monday nights infiltrating the fixture list as well.

The supporters were still important but only in so much as they became the product rather than the customer. 'A packed house' was suddenly a selling point with the atmosphere generated inside the stadium as a measure of the match rather than a measure of support. By being outside of the Premier League and therefore excluded from that it made it clearer to see. Or maybe I was just jealous.

Just like those epic Cup matches in the 1993–94 season when we held eventual finalists Sheffield Wednesday and Arsenal to draws at the Baseball Ground, that famous old stadium again witnessed a classic encounter. Leeds went ahead but we clawed our way back into the game and despite having a man sent off we continued to press, taking to our role as the plucky underdogs that continued to drive forward in the face of adversity. I was reluctant to be a part of the Sky Sports experience but the reality was that we were a producer's wet dream. Derby, from that place that existed far away from the Premier League, tried their hardest but ultimately came away as the gallant loser. Leeds won by four goals to two.

*****

The FA Cup defeat did not put us off our stride and we continued to remain unbeaten in the League for a further 10 games, stretching the run to 20 matches without defeat. On 9 March Sunderland had their chance to exact revenge though and without my Dad to thwart any attacks Derby fell to a three nil defeat at Roker Park, the result of which allowed Sunderland to pull the gap back to four points at the top of the table.

Derby's success was a source of pride for me at university but it also eased the banter with Ian at home. Nottingham Forest had finished the 1994–95 season in third place in the Premier League, behind Manchester United and champions Blackburn Rovers and had therefore qualified to play in the UEFA Cup. It wasn't until the 1997–98 season that the Champions League expanded to become the 'Champions, Runners-Up and Also-Rans League' and spread its way to include fourth place in England's first division.

That season Ian travelled to Malmo in Sweden, Auxerre and Lyon in France, and finally to watch his team play Germany's Bayern Munich. He later told me that one of his mates spent the entire bus trip to Lyon convincing everyone that buying food would not be a problem and so he naturally thought that the guy could speak French. The group entered a restaurant but instead of asking, 'Bonjour, pourrais-je s'il vous plaît ordonner un poulet pour moi et mes amis de Nottingham?' the fan simply re-enacted the Birdie Song dance and shouted, 'Gorranny chicken?'

I respected Ian and his following of Forest that season but I would never let him know. Instead I would criticise the slenderness of his team's victories or the quality of the opposition, and when he proudly showed me the Bayern Munich scarf he had swapped with a fan outside the Olympic Stadium my rusty German translated, 'Die Europäische Cup Final '74, '75, '76, '82, '87' as the years in which the team had either been winners or runners-up in the European Cup. Having beaten Forest by five goals to one at the City Ground though I couldn't resist asking Ian if they were the times that Bayern's goals had gone in.

After being beaten by Sunderland, two more defeats in the next four matches left us looking over our shoulders instead of ahead at the finish line. The Wearsiders overtook us at the top while Crystal Palace started sniffing just two points off us in third. However, the Rams were unbeaten in the next five, including a home victory against Palace on Sunday 28 April that ensured our return to the top-flight.

This time I wasn't at the match to celebrate with my Dad. I assumed that it would be shown on television but Tyne Tees was showing *Gone With the Wind* instead. Being a Sunday the bar was closed until the evening and so I couldn't laugh loudest at those who had good-naturedly ripped me to pieces in October. I didn't have to wait long though and as soon as the bar opened at seven o'clock my university friends and I went in to take part in the weekly quiz. I was in high-spirits and drank far too much Carling before playing football in the halls of residence car park while someone played John Denver's *Country Road* repeatedly out of my window.

It was a surreal end to a strange period of time. These friendships I had made at university were those I had formed while taking my first degree and while I was about to head into my second year they were just about to leave their third, and the university for good. I would be treading among unfamiliar faces while Derby's promotion would see them too trying to cope in strange surroundings. The Premier League could be an unforgiving place and trying to fit in with new peers who had already become acquainted in their first year might mean me finding it difficult to adjust as well.

Endsleigh League Division One 1995–96

Pos		Pl	W	D	L	F	A	GD	Pts
1	Sunderland	46	22	17	7	59	33	59	83
2	**Derby County**	**46**	**21**	**16**	**9**	**71**	**51**	**71**	**79**
3	Crystal Palace	46	20	15	11	67	48	67	75
4	Stoke City	46	20	13	13	60	49	60	73
5	Leicester City	46	19	14	13	66	60	66	71
6	Charlton Athletic	46	17	20	9	57	45	57	71
7	Ipswich Town	46	19	12	15	79	69	79	69

1996–97

Derby County 3 Leeds United 3
Saturday 17 August 1996

The night before our first game in the Premier League I was drinking in the pub at the top end of Old Sawley. As it stands at the edge of the village just before the countryside opens out to reveal the floodplains of the River Trent, the pub retains the feel of one of the taverns in the Peak District and it wasn't uncommon for someone to run in on occasion and coax the regulars into leaving their pints to help retrieve escaping livestock.

James England worked there in the evenings during his summer vacations from university as well as working throughout the day at his Dad's mate's paint shop in town. As such he not only emerged from university debt free but also managed to buy a red Vauxhall Nova for the final fourth year of his Masters course.

Our advent in the Premier League coincided with the capacity at the Baseball Ground at an all-time low and so I had given up on getting a ticket for our opening match with Leeds United before they had even gone on sale. Dad was away on holiday with Mum, James was working and as the Goodhall brothers had season tickets I would have been sitting on my own anyway. I was therefore satisfied with the improved coverage on television and radio that being in the Premier League brought.

Talk of the match had been rife in the pub though and the excitement of our return to the top-flight soon gave way to disappointment that I wouldn't be attending. At a quarter past 11 I went to the toilet for the last time before the two mile trek back home and, once there, the headiness of the real ale offered by the Harrington Arms made me break the first rule of urinal etiquette and I spoke to the guy next to me.

'I don't suppose you have a ticket for tomorrow?' I asked, vaguely knowing the chap just by the fact that he was often in the pub when we went there.

'As a matter of fact, I think I do.' came the reply.

And so from the toilet I returned to the bar with my new friend, which is never something one usually likes to disclose and confirmed that his mate did have a spare ticket and that if I came to the pub at 12 the following day I could go along with their group.

Outside the ground we got our first taste of life in the Premier League as representatives from *The Sun* newspaper gave out plastic bowler hats to every supporter who went past. I still didn't want to be a part of the cabaret but it was difficult not to be swept along. I still had memories of playing Leeds in the Cup the previous season and how, on going ahead in the game I had been as guilty as the next fan in reacting to the television cameras, cheering into the lens and subsequently becoming part of the football product.

The tickets were for the Osmaston Upper, above where the away fans were housed and so once inside the stadium I couldn't avoid the full verbal assault from the Leeds support. Chants of, 'You're in the wrong division.' and, 'Derby's going down.' had begun and we hadn't even kicked a ball yet. Things only got worse as the visitors steamed into a two-goal lead and it looked like dark days ahead for the Rams.

Derby didn't give in though and instead of crumbling under the pressure we pulled the game back to two-all, turning the Baseball Ground into an ocean of flailing limbs that high in the Osmaston Upper lay on the brink of stupidity. For so long I had looked up at the supporters in this area and berated them for their lack of animation but now I realised that anything more vigorous than a brief period of applause made it highly likely that you'd end up over the side of the stand.

Leeds soon ruined the party though by taking the lead again, reigniting the songs of their travelling army and their belief that we didn't deserve our place in their League but again the Rams fought back and tied the match once more. Despite there being around 18,000 supporters in the old stadium the noise generated was immense. The steep stands simply wouldn't let the noise out and it seemed to swirl among the eaves like a howling wind.

*****

At the end of the summer holiday I returned to Stockton-on-Tees and again forsook my place at the Baseball Ground. I left with the feeling that the team were in good hands though and no longer needed my support, having some grand belief that my attendance was something more contributory than simply that of a mug punter who had remained blindly loyal through the turgid years.

Despite what those from Leeds had said, our results compounded our right to be in the division. We drew against Tottenham Hotspur at White Hart Lane and at home against Manchester United, in which summer signing Jacob Laursen fulfilled the dream of all journalists by scoring a 20 yard free kick and handing them the headline, 'Jacob's Cracker' on a plate. We also managed wins against teams that my Dad described as, 'those you have to beat if you want to stay in the division' as Blackburn Rovers and Sunderland were also beaten in those early Premier League encounters.

Ian was doing his best to dampen my mood by citing the fact that the League was, '…a marathon and not a sprint' but this was understandable seeing as though Forest were languishing way down in 16th and just two points above the relegation zone.

For my second year at university I moved into a rented house in nearby Thornaby-on-Tees along with three other students and four others who lived next door. One guy, Tom, I didn't know at all and actually had turned up that first weekend back expecting someone else who it turned out was called Guy.

Explaining in the past that I supported Derby County had often brought looks and expressions of sympathy from strangers similar to how my Mum looked at me and my Dad when we returned from a defeat. It always seemed like I was conversing with someone who thought I was in some way disadvantaged and that I would soon be expecting them to stand aside for me to accept alms from the Queen. Since becoming a Premier League team though, and one that was acclimatising well to their new horizons, the badge of honour that had been mine had somehow lost its shine. I was now regarded in the same manner as those who supported Manchester United, Liverpool and Arsenal by those who came from Barnsley, Darlington and Norwich.

As Derby progressed my Dad continued to send me copies of the green *Derby Evening Telegraph* as well as any other reports that he happened to come across in the national press. He still went to some matches with my Uncle Paul, reliving those games at the Baseball Ground that they went to in the 1960s before Derby emerged from 80 years of going through the motions to become a recognisable name in English football.

On 1 December Derby came away from Highbury, the home of League leaders Arsenal with a point, which gave me a great deal of encouragement as our televised home game against Everton approached. For months I had had to settle for the videprinter action when Derby's afternoon fate was played out on screen in a jerking motion, but here was a full 90 minutes at the Baseball Ground for me to enjoy, beamed live and exclusive into the student union.

My excitement never faltered as I sat beneath the television in the small bar, which was sufficient for our quiet university campus. At first I had an army of students around me who through their friendship with me had found an allegiance to my cause. Gradually though the interest of my friends waned as the game seemed to be petering out into a goalless draw.

As Everton were pushing for a place in the UEFA Cup I was picturing a fine result while the neutrals around me started conversations on whether they would end the night at the Millenium nightclub on the Teesside Retail Park. That was until Everton scored a last-minute winner and suddenly the whole bar were focussed on the television screen once again.

Without an Everton fan among them they still managed to cheer as if Earth United had beaten bitter rivals Mars Wanderers in the Inter-galactic Cup Final. Even those who had never expressed an interest in football joined in as they took great pleasure in my demise. I turned to face them and once again found myself looking into the many faces of sympathy that had accompanied me on many days of watching Derby County. If I had come to witness a submersion into the Derby experiences of the past then this disappointment certainly didn't let me down.

A bitterly cold Christmas threw the fixture list into chaos. We only had one home match in the League between that televised game in early December against Everton and when Liverpool came to the Baseball Ground on 1 February. Subsequently our League position dropped dramatically and we fell to 16th position, just three points away from the relegation zone. Ian, who could never usually be bothered to answer the home phone suddenly started picking it up on every occasion and proceeded to sing the theme tune to *Chariots of Fire* in reference to his earlier insistence about marathons and not sprints.

One loss in the next five saw us climb up the table and after beating Chelsea on 1 March we were back up to 12th. Meanwhile Forest remained in 17th and Ian's telephony skills reverted back to normal.

Middlesbrough 6 Derby County 1
Wednesday 5 March 1997

Middlesbrough's Riverside Stadium was just over five miles from my student house in Thornaby but this was the first opportunity I'd had of going to see Derby play there. In my first year we had played the Boro in August before I had arrived in the North East whilst in the second first year the two clubs had been in different divisions.

James England drove up in his Vauxhall Nova from Leeds and Ryan Goodhall who had started a degree course in history at university in Newcastle caught the train down.

On a bitterly cold evening in Middlesbrough we set off with layers of clothes around us, supplemented with layers of alcoholic drinks inside of us, neither of which were any defence against the North East winter that lasted from when we arrived in mid September right through to May. That Middlesbrough's stadium stood on the banks of the River Tees further added to the cold as the wind blew uninvitingly and directly into our faces from off the black water despite being in the enclosed stadium.

With Derby in 12th and Middlesbrough languishing at the foot of the table it looked like my visit might coincide with the football supporter's Holy Grail of an away win, despite the Ram's only having secured one away victory over Blackburn

Rovers way back on 9 September. Middlesbrough, however, had developed somewhat of a siege mentality after being docked three points by the FA for failing to fulfil a pre-Christmas fixture against Blackburn, even though they apparently phoned the Premier League and were told it would be fine to do so.

As the match progressed any notion that Derby were going to reward us with the desired three points was blown out of the stadium on the blustering Teesside wind. By the time we scored we were already six down and with the blanket of ale wearing off both the cold and the fact that we were being roundly beaten by the worst team in the division combined to create a truly miserable night.

I didn't appreciate it at the time but with only a five mile trip home I was perhaps the luckiest Derby fan in the stadium that night, with most supporters having to face a 260 mile round trip to watch the game. This daunting return home must have been what gave the Rams fans a melancholic dark humour that night and as we scored our consolation goal the rest of the supporters started goading the home support with chants of, 'You're not singing anymore!' but I wasn't singing either. It was becoming apparent that Derby seemed to find their best form when I wasn't around.

Supporters own strange superstitions and while most can attend matches in a detached atmosphere some will go to great measures in ensuring that they do everything they can to help the team. Clothing suddenly becomes lucky and fans will veer out of their way to buy programmes from a particular vendor just because on one occasion this was seen as being the ignition that sparked a victory against local rivals.

Maybe this comes from the supporters' desire to be a part of the game as before the Football Association was founded in 1863 football largely resembled the annual Shrovetide match played near Ashbourne in Derbyshire each year where every man and his dog takes part. But when strict rules, which included restricting team sizes came into force, suddenly each team was reduced to 11 men and relegated the rest of the mob to mere supporters who could only dream of playing.

Believing in luck and thinking we can affect the game allows supporters to retake ownership and as such be a part of the team once more. Maybe before the Middlesbrough match someone was going so far to put on a pair of lucky underpants in their bedroom with as much pride and purpose as Igor Stimac was putting on the Rams shirt in the Riverside Stadium dressing room.

Luck can go both ways though and sometimes we believe that our actions can provoke failure rather than bring on success for our team. When Derby moved permanently to the Baseball Ground in 1895, moving a group of gypsies from the site provoked a curse that was made to prevent the club from winning any major trophies. That their dispersal from the site would have happened anyway with the very essence of gypsy culture being that they are free to roam without laying down any roots was not pointed out at the time or maybe it was, alongside suggestions from Sir Francis Ley and the Derby County Board as to where exactly the gypsies could stick their lucky heather.

Watching from high among the Derby supporters that night in Middlesbrough I started to think that maybe I was the curse on the team that was stopping us from maintaining the successes of the seventies. My first season had resulted in our relegation while our brief flirtation with top-flight football had been tainted by the fact that only winning the League brought any glory with no European football for those just missing out.

The final whistle was our signal to depart and without even an applause of recognition to the team leaving the field we descended the stairs to the concourse behind the stand. The lads were staying at my house and so we consoled ourselves with a race to get back to the student bar and tackle some more drinks before closing time.

We wandered for what seemed like hours back to Middlesbrough train station for the short trip back to Thornaby. The locals were in good spirits and as they circled around us on their own journeys home their excited chatter started to grate. By the time we got back to the bar though I felt stoic after chatting through the developments of the game with the other two on the train like we were some women's counselling group off *Jerry Maguire*.

Entering the student bar was like a repeat of the Everton match with almost everyone looking up from their drinks to jeer me through the door but far from feeling embarrassed I recognised that it was all done in good spirits. My childhood tantrums at losses had deserted me and largely thanks to my Dad I could now face defeat with good grace. That I was able to mimic his grin and smile into the face of the crowd was a testament that despite being away from my family I had brought some of the best of it with me.

Derby County 1 Southampton 1
Wednesday 9 April 1997

The 1996–97 season was the last year that Derby County played their first team action at the Baseball Ground. The ambitions of four club directors, Lionel Pickering, Peter Gadsby, Stuart Webb and John Kirkland, had become a reality and the club had announced that they would be moving to a 30,000 seated, purpose built stadium in the February of 1996. With Derby top of the Championship and 15 matches into their run of 20 games unbeaten they probably also had a quiet word with Jim Smith to see if he could postpone promotion for a year to avoid crowds in our first season in the Premier League being constrained by the small capacity at the Baseball Ground.

As work progressed on the impressive steel structure on the site of former railway sidings and gasworks just a mile away I continued my pilgrimage to the Baseball Ground for a home match against Southampton. All season we could only dare to hope that we could steer clear of relegation so that the new stadium would host top-flight football in its first year but as the season progressed Derby had us believing.

Despite the terrible defeat at Middlesbrough, which had dropped us down to 14th, we had since triumphed over Tottenham Hotspur at home and after Jim Smith introduced Paulo Wanchope to English football we had also beaten the League leaders and eventual champions, Manchester United, at Old Trafford.

Wanchope had joined Derby as part of a combined deal with fellow Costa Rican, Mauricio Solis, for £1.2 million and was an instant hit, least of all due to his mazy run which led to one of the three goals scored at Old Trafford. His unpredictable style had supporters guessing for the entirety of his time at Derby whether he was actually any good or just too difficult to defend against. The Premier League thought the former and in October 1997 he was their Player of the Month, and having later furthered his career at West Ham United and Manchester City, as well as scoring four goals in one match at international level where apparently there is never an easy game, those who continued to question his ability found themselves in the minority.

Solis enjoyed less success at the club, being left out of the side mostly because teams could only field three players from non-EEC countries at the time and the Rams already boasted Croation Igor Stimac and his countryman Aljosa Asanovic who had signed from Hadjuk Split in the close-season of 1996. We also had goalkeeper Mart Poom who had apparently won Estonia's equivalent of the Sport's Personality of the Year on numerous occasions.

Many at the time complained about Derby's tendency to recruit foreign players but the fact was that those from abroad were far cheaper than those with similar or less talent of English descent. It was also difficult for newly promoted teams to attract established Premier League players as the tendency to return straight to Division One was not something players were looking to have on their CV, presuming they have CVs and not just copies of a Panini sticker album that they hand over at every transfer.

As I was home for Easter my Dad had given up his ticket so that I could enjoy my last match at the Baseball Ground. Simon Goodhall had driven but with him having a season ticket on the Pop-Side I again sat alone in the Osmaston Upper. The lack of atmosphere up there was balanced by the incredible views, not just of the match but of the supporters who mark each matchday by flocking back to the stadium like sand in an hourglass.

It was up in that lofty position that I watched my final League match at the Baseball Ground, sat forward with my elbows resting on my knees and my hands covering my mouth. It was easier to then cover my eyes if things turned against us and the mouth if things turned really bad.

Through my eyes and my hands I looked into the stands trying to work out which people had come together and how many, like me, were watching the match alone. I tried to spot the fathers and sons over in the Pop-Side where me and my Dad had seen so many matches or in the lower part of the Normanton End opposite where I used to meet him after he'd finished a shift at work. I tried to make out the figures in the darkness of the middle tier, wondering whether some father was taking his lad to his first match like mine had done almost 20 years before.

Maybe it was the end of the era that was making me outrospective or maybe it was my Human Sciences course but for once the crowd, who had always seemed one to me, became a group of individuals. I started to consider what lives they left to come here and where they returned after the final whistle. Did they come from understanding spouses who would welcome them with sympathetic looks when they returned from defeat or was watching Derby County a guilty pleasure upon which none of their acquaintances knew?

My eyes rested on a figure in the C Stand just below me and to the right. Everyone else in the ground was sat upright, eyes intent on the game before them like meerkats. But just like me this one figure was sat forward with his elbows resting on his knees and his hands covering his mouth. And I realised it was Uncle Paul.

Part of the deal with me having the ticket that day was that I'd queue up and get a ticket for Dad for the final match of the season, which would be the last League game at the Baseball Ground. I would be back at university and after all the memories that Dad had been responsible for giving me, it was the least I could do. To make sure of getting the ticket I left with a quarter of an hour to go and descended the many steps at the back of the stand to get to the exit.

Holes were already appearing in the old stand and while it wasn't as bad as what the Germans had done during World War Two, or as hurtful as the comment from Matthias after being thrashed by Liverpool, it wasn't pretty. Now in the Premier League with its glamorous television coverage and foreign stars it was obvious that a move was needed, otherwise those Leeds supporters who had greeted our inaugural match with such derision would have been right.

People complained that many memories were contained within the old ground but memories exist in the mind. We don't have to return to a place to remember and I can recall the images that came flooding back that afternoon no matter where I am. The alternative to moving was to redevelop three sides of the Baseball Ground, which would have rendered it unrecognisable from the one that had seen over 100 years of history. Trying to welcome 26,000 of the new breed of fan, the ones who came in cars now rather than on trains or directly from the foundries and factories would also have been impossible when hemmed in by the tight Normanton Streets.

Three years previous the British male/female duo, Everything But The Girl, so called because apparently every record company they approached liked, 'everything but the girl,' released their best-known track, *Missing*. It was a song a little removed from the usual stuff they played in the student bars and created a new dancing style akin to a one-armed man attempting to clap. Although not about the relocation of football clubs the lyrics were so pertinent to Derby's situation that I used them as the introduction to my dissertation, which was written on the effect that the relocation of football clubs can have on their communities.

Sometimes you have to accept change, even that as big as moving away from a home that has provided much joy, excitement and even heartbreak and despair as both necessary and unavoidable. You just have to be prepared to take those emotions with you.

As I emerged from the grand old stadium for the last time into the chilled streets the beast of the crowd still rumbled within the belly of the ground. People said that the roar inside was loud because the noise couldn't escape but I realised then that it could. It spilled out and over like water out of a bath and drenched me with its sound.

Despite not being for me the ticket that I bought was probably the most important I had ever purchased. One of only 18,287 it was for my Dad and went some small way in repaying him for all that he had given me by introducing me to the life of a football supporter.

People joke that those who take their kids to football matches should be arrested for child cruelty and that watching Derby in particular should carry a harsher sentence than most but in his defence when Dad started taking me we were in one of the best Leagues in the world and had even won the Championship twice throughout that decade. It must have been obvious to all at the time though that we were on the decline and if the League table didn't show it then Dad could always rely on Ian to tell him we were rubbish.

It must be tempting to wrap our kids in cotton wool and tell them that the world is perfect and that everything will be alright but the truth is that it is a cruel place and sooner or later if their parents don't let them know, then the kids will find out for themselves. In taking me to football Dad helped me witness despair, heartbreak and a sense of injustice in a controlled environment, one that we could turn our backs on at full-time as we walked back along Cambridge Street to the train station. After almost 20 years of watching Derby County I could honestly say that the experience was akin to a parent buying a pet with a short life expectancy so as to introduce their children to the concept of death.

A draw at home against Nottingham Forest on 23 April all but secured our Premier League survival. With two matches to go and six points clear of Sunderland, who were third from bottom and with a goal difference of minus 20, it would take one hell of a gypsy's curse for us to be relegated. To make sure, we won our last away game at Coventry City and could look forward to celebrating the final match at the Baseball Ground without having to worry about the result on the pitch.

Derby County 1 Arsenal 3
Sunday 11 May 1997

Some of the club's greats attended the final League match at the Baseball Ground on Sunday 11 May 1997. My Dad was there along with my Uncle Alan and Auntie Sylvia, his wife, who always took the most amazingly aromatic coffee to matches in a flask. Uncle Paul was there too. The club also introduced legends from the past like Dave Mackay and Charlie George, who by now looked less like a footballing legend and more like that bloke out of the Chemical Brothers who that March had released *Block Rockin' Beats*.

It must have been like a death to the old ground with its life flashing before it as it agonised in its final moments. Further agony was to come when, despite Ashley Ward giving the Rams a sixth minute lead and Arsenal defender, Tony Adams, being sent off for two bookable offences after only 10 minutes, Arsenal responded with three goals to win the match.

The Gunner's all-time top marksman, Ian Wright, scored twice, with Dutch international, Dennis Bergkamp, getting the other. Meanwhile at the other end England goalkeeper, David Seaman, thwarted the Derby attack. These were great players who have since become legends and while some were disappointed at the final result, least of all manager, Jim Smith, that the ground was graced with legends of the past before the match and those of the future, such a presence as part of its farewell was nothing other than fitting.

Meanwhile I was still up in Stockton-on-Tees trying to find coverage of that historic day at the Baseball Ground on television. Despite the fact that there was one hell of a relegation scrap going on, with Blackburn Rovers in a position of 13th and about as respectably mid-table as you can get still within two points of relegated Sunderland, Sky Sports concentrated on the 'Championship party' that saw Manchester United beat West Ham United in a match that meant nothing.

I had resigned myself to listening to snippets of Derby's game coming through on Radio 5 where despite our defeat we finished the season in 12th position and with 46 points. This was just one place below Leeds United who finished with the same points total as we did and so it looked like we weren't in the wrong division after all.

As me and my Dad remotely basked in the relative success of retaining our Premier League status it occurred to me that this was one of the rare occasions when being a Derby fan actually made any sense. All too often I had applauded the appalling and tried to find reason to excuse the poor performances that me and my Dad had witnessed. But it is this irrational behaviour that sets the sports fan apart from the sane majority and we welcome and revel in the eccentricity.

That season while Derby breathed a sigh of relief at not falling from the Premier League juggernaut at the first attempt, Ian's Nottingham Forest were relegated long before the last game of the season. Despite this, when the Reds played Newcastle at St James' Park at the end of the year Ian took the opportunity to take in the game anyway and to come and visit me in the North East for the weekend. The night before the match we were sitting in the student bar with Ian revelling in supping pound pints compared to normal prices that he was used to paying in the pubs and clubs back home.

'How have Forest been doing this year?' asked a friend of mine, who knew little about football.

'Not so well, we've been relegated!' Ian replied.

Her response was incredulous, 'What…and they're still making you play?'

FA Carling Premiership 1996–97

Pos		Pl	W	D	L	F	A	GD	Pts
1	Manchester United	38	21	12	5	76	44	32	75
9	Leicester City	38	12	11	15	46	54	-8	47
10	Tottenham Hotspur	38	13	7	18	44	51	-7	46
11	Leeds United	38	11	13	14	28	38	-10	46
12	**Derby County**	38	11	13	14	45	58	-13	46
13	Blackburn Rovers	38	9	15	14	42	43	-1	42
18	Sunderland	38	10	10	18	35	53	-18	40
19	Middlesbrough	38	10	12	16	51	60	-9	39
20	Nottingham Forest	38	6	16	16	31	59	-28	34

1997–98

As ever there were comings and goings in the close season, the most notably of 1997 being Paul McGrath. Despite playing only 26 times for the Rams McGrath is still regarded as one of the club's most important players, as not only did he help Derby stay up in that first year in the Premier League but he also inspired those around him to become better players. Most of the team that took to the pitch as part of the opening ceremony of the new ground on 18 July, however, were the same that had admirably avoided relegation the previous year.

The manager was the same, the Board were the same and there was even a suggestion that the club had been required to move a new band of gypsies off the building site at Pride Park, culminating in another curse that was by now looking more like a convenient excuse for a relatively bare trophy cabinet.

The supporters came too, and then some. The last match at the Baseball Ground had seen just over 18,000 attend whereas when the new stadium opened there wasn't a spare seat among the 30,000 capacity.

Derby County A Wimbledon A

Wednesday 13 August 1997

As Derby County took to the pitch for the first home game the club were almost unrecognisable from the team that had existed for the previous 113 years. Under the backdrop of a stadium that stood proud on the wasteland of Pride Park unhindered by any surroundings, it shone like a beacon at the edge of the city. Meanwhile on the pitch some of the finest players from Europe and the rest of the world sported the famous white shirt with only the Derby Ram there to convince us that this was still our team.

The first visitors in genuine competition were Wimbledon, a team who later moved to Milton Keynes in 2003 after sharing Crystal Palace's Selhurst Park for over 10 years. In June 2004 they became the Milton Keynes Dons while back in South London the spirit of the old club, which famously beat Liverpool in the 1988 FA Cup Final, remains in the admirable attempts of the supporters to form AFC Wimbledon.

With nothing in the surroundings apart from a couple of buildings and the gasworks the site of Derby's new stadium seemed remote and the lack of pubs in the vicinity led many to believe that the matchday experience would become sterile. However, the stadium was barely a mile from the train station and the pubs along Railway Terrace and the supporters simply needed to change their habits.

Dad was at work on the evening of that first League match at the new stadium so I borrowed his car and drove to Derby, via Shardlow to pick up the Goodhall brothers. With nobody quite sure where we could park the journey was like travelling to an away match although Simon had an inkling that we could leave the car at a small recreation ground about a mile and a half from the stadium and walk along the riverside.

We kept to the usual route, travelling out of Shardlow along the A6, through Chellaston and into the city but that night instead of taking a left at the Blue Peter pub to continue along the ring road towards Normanton we continued straight ahead along London Road and further in towards the city centre.

The local college was offering parking spaces but Simon stood steadfast in his belief that we would be fine in the park, so with traffic building up I took a right turn down the narrow lane that led to an area of secluded trees surrounding several football pitches and a bmx track. Severe speed-bumps competed with the car even though I was already down to five miles-per-hour and I cringed every time I heard the scrape of metal from beneath Dad's Rover.

As we parked by the changing rooms, which through years of neglect had lost their windows and become a blank canvas to graffiti artists, the floodlights of the stadium glowed above the trees in the distance like a scene from *Close Encounters of the Third Kind*. It was an eerie sight with grown men gingerly walking towards it as if some ethereal message was calling them. Usually the familiar streets made the reason for these journeys obvious but tonight we were all walking into a strange land.

Simon was right, which was unsurprising coming from someone who would tell you the time in hours, minutes and seconds, and it was a simple walk along the river that saw us emerge at the back of the East Stand. Once within actual sight of the stands the stadium acted like a vortex, pulling us towards it, understanding our reticence and overcompensating with its welcome.

The turnstiles were huge compared to those at the Baseball Ground, which had resembled a country gate and reached from the floor to the entrance roof like those I had encountered at Wembley Stadium when watching the Merseyside FA Cup Final of 1986.

Once inside we were left aghast at the amount of space actually within the confines of the arena, where people could wander to find the stairway to their new seats. The Baseball Ground was a rabbit-warren of tight corridors, dead-ends and tiny food outlets the size of small caravans whereas inside Pride Park Stadium wide avenues allowed supporters to mingle freely with beers and burgers that they purchased from the gleaming kitchens.

With the Goodhalls having bought season tickets they were eager to find their view for the forthcoming year and so declined the offer of a drink and went straight inside. My seat for the night was further back but in a similar location in the East Stand, halfway between the centre spot and the goal line. The view was incredible, almost like the Osmaston Upper yet instead of feeling estranged from the rest of the crowd I was right among it.

The original plan for the Board had been to have the West Stand separate from the rest of the stands, which would form a horseshoe. The corners would be filled in at a later date but such was the huge interest from corporate sponsors that a huge bank of executive boxes linking the West Stand to the North Stand was already present. This left one gap in the South West Corner through which we could still see people streaming towards the ground from the direction of the college where we had been told to park.

The fairytale continued when Ashley Ward, the Derby forward who scored the last goal for the Rams at the Baseball Ground, opened our account at the new stadium and any fear that we would find the new surroundings as suppressive as an away ground were dispelled. It was easy to forget that most stories at Derby often had an unhappy ending.

Almost in protest at the fixture computer, as if the new stadium wanted a grander opening, the new floodlights that peered like eager supporters over the edges of the side of the West and East Stands extinguished themselves with 34 minutes still to play. After a delay of half an hour during which time 11 electricians attempted to rectify the issue, referee, Uriah Rennie, abandoned the match with the Rams leading by two goals to one.

It was an embarrassment to the Board who had understandably been proud of the club's transformation but it was not an isolated incident. A spate of floodlight failures followed when West Ham hosted Crystal Palace on 3 November and at the match between Wimbledon and Arsenal on 22 December, which must have seen Wimbledon manager Joe Kinnear dine out on humble pie for a month after his unstinting criticism of our own stadium.

Police were called in to investigate but found no signs of sabotage and so the conspiracy theorists soon trundled off to spout their thoughts on alien abduction and Gillian Anderson instead.

On Saturday 30 August Pride Park opened its new turnstiles again, this time to Barnsley and this time the floodlights held out as the Rams won by a single goal. Italian Stefano Eranio, who played 20 times for his country and appeared in two European Cup Finals for AC Milan left most of the 27,232 crowd smiling as we

SON OF MY FATHER

walked away from our new home. It was the biggest home attendance for a Derby match since playing Manchester United at the Baseball Ground on 2 February 1980.

Further wins at home against Everton, Southampton and Southend in the League Cup saw 12 goals scored by the Rams with only one goal conceded. It seemed like the team had took to their new surroundings in their stride, as had the supporters, with the Pop-Side transferred to the corner of the East and South Stands and the C-Stand relocated to the corner opposite, hemming in the away supporters with noise as they had done at the Baseball Ground for the previous 102 years.

Meanwhile I was entering my final year at university and could only look at the highlights of matches with envy. On 18 October Manchester United were held to a 2–2 draw at the new stadium and while the rearranged home match with Wimbledon ended in a disappointing draw, when Arsenal arrived on 1 November they were blown away emphatically as the Rams recorded a three-nil win over the second-placed Gunners and climbed to sixth in the Premier League table.

Leeds United 4 Derby County 3

Saturday 8 November 1997

The week after the Arsenal match we played Leeds United at Elland Road. It was only a 40 mile trip from Stockton-on-Tees and so I travelled down to the game along with Ryan Goodhall, who I met on the train from Newcastle. These were great times to be a Derby fan and watching the team play seemed light years from the previous 22 of the brief highs that had punctuated our steady downfalls.

For a club with such a stature in the game Leeds United are a relatively new football club among those founded in the late 1800s. They were formed in 1919 after the Football Association disbanded Leeds City for making illegal payments to players throughout World War One at a time when you would have thought people had more important things to worry about. United were elected to the Football League on 31 May 1920 and in 1924 won promotion to Division One.

In 1961 Don Revie became manager and had a similar affect on the club to that which Brian Clough had with both Derby County and Nottingham Forest, taking the team from the brink of Division Three and making them English Champions. In 1974 Clough actually took over from Revie as manager of Leeds in a reign that lasted just 44 days. Leeds obviously didn't think too much of Brian Clough so instead he went to Forest and between 1975 and 1993 won two European Cups, the European Super Cup, the Football League Championship, four League Cups and the FA Charity Shield. During the same period Leeds won the Football League Championship once and the Charity Shield.

140

When Derby arrived at Elland Road Leeds were just below us in the table in seventh, sharing the same points but with an inferior goal difference that was currently edging Derby into a place in European competition. As I continued to progress successfully at university so the Rams were casting old failures aside and punching their weight among some of the best teams in the country.

In spite of our current form we weren't expecting anything from the game and the old cliché that, 'A draw would be a good result.' was uttered many times among the supporters that congregated in the concourse beneath the South Stand before the match. The team had different ideas though and quickly sped into a three-goal lead. Our constant chanting was only interrupted when a supporter arrived late to the match and I turned round half expecting to see my Dad, but on this occasion it wasn't him.

At home Dad still seemed to be doing his famous juggling act, carrying out tasks and jobs that the day just didn't have time for. Many times I had returned back from Stockton to find a list of chores with only half crossed off, more amazed at those he had done as opposed to criticising the ones he still had to do, all while maintaining his contribution to the Long Eaton Sunday League, his work at Rolls-Royce and to his family.

By this time my Dad had competed in the London Marathon four times and could regularly be seen running through the streets of our town and the lanes that led to the surrounding villages. For his age he was a talented athlete and was hovering around the three-hour mark for the 26 mile course but he would deny that this milestone was his target and instead insisted that his only aim was to keep on running until overtaken by a man with a bucket of change dressed in a rhinoceros suit.

If any fan ever believed in the curse of themselves which I had contemplated at the Riverside Stadium the previous season it should have been this man, who missed our three-goal surge into the lead and instead witnessed Leeds score twice before half-time to bring the score back to 2–3. The ground was now an ocean of noise coming from the home support, which had swept away our own voices as we cheered on what we thought was to be only our third away win of the season. The inevitable equaliser came from Leeds and by the time they scored their fourth our turnaround from joy to abject despair was complete.

It would have been easy for the team's confidence to be dented but we responded by going on an unbeaten run at home that lasted for six matches, five of which were won, leaving us again in sixth position and dreaming of Europe. Even though I wasn't living in the region at the time it was easy to pick up on the buzz that the success was creating. Supporters who had been tempted by the new stadium and its pristine surroundings were speaking of a new era while those who had been present at the close of the 1980s were talking of another Derby County resurgence, this time with the promise of European action that only those who had been witness in the mid-seventies could relate to.

When I came back from university at Christmas and Easter the conversations at home and in the pub were animated. The likelihood of Derby in the UEFA Cup meant that Dad could talk openly about the balmy nights at the Baseball Ground that he had seen before I was born. Before when he spoke something had stopped him as maybe he thought it was unfair to rekindle a past so elevated from that which I had seen at our club, or maybe he thought it would drive some sort of wedge between himself and our group of friends that now met and were now anticipating great wins before each match.

But that was Dad, usually opting to say nothing at all rather than something that would offend anyone. It was appropriate that he took to refereeing as opposed to playing the game as what concerned him most was enjoying the sport rather than the winning. He was the man behind the scenes, watching and making everything work rather than the one on the frontline and taking the headlines. The self-satisfaction that he had done his job well was all the reward he needed and the trophies that lined the cabinets could always have someone else's name inscribed upon them.

That's what he was now doing with me, and also with Ian and Daniel. Ian had already passed his diploma and was forging a career in IT when most of us were still calling it 'computers'. Meanwhile Daniel was academically sound and heading towards his own university days as well as making his own strides in athletics. Meanwhile there was always my Dad, either sitting at the back of the graduation hall or quietly encouraging from the side of the track allowing his boys to shine on the various paths that he had let us find.

On 5 March Leeds arrived at Pride Park and we all felt that we had a score to settle, that score being 4–3, but things at Derby County never turn out how you want them to. Far from being avenged Leeds piled on more agony and returned to Yorkshire on the crest of a 5–0 win. This time defeat did dent the confidence and Derby only won one game out of the next seven, a four-nil win at home against Bolton Wanderers who had themselves moved into their brand new Reebok Stadium in 1997 from the old Burnden Park.

The slump left us in 10th position, six points behind Blackburn Rovers who held the final European place that had been tantalisingly ours throughout the year. With only two matches still to play it was only mathematically possible that we would further our ambitions and complete a massive turnaround in the club's fortunes. Despite the disappointment though the sensible fans, of which Dad certainly sat among, were able to convince themselves that these were still great times for the club.

A win in the penultimate match had us dreaming of Europe again as we were still within touching distance of Rovers. With a goal difference of just two separating the teams a win for us and Blackburn's own demise would mean we would end the season above them. But we were also relying on too many other teams to slip up and whereas in relegation battles you are vying with teams who have a tendency to lose matches, at the top more often than not they win. The fact that we were hosting third-placed Liverpool didn't help.

Derby County ended the 1997–98 season by beating the Anfield side by a single goal. We finished ninth in the Premier League, the highest we'd been for almost 10 years, in a season that had seen the biggest upheaval in the team's history. The season had also encompassed wins at home against eventual champions Arsenal and a draw against second-placed Manchester United. Despite bitter disappointment I was starting to see Dad's point that these were days to be enjoyed.

FA Carling Premiership 1997–98

Pos		Pl	W	D	L	F	A	GD	Pts
1	Arsenal	38	23	9	6	68	33	35	78
6	Blackburn Rovers	38	16	10	12	57	52	5	58
7	Aston Villa	38	17	6	15	49	48	1	57
8	West Ham United	38	16	8	14	56	57	-1	56
9	**Derby County**	**38**	**16**	**7**	**15**	**52**	**49**	**3**	**55**
10	Leicester City	38	13	14	11	51	41	10	53

1998–99

In the summer of 1998 I had other things to occupy my mind as well as football. It had been three years since I returned to university and the second spell had been far more successful than my first encounter. I was achieving decent results throughout my coursework which had put me on course for a 2:1 although the dissertation was worth a huge percentage and so the final result hung upon my subject: How Derby County's move across the city had affected the wider community of Normanton and the gypsies of Pride Park.

It had been a tough assignment as I'd had to stay focussed on the subject in hand, which had so often been my downfall in previous exams. Throughout my educational history it seemed that my parents and teachers often lamented at how I had failed to answer the question, while looking at me in a way not dissimilar to how Mum looked at me and my Dad when Derby had lost. As I faced my final academic result, despite the recent success I wondered why anything would be different now.

Our final grades were to be placed on a noticeboard in one of the corridors of the first floor of the main college building. This meant that anyone could come along and see them, which drew some protest in the student bar the night before our futures were revealed. As it was, when I arrived to see the swarm of students buzzing within the clinical white walls of the college I was so transfixed on finding my own result that I didn't see anyone else's. My peripheral vision deserted me much as it had done when I scored the only goal of my football career at junior level. Through a pinprick of light among blurred vision I scanned down the names.

Craig Trembirth – 2:1.

Suddenly it felt like everyone milling around the board disappeared and I was left in the centre circle with Pride Park Stadium spinning all around me. Supporters in the stands were wild with excitement as I stood with the trophy resting tight in my fingers yet limp in my hand. As I exhaled a breath of steam came from me, at first shadowing the scoreboard but when it dissipated I could see my name in lights and the result emblazoned into the dark recesses of the cantilevered stand.

One of the students who lived next door was the first person to speak to me, then it just seemed like everyone was mingling, asking how each other had done and congratulating successes and commiserating with what other people saw as underachieving.

It was difficult to gauge what to say to people, not knowing whether they were pleased with their result or not. Some were ecstatic about getting thirds whereas for others 2:2s were nothing short of failure. Judging their mood was impossible though as the blurred vision at the edge of my eyesight had only lifted slightly such was my relief and joy at passing the degree.

I was pleased with myself but was also pleased for Mum and Dad who had backed me even though I had failed before. I had repaid their faith in me and felt like the kid back at the cub's Cup Final almost able to see that child that used to be me standing small in the yellow jersey on a cold Saturday morning field in a place and time so very distant from here.

I remembered too what Dad had said to me many a time. I heard his words and tone and suddenly I knew what to say. One lad who I recognised as being more than just a regular at the student bar approached and instead of prolonging the conversation through being unable to think of what to say I asked him calmly what he'd got.

'2:2.' he replied.

'And are you pleased with that, because you should be, that's a really good result.' I responded. I don't know if he was pleased with the mark before I saw him but he was certainly happy after.

I had started university wanting to be a teacher but that was no longer something I aspired to be, so instead of forging forward into a career or a graduate training course I joined a recruitment agency and started working on a temporary contract for Rolls-Royce in another of those towns that sit within sight and sound of the M1.

In the twilight weeks of my time in Stockton I had started a relationship with a girl who still had two years left to study. We would continue this relationship with me returning north every four weeks with Melissa completing the return fixture in between by coming to Long Eaton.

With me not being around every weekend, Dad not wanting to commit to a full season and Uncle Paul often working on Saturdays it seemed convenient for us all to buy a season ticket between us. The downside was that we no longer went together, with either one of us occupying the lone seat in the North East Corner of the stadium. The surroundings were superb and the football sublime but with only strangers to share it with I find myself somehow missing the drab Baseball Ground years.

Swansea City 0 Derby County 1

Saturday 23 January 1999

I was not the only one reminiscing about those days of watching the match from behind someone's head on a cold blank bank of concrete. When we were drawn away at Plymouth Argyle in the FA Cup, despite the distance the clamour for tickets to be able to relive those days on the terraces was incredible.

For me the prospect of a 420 mile round trip on 2 January coupled with previous FA Cup encounters with Plymouth Argyle in the past dissuaded me from going. The two Goodhalls took the trip down though and helped add to the crowd of 16,730. The attendance was only half that which had turned up to the sixth round match back in 1984 but it was still four times the number who had attended previously to see Plymouth beat Wycombe Wanderers in the second round.

Plymouth were now in the fourth division and looking for an even bigger upset than they had done when Derby were sinking to their lowest ebb 15 years before. It was not to be for the south coast club though and Derby ran out convincing winners by three goals to nil.

That victory set up another away tie against another team in the basement League, Swansea City. The Welsh side had already caused an upset by beating Premier League West Ham United in the third round, holding them at Upton Park before disposing of them at the Vetch Field 10 days before our visit.

The Vetch was where Swansea played until moving to the Liberty Stadium in 2005 when the relocation resulted in the club moving within half a mile of one supporter who had previously received an ASBO banning him from being within one mile of Swansea's stadium.

This time the 138 miles was more palatable than the journey to Plymouth, plus the lack of history between the two clubs meant that I was more inclined to go. With Ryan Goodhall back in Newcastle there was just Simon and I travelling to Wales and having arrived in plenty of time we were directed to a car park on the outskirts of the city. It was only just gone 12 but when we got out of Simon's bright red Ford Fiesta we could already hear the chants of the Derby faithful coming towards us upon the Welsh breeze. At first we thought that we'd mistaken the kick-off time and that the match was due to start at one o'clock but as we looked towards the source of the sound, instead of seeing the ground we saw that the sound was coming out of the nearby pub.

The bar was already rammed with Derby fans with one exuberant chap beating the hell out of a knackered old piano in the corner furthest from the door. With several keys missing and the fact that the pianist had no training whatsoever the crowd was encouraged to sing louder to drown out the din. Even the pub dog turned away, taking one look at the piano before wandering back behind the bar.

After one pint we went for a walk into the city to find somewhere to eat. As he wasn't drinking Simon didn't fancy spending two hours in the pub and so we ended up in Burger King. The city was awash with black and white, that being the colours of Swansea as well as our own, and most fans had painted faces and scarves or flags wrapped around them. Newspaper headlines pinned to A-boards outside newsagents carried messages about the 'big match', a sell-out was guaranteed and there was talk of this being one of the biggest matches since Swansea had dipped out of the top-flight almost 17 years before.

If we hadn't realised the great steps our own club had taken in recent years this was certainly our wake-up call. The local fans were welcoming us like we were some footballing giant, one of the plum draws that the lower League teams love to get but by being so engrossed in Derby County we had failed to see the big side that we had become.

After a Whopper meal Simon and I strolled away from the city centre and back to the ground, leaving early and resorting to the old routines with which we used to abide before seats claimed the terrace. The re-enactment of history didn't stop there with the Derby support being housed in the Vetch Field's West Stand behind the goal, which was still fronted by a seven-foot perimeter fence like some modern-day Offa's Dyke to keep the English out. This structure was probably what prompted Simon to surmise that we were housed on the west of the ground because an ancient law still stood allowing the English to shoot a Welshman with a bow and arrow if he is walking towards England.

With the pitch looking more like a recreation ground rather than the plush Pride Park pitch we had come to know it was easy for those old Baseball Ground years to come flooding back. Having moved forward though, even with the most rose-tinted of glasses it was impossible not to be glad of the fact that those old days were gone for us.

As more people entered the terrace we were left standing on our toes so as to get any view of the pitch and after indignantly tying a huge cross of Saint George on the fencing right behind the goal, much to the derision of the locals, one fan was forced to move it when Derby supporters on the terrace behind pointed out that it was blocking our view of the goal itself.

I used to find the swaying of the crowd exciting and the fact that you could only glimpse pieces of the green turf between necks and shoulders never used to bother me when standing on the Pop-Side. But I had since been introduced to a more civilised way to watch football and the terraces no longer held their appeal. Even when Derby scored, a fluffed effort at the other end of the pitch that limped apologetically over the goal-line, it took a while to register at our end as if the news was being telegraphed from Victorian Australia. When the news did reach us the players were almost back in position to take the kick-off and subsequently the cheering and dancing was more like a Sunday morning hangover than Saturday night fever.

Our reward for beating Swansea was another away fixture, this time at second division Huddersfield Town. Although not as far as Plymouth and Swansea the trip still added another 100 miles onto the dashboard. Derby drew the match and ensured both teams were in the draw for the sixth round. Meanwhile an argument was raging at Arsenal where Sheffield United were feeling aggrieved after coming away from Highbury on the wrong end of a 2–1 defeat.

The Gunners' winning goal had come after one of the visitors kicked the ball out of play for a teammate to receive treatment. At the restart Nwankwo Kanu received the ball in acres of space with the United players not pressing as they expected to receive the ball back, such was the sporting manner at the time. Instead Kanu sprinted down the wing and crossed the ball for Marc Overmars who promptly buried it in the back of the net.

The footballing world was far from impressed and Overmars had barely returned to his own half for the kick-off before people were asking which three people associated with Arsenal have swearwords in their names, with the answer being Nwankwo Kanu, Arsene Wenger and That Twat Marc Overmars.

Had the internationally popular and all-round nice guy Neil Warnock, who would take over the managerial role at Bramall Lane at the end of the year been in charge, then United probably would not have drawn the sympathy that they did. As it was, manager Steve Bruce was from the North East and had a funny-shaped nose and so the clamour for a replay gradually grew.

Under the howling chants of, 'Same old Arsenal, always cheating.' Arsene Wenger graciously agreed to replay the game and a subsequent rematch was held at Highbury 10 days after the original on 23 February. The result was predictably the same with Overmars opening the scoring with a conventional goal and Dennis Bergkamp grabbing the winner.

A day later and with the mouth-watering prospect of a sixth round tie at Highbury waiting for the winners, 28,704 fans turned up at Pride Park Stadium to see Derby beat Huddersfield by three goals to one and we were due our day in the capital.

Arsenal 1 Derby County 0
Saturday 6 March 1999
That morning a cruel cold snap reduced the M1 to two carriageways with the outside lane still covered in snow as me and my Dad drove south. The plan was to travel as far as junction 4 and then park at Stanmore tube station, making the rest of the way on the underground.

Dad took the journey cautiously, as did everyone else and it could have appeared that we were reticent to get to the match whereas in reality we couldn't wait to get there. Earlier that season Derby had played out a creditable draw against Arsenal at home in the League although we had succumbed to the Gunners in the League Cup. In the League we were fairing well and having recently drawn with Tottenham Hotspur just down the road from Arsenal we were dreaming of a similar result and a replay in our new stadium that was gaining its reputation as a fortress.

Fortunately that day Mum had trusted me to dress myself, which was perhaps a good job with me being 24 years old. I proudly wore the replica shirt of the one worn by the team in the 1946 Cup Final, which Derby had won by beating Charlton Athletic 4–1.

That Cup Final was the first after World War Two and went some way in convincing the 98,000 supporters inside Wembley Stadium, as well as the population outside that the planet was getting back to some semblance of normality after six years of bombs and blitzes.

Bert Turner, the only Welshman among the two Scots and 17 Englishmen which made up the two line-ups deflected the ball into his own net to give Derby the lead just five minutes from time, thus becoming the oldest player to score in a Cup Final, aged 36 years, 312 days and 85 minutes. A minute later Turner again became the oldest person to score in a Cup Final, aged 36 years, 312 days and 86 minutes when he scored into the correct goal to draw parity with the Rams.

In the short break before extra-time the Derby manager, Stuart McMillan, instructed the players to put longer studs in their boots, which they did and subsequently won 4–1 with one goal from Peter Doherty and a brace from Jackie Stamps.

Derby County had reached the FA Cup Final on three other occasions before this but on each they had left without the prize. This included suffering the heaviest defeat in the final of the competition, losing 6–0 against Bury in 1903 just five years after ingloriously losing to neighbours Nottingham Forest.

It was on 16 April 1898 that Derby played Forest in the Final with the history books recording a 3–1 victory for the Reds, although post-match photographs of the victorious Forest team with the trophy actually show the winners in the unmistakable white shirts of the Rams. The story goes that in those early years, when photography was in its infancy, the red shirts of Forest didn't show up well against the dull background in the black and white picture and so they were told to wear the white of Derby. Other theories are that Derby Country actually won that game and this rather tall story about photography was invented on the coach home by unscrupulous men of a city whose most famous citizen is a homeless armed robber.

Fifty-two years after we had beaten Charlton to lift the trophy me and my Dad were hoping for further FA Cup glory. Heading along the Jubilee Line from Stanmore and into London added extra spice to the fixture as we rubbed shoulders with theatre-goers attending the matinees in the West End and shoppers alighting at Bond Street station for the stores on Oxford Street.

The train emptied most of its passengers at Leicester Square and Covent Garden only to fill up again at King's Cross and it was here that most other Derby fans who had travelled down to Saint Pancras got onto the train. That familiar sense of camaraderie of an army outnumbered and far from home invaded the carriages along with those travelling fans. With our new battalion we headed out of the city northwards along the Piccadilly Line to get off at Holloway Road. This stop was more convenient than trying to alight at Arsenal tube station, which was originally known as Gillespie Road until 1932. Arsenal station is the only one on the underground to be named after a football team although fans of London clubs often disagree and believe that Cockfosters was named after their nearest rivals and their tendency to adopt a load of pricks to support them.

Me and my Dad entered the stadium and found our place wedged in one corner of the Clock End. Huge double-decker executive boxes hung in the space above us while opposite the North Bank loomed ominously. Meanwhile on either side stood the art deco East Stand, opened in 1932 and the identical West Stand that was built in 1936. Both these stands made the occasion like watching football in a gallery rather than a stadium.

The surroundings seemed to place a refined aspect to our experience of being spectators although after years of me trundling in the wake of my Dad carrying an array of objects to help me see above the shoulders of the men around me it could have been me who was more grown up. Despite the disagreements we may have had or the years of desperation that Dad had had to endure while I argued with Daniel or failed to apply myself to my studies I had made it into the adult that I hoped my Dad had always wanted me to be and one that did justice to him.

Despite only losing by a single goal Derby never looked close to getting anything from the game. Arsenal were in full control with our own team resigned to taking speculative shots from the edge of the area. As ever Dad remained philosophical and as such made me so too, taking comfort from the fact that to even come to a place like Arsenal and think you were in with a chance of winning showed how far we, as a club, had come.

Outside the stadium was a melee of people as we tried to find our way back to the tube station but we were in no real hurry to get back home. Instead we hung back from the frantic pace of London life and breathed in the atmosphere of the occasion.

Whenever I came to the capital it always seemed to hold a vibrancy that some people understandably interpret as hectic, but if I found myself within the city's suburbs and to me the place seemed to whisper its potential to offer great things if you were just willing to let it.

On that occasion Derby failed to rise to the challenge and left almost chastised for trying to reach too far too fast but the history of Derby County had shown us what was possible. The team of the seventies were a testament to the fact that a small team from a provincial city with only one FA Cup victory to its name could thrive, and under the Highbury skyline with the floodlights still cutting ribbons into the darkness me and my Dad could still dream.

Arsenal went on to play Manchester United in the semi-final, with the first match ending in a draw. In the replay the Gunners were knocked out in extra-time and left in a strop, beating Wimbledon 5–1 and Middlesbrough 6–1 in their next two games. The results failed to help them in the Premier League though as Manchester United went on to win the League by a single point.

This was the year of Manchester United's historic treble, with them defeating Newcastle United in the FA Cup Final and beating Bayern Munich in the Final of the Champions League, scoring two goals in injury time to turn round a 1–0 deficit. It was a unique achievement although critics and sore losers suggested that teams in the past did not have the advantage of entering what used to be the European Cup unless they were champions of their own League, which United had not been the previous season.

Meanwhile Derby also emerged from the disappointment of being knocked out of the Cup by winning their next two games, against Aston Villa who ended the season in sixth and Liverpool who finished seventh. But a disappointing run-in saw us win only two of the remaining nine matches, although this was softened by the fact that one of these was against Forest who had been promoted the previous season after one year in the second tier.

The poor end to the season left us in eighth position, 15 points short of Leeds in fourth place, which secured them a UEFA Cup place. Tottenham Hotspur also secured a slot after winning the League Cup, as did Newcastle whose honour that season was to be beaten by Manchester United in the Final of the FA Cup. Still, eighth was one position better than the previous year and Derby County were still on the up.

FA Carling Premiership 1998–99

Pos		Pl	W	D	L	F	A	GD	Pts
1	Manchester United	38	22	13	3	80	37	43	79
2	Arsenal	38	22	12	4	59	17	42	78
4	Leeds United	38	18	13	7	62	34	28	67
5	West Ham United	38	16	9	13	46	53	-7	57
6	Aston Villa	38	15	10	13	51	46	5	55
7	Liverpool	38	15	9	14	68	49	19	54
8	**Derby County**	**38**	**13**	**13**	**12**	**40**	**45**	**-5**	**52**

1999–2000

It was with great anticipation that Derby supporters approached the season that would incorporate the new millennium. A gradual improvement over the last few years had culminated in full houses watching from a stadium that was almost twice the size of the Baseball Ground, which we had left just two years before.

The expectation of victory was in the air as soon as we walked through the turnstiles and into the concourses at the back of the stands, mixed with the sweet scent of hot dogs and lager now being served alongside the traditional pies and Bovril.

Family relationships flourished in the new surroundings with the sight of young children weighed down by milk crates replaced by those laden with coke and chips disappearing with their fathers, and often their mothers and sisters into the light at the top of the many stairways that led out into the gleaming black and white seats like little astronauts boarding a spaceship.

It was labelled as the new generation of football yet the old generation was still in attendance, passing on the baton like my Dad had done to me back in 1979. But this wasn't a race in which only one member of the team crossed the finish line. The beauty of this game was that it took everyone through the tape and we could enjoy the victories together.

If the transformation of football over the last 20 years could have been summed up by one club it was here at Derby, now playing our matches on a pitch fit for bowling and in front of families as opposed to mud flats and fences.

But I could not help but look upon those old times with affection. Me and my Dad could have had the same relationship over a different pastime or even a different club, it didn't have to be Derby, and often I wondered for the life of me why it was, but the awareness of this fact didn't make me love our club any less.

The football product was the same as it always had been but somewhat repackaged, in a similar way to that which George Lucas had just released *Star Wars Episode One*, 22 years after the original, and since outdated, third episode in a series that was now becoming as confusing as the rebranding of the football divisions. Meanwhile other moviegoers were petrified by the *Blair Witch Project* and nobody was talking about *Fight Club*.

Unfortunately, unlike in those movies that hit our screens at the end of the second millennium Derby County were failing to follow the script. Our first four matches bought just one solitary point, won on the first day of the season at Elland Road and while we were selling the players that had seen us rise from the ashes of the second tier they were simply not being replaced with men of a similar standard.

The mercurial Aljosa Asanovic had left in January 1999, unhappy at not having the starring role in a team that contained too many major players. Dad blamed what he called Asanovic's Latin temperament, disregarding the fact that he was from Croatia but we knew what he meant.

Dad had missed out on attending Grammar School in 1960 but his intelligence was never far away, even if it was rarely demonstrated. His understanding and compassion would probably have been better suited to the Human Science course that I had taken at university but blokes didn't do stuff like that back in his day. Instead after failing the exams after Primary school he was trundled off into a trade and compartmentalised as a labourer like everyone else of that generation who didn't get the required grades when they were merely 11 years old.

Aljosa Asanovic, a name forever changed to Al Jolson in predictive text, was not the only departure to put a halt to Derby's current high standing in the Premier League. Lee Carsley, who never succumbed to auto-formatting software was sold to Blackburn Rovers in March for £3.3 million, which was seen as good profit for a player who had come through the youth team ranks. His footballing ability was underrated by Derby though and his battling presence in midfield was sorely missed.

The sales continued and saw Derby's iconic centre-forward, Paulo Wanchope, sold to West Ham United in July 1999 for £3.5 million after being bought less than two years previously for around £700,000. In August our most influential player at that time, Igor Stimac, was also sold, again to West Ham.

Four months into the 1999–2000 season Derby then had to do without the services of the two influential Italians, Francesco Baiano, who returned to play in Italy's Serie B and Stefano Eranio, who was tackled late in a game at Anfield and didn't even receive a free kick for the foul that broke his leg. Still, as one newspaper reported, 'it was nice to see Liverpool regain some of their ruthless streak.' Obviously our rise into a fashionable team had yet to filter down to Fleet Street.

The replacements for those departing Derby County looked good on paper although most people will tell you that football is played on grass. In December Branko Strupar was bought for £3 million from Belgium side Genk, having helped them to secure the title while on the way to becoming the country's player of the year. At the time he was the nation's third most famous person behind Audrey Hepburn and Hercule Poirot and arrived to hear the Derby crowd adapting Abba's Super Trooper as well as a chorus of people commenting, 'I didn't know Audrey Hepburn was from Belgium?'

Unfortunately injury plagued Strupar's career at Derby and subsequently he failed to show the form that had made him more famous than Jean Claude Van Damme, who most people know as a filmstar having been told by film buff Jonathon Ross, and Adolphe Sax, who most people know as the inventor of the saxophone having been told by a bear shitting in the woods.

Giorgi Kinkladze who had already been signed on loan in November also failed to repay the £3 million transfer fee that was eventually paid for him despite manager Jim Smith being told by Joe Royle, Kinkladze's former manager at Manchester City and part-time director of traffic while at Oldham, that while undoubtedly talented the Georgian was largely ineffective.

Two wins in four days at the end of August saw Derby end the month in 13th position but by the end of September we were one place off the relegation zone. Optimistic thoughts that usually accompanied the start of the season were further dispelled in October when we only managed a single victory against a Chelsea team who were yet to benefit from Roman Abramovich's injection of cash.

Me, my Dad and Uncle Paul continued taking it in turns attending matches and so it was still largely a solitary affair sitting in the stands. James England had not come back to the East Midlands after university and instead found a job in Wimbledon and so usually I would travel with the two Goodhall brothers to games.

Saturdays would see me wander down Fields Farm Road towards the train station in a similar way to that which me and my Dad had travelled so many times before, but I'd be earlier, replicating the boy who had been too excited to stay at home in the late '80s. Instead of catching the train though I'd take a left at the roundabout and meet the Goodhall brothers in one of the pubs in Old Sawley.

The conversations would slip easily from football to life and back again while in one corner several blokes would huddle around the small television screen watching the horse racing, occasionally nipping out to place their bets at the bookmakers. I sometimes went too so as to make the less glamorous games more interesting, and accompanying me on those occasions was always one of Dad's mantras echoing in my ears, 'You can only afford to bet what you can afford to lose.'

The bookmakers was located next to a launderette above which my Dad and Mum had made their first home together after they were married. In hearing his voice I was never sure whether it was his continual presence or the ghost of his past that was looking over me.

Back in the pub there was always a game scheduled for lunchtime and shown live on Sky, which often became the precursor to our own fixture. The introductions by ex-players turned pundits coincided with the arrival of our cooked breakfast, which we polished off before the televised match got under way. If it was a poor game then we'd pass the time on the quiz machine but more often than not the featured game would be the support act of our own game later that day, like watching PJ Harvey at Wembley Stadium before U2 take to the stage.

At about half past one we'd set off, driving out of Old Sawley and along familiar roads to familiar places to leave the car. We'd then get into the stadium with enough time to sink one more pint before going our separate ways, with the Goodhalls and I sat at opposite ends of the East Stand in our allocated seats.

This often created a sterile affair with nobody to talk with apart from the odd grunts from the guy next to me who spent the matches listening through earphones to his radio. The football may have been first division standard but this was not what the game was about to me. I was brought up on the closeness of the crowd, not just physically as they pushed and pulled you across the terraces but also in the way that it made you feel a part of something larger than just you. There was some hidden bond that existed before, both with my mates who I used to go with and the strangers who used to share the terraces, even with the father and son who we took the piss out of by making them stand up five minutes before the teams came out for the second half back in 1990 when we stood on the Pop-Side.

As Derby's form collapsed in front of my eyes I had nobody to turn to and explain the demise and it seemed like everyone else around me felt the same. We were no longer supporters but spectators, an audience rather than an attendance and with all eyes on the field expecting a performance it divided those from the pitch with those in the stands in a way that even the old fences failed to do. Suddenly I felt an immense sense of nostalgia, wanting once again to be standing on that godforsaken plank of wood with my Dad's arms either side of me and his sensible words in my ears.

November 1999 was even worse than October with Derby recording three losses out of three. Having coincided with games against Liverpool, Manchester United and Arsenal, as well as Eranio's injury it was easy not to feel too dejected, or maybe we were just too optimistic. Appropriately for a team whose away strip was purple we ended the month marooned in the bottom three.

*****

Having supposedly not been programmed to cope with the date changing to the year 2000 the world watched with baited breath to see whether the planet's computers would turn into Terminator style robots and kill us all. However, when the clocks turned to 00:00:00 we all realised that things would be exactly the same as the previous millennium. Most of us had the same jobs and relationships, Westlife were still at Number One and Derby County were rooted in the relegation zone.

By January we were out of immediate danger but also out of the FA Cup having already been disposed of by Burnley in December in a third round that the Football Association had brought forward from the traditional first weekend in January. The Clarets were then in the third tier of English football but with Armageddon on the horizon it was easy to be distracted, although after defeat the tried and tested cliché that we could concentrate on the League held little weight when that was due to finish five months after the world's end.

A season is a long time to be embroiled in a relegation battle but that is what we were treated to throughout the entirety of that year. I spent so much time looking at the table that I failed to recognise what was really happening out on the pitch. Subsequently all the games seemed to roll into one long memory of a season that we tried to forget. Derby finished with 38 points, which often will see a team relegated although that season's third from bottom team, Wimbledon, only accrued thirty-three.

*****

In the summer of 2000 I again moved away from the East Midlands and this time went to live in Bristol. My long distance relationship that had started after I left university had lasted and Melissa had finally graduated and returned south to her hometown.

We stayed with friends for a few weeks before renting the top floor flat in a three-storey block in the Montpelier district of the city, which sounds nice although it was just off Stokes Croft, which was not. On one wall of an alleyway that acted as a shortcut into the city centre someone had scrawled the legend, 'Jah Liveth' in huge red paint, below which someone had added in smaller black font, 'Not round here he doesn't!'

Just as it had done when I moved to the North East the club were not inclined to give me a fond farewell but maybe this was a good thing. It was hard enough leaving family and friends once more without a fantastic football club to try to make me stay. There was also the possibility that Derby County would do what they had often done in the past and save their best form for when I wasn't there.

FA Carling Premiership 1999–2000

Pos		Pl	W	D	L	F	A	GD	Pts
1	Manchester United	38	28	7	3	97	45	52	91
2	Arsenal	38	22	7	9	73	43	30	73
15	Southampton	38	12	8	18	45	62	-17	44
16	**Derby County**	**38**	**9**	**11**	**18**	**44**	**57**	**-13**	**38**
17	Bradford City	38	9	9	20	38	68	-30	36
18	Wimbledon	38	7	12	19	46	74	-28	33
19	Sheffield Wednesday	38	8	7	23	38	70	-32	31
20	Watford	38	6	6	26	35	77	-42	24

2000–01

If the North East of England had been a hotbed of football then Bristol was probably the cold sofa, bought from the IKEA superstore that had been built on the site of the city's old Eastville Stadium in 1998. Despite having two teams within the city both were in the third tier of English football, which probably attributed to the apathy towards football that seemed to exist there at the time.

Situated on the River Avon, which acted as a gateway to the Atlantic Ocean, Bristol's history has been largely dependent upon all things maritime. In 1497, John Cabot sailed from the city across the Atlantic, landing in Canada and calling his new found land Newfoundland. The annuls of time are then blotted by the slave trade, pirates and privateers although stealing gold from the Spanish, who themselves had nicked it from the Americas, somehow made their work acceptable. It wasn't until halfway through the 20th century that two wrongs stopped making a right.

Bristol's more palatable claim to fame comes from Isambard Kingdom Brunel and his feats of engineering. The Clifton Suspension Bridge, which spans the Avon Gorge was completed in 1859 and is a popular spot for tourists and people attempting suicide, the latter of which often jump from the bridge only to be saved by landing in the soft silt and mud at the river's edge where they later drown when the tide rises in the morning.

It had been eight years since I had travelled down with my Dad to see Derby win at Ashton Gate, the home of Bristol City. Since that visit the Robins had been relegated to the third division in 1994, promoted in 1998 but relegated again the following season.

The history of neighbours Bristol Rovers was no better. The club was formed in 1883 and originally called the Black Arabs after the local rugby team and their black kit. Fans of political correctness gave a huge sigh of relief the following year though when the name was changed to Eastville Rovers. A further name change came in 1897 when the club added the name of the city to their moniker, becoming Bristol Eastville Rovers but the Eastville was dropped in 1899 after one too many fans on the terraces started chanting, 'Give us a B...'.

By 1986 the club were sharing their Eastville Stadium with speedway and greyhound racing, as well as an American Football Team called the Bristol Bombers who were true to their name and folded after just one year. Financial trouble was also brewing at Rovers and that year they were required to embark on a 15-mile relocation to Bath, which added insult in a history of underachievement.

Ten years later Rovers returned to the city, renting the rugby club's Memorial Ground before buying it in 1998, which was the same year that the Eastville Stadium was finally demolished in place of a Scandinavian furniture warehouse. While Saturday afternoons in Bristol used to be spent cheering on the local team, now it was Sunday afternoons looking at wooden tables with names like Taybl, metal chairs called Stuhl and useless bits of plastic named Frskn.

I could only watch from afar as my own club spent the 2000–01 season in another fight against Premier League relegation. Even from my distant viewpoint it was all too clear to see why we were struggling with the Rams conceding 26 goals in their first 10 League games, after which Derby were rock bottom of the League with just five points and without a win to their name. It was actually a blessing that nobody in my new hometown were interested in football, which meant I could sulk in the Cadbury House pub on a Saturday night without a finger of fun pointed in my direction.

In November Colin Todd arrived at Derby as assistant manager to Jim Smith, 23 years after leaving the club after playing in both Championship sides of the seventies and winning the PFA Player of the Year award in 1975. Brian Clough had signed Todd from Sunderland in 1971 for a British record transfer fee for a defender of £175,000, therefore lifting the gloom of a city that was under a cloud after one of the major employers in the region, Rolls-Royce, had gone into receivership.

With another relegation fight being played out at Pride Park Stadium the addition of seats into the South East Corner, which saw the capacity of the stadium increase to 33,597 seemed premature. However, on Saturday 18 November 31,614 supporters were in attendance to see the two worst teams in the division, Derby and Bradford City, battle against each other and see the Rams record their first win of the campaign after 14 attempts.

A positive festive period saw us achieve victories over Coventry City and Newcastle United at home, and record a goalless draw at Manchester City, which coincided with my brief return to the East Midlands for Christmas. It seemed that I had reversed my earlier curse and Derby looked to be on the up, but after I returned to Bristol, Derby reverted to flirting with relegation.

Liverpool 1 Derby County 1

Sunday 18 March 2001

After coming through the angst of the three-way relationship made up of me, my Dad and my adolescence there was still one person back at home with which I had some bridges to build. The bond between Daniel and I had been at the root of many problems at home but since we had both moved away to university the pair of us had grown up a great deal. Like Derby and Forest existing in separate divisions mine and Daniel's rivalry had subsided somewhat and when I returned home it was like both of us had forgotten what we were fighting about, until Mum reminded us of the A-Team incident.

Daniel had matured into the person he needed to be without trying to follow in my footsteps, which were quite honestly not the most ambitious, and he was doing well forging his own life. While most of his friends left the sixth form at his Secondary school to go straight into work Daniel still remained resolute to his own path and went to study Maths and Sports Science at Liverpool Hope, presumably to answer questions such as, 'Small, round, spherical object hurled in athletics: Discus.'

Back in 1986, aged almost six years old Daniel had quickly scrawled a birthday card message to Ian that he'd signed, 'To Ian, from Daniel the Derby seporrter!' but despite this, and being taken to the Baseball Ground, Bramall Lane and Turf Moor, Daniel had never fully caught the Derby County bug and turned to supporting Liverpool. Obviously Ian and I were quick to point out, 'Daniel, if you are going to support a team because of the glory, at least support a team that will give you some bloody glory.'

Liverpool were the team of the 80s but since that decade the re-emergence of Manchester United, along with the continued relative success of Arsenal had relegated Liverpool to also-rans, especially when it came to the Premiership title. Still, Daniel's allegiance to Liverpool had remained and as such he endured as much heartbreak as if he had stayed supporting one of his local teams.

With Daniel studying in Liverpool I had the perfect opportunity for when Derby played at either Anfield or when they were up against Everton at Goodison Park and so on Friday 16 April 2001 I hired a car and drove up the M6 for a weekend in the future City of Culture. Meanwhile Ryan travelled along from the Midlands and we all met up in Daniel's student house in the Wavertree area of the city.

Friday night was a quiet one with us getting a few beers and fish and chips from the shop at the top of the street, inside which was a child of about two years old who looked remarkably like Sting from the Police. Saturday proved to be a little more raucous.

As our match wasn't scheduled until the Sunday and with Saturday being St Patrick's Day, Daniel had developed an itinerary for the following morning that started with us going to the Student Union bar to watch Ireland play France in the Five Nations Championships. Feeling somewhat guilty of our past relationship I was attempting to act like the older, concerned brother as Daniel, Ryan and I walked towards the bar, via the halls of residence that Daniel had to go to in order to drop a textbook off with a friend. It was impossible to string a sentence together though as every person we passed seemed to know our Daniel and we would have to stop on each occasion as a new conversation started with each. It soon became obvious that Daniel was a very popular member of the community there and reminded me of the times when Dad took three hours to go shopping in our local Asda store, having to stop in every aisle to speak with someone he knew.

Eventually we made it inside the bar and I swiftly declared that there was no way I would be wearing one of the huge foam St Patrick's Day hats that had found their way onto to the heads of some early revellers. Despite being given away for free with every purchase of six pints of Guinness and the highly likelihood that each of Daniel, Ryan and I would reach that quota by the evening I vowed that I wouldn't be seen dead in one.

Eight hours later we emerged from the bar, each with our own huge foam St Patrick's Day hat to continue our drinking spree in the city. After a beer in one of the pubs close to the union bar I asked Daniel whether we'd be getting a cab back to his home or catching the bus.

'I don't know mate,' Daniel said, 'but the next pub's just down the road.'

I was a bit surprised, 'Daniel, they won't let us in! It's closing time!' I argued, but then looked down at my watch and realised it was only five past nine.

I was shattered and decided to leave Daniel and Ryan and after taking Daniel's house keys I headed back. I knew that he lived on Cretan Road, which Ian and I had obviously renamed Cretin Road in honour of our Daniel and so headed to the nearest taxi rank, assuming that the drivers would have 'the knowledge'.

After three quarters of an hour queuing up it was finally my turn to stumble into the back of one of the city's Hackney Carriages, during which time I had sobered up slightly enough to ask, 'Cretan Road, please?'

'Whereabouts is that, mate?' came the reply and I knew then that I had a problem.

The taxi driver needed more information that I simply didn't possess. All I knew was that Daniel lived on Cretan Road but as mobile phones were the reserve of London city traders at the time I had no way to call him to find out where he lived or where he was. Instead I wandered helplessly around Liverpool until eventually I recognised one street that we had been down earlier and traced my earlier steps to the halls of residence that we had briefly visited that morning.

I buzzed the intercom but the lad we had seen earlier was out and instead someone else answered.

'I'm sorry but I don't suppose you know Daniel Trembirth do you?' I asked.

'Yeah, of course I know Daniel.' came the reply, as if I'd asked for the Pope. With his full address in hand I went back to the taxi rank and again queued for three quarters of an hour for a ride home.

This time I was able to get back to the house but by now it was getting on for 12 o'clock. As Daniel and Ryan had not stayed out much longer than me, and I had the key, they hadn't been able to get in, forcing Daniel to wake his landlord who lived next door to gain entry.

The following morning I awoke sheepishly, wedged into Daniel's sofa in the living room with a sleeping bag wrapped over me. Ryan was on the floor just inches from a huge ball of something covered in fluff, which shifted slowly with the movement of his breath. I couldn't look and so went into the kitchen and poured myself a glass of water, which seemed to orchestrate the piping into a cacophony of sound that awoke the rest of the house.

With my popularity getting ever smaller I got dressed and waited for Ryan to wake and for the others to come downstairs. We were all in a hazy state and watched easy Sunday morning television as the hours ticked towards kick-off. Almost out of the blue one of Daniel's housemates, a lad from Barnsley, asked, 'I thought you lads were going to the match, like?'

After resisting the temptation to ask, 'Like what?' I replied, 'Yeah, we are.'

'But it's a quarter past two!' he continued.

Daniel quickly called a taxi, which turned up in 10 minutes and drove us into the Anfield area of the city. The plan would have been to have a few drinks before the game but after the night before nobody was interested in a top-up. Instead we headed straight into the ground and took our places in the Anfield Road Stand behind the goal, which stood opposite the famous Kop.

It seemed that the whole of Liverpool had been celebrating St Patrick's Day the night before and there were more than a few huge foam Guinness hats in the crowd that afternoon to prove it. Subsequently the atmosphere inside the stadium was muted, especially for a crowd of 43,362. Liverpool were in sixth position in the League and only three points off Ipswich Town in third but eight points behind Arsenal in second and a staggering 24 away from rivals Manchester United.

Even a draw at Anfield was beyond our expectations and so Ryan and I took our seats more for the experience than the joy of returning with any points. Daniel had managed to find a ticket in with the Liverpool fans and must have been glad he wasn't with us after seven minutes when Deon Burton found himself on the end of a Derby corner and headed us into the lead. It was hard to believe in our end and our silence was akin to the Liverpool fans all around us who were looking on in their own state of disbelief.

We were expecting a backlash but like the crowd that afternoon there seemed to be something missing from our opponents that day and we went in at half-time leading by that one goal to nil. Our luck could not hold out though and 10 minutes into the second-half Michael Owen equalised and suddenly the ground woke up. We had been hoping we could have held out for longer, thinking that the more time it took Liverpool to equalise the less time they would have to get the winner but we didn't have to worry. The Rams held on for a precious point and we celebrated as if we had won the League.

*****

Despite only one win from the five matches in April Derby still remained one place out of the relegation zone and we were still believing. Our next trip saw us up against Manchester United who were already champions and so this was not a place we went to hoping to secure top-flight football for the following season. Malcolm Christie's 34th minute strike was enough to see the Rams come away with all three points though and we were safe for another year.

We finished the season on 42 points, just one place off the relegation zone but with three other teams with the same tally one more draw would have seen us finish lauding it in the relative respectability of the mid-table. Still we had ended the season eight points from the relegated teams and another year in the Premier League beckoned.

FA Carling Premiership 2000–01

Pos		Pl	W	D	L	F	A	GD	Pts
1	Manchester United	38	24	8	6	79	31	48	80
2	Arsenal	38	20	10	8	63	38	25	70
14	Middlesbrough	38	9	15	14	44	44	0	42
15	West Ham United	38	10	12	16	45	50	-5	42
16	Everton	38	11	9	18	45	59	-14	42
17	**Derby County**	**38**	**10**	**12**	**16**	**37**	**59**	**-22**	**42**
18	Manchester City	38	8	10	20	41	65	-24	34
19	Coventry City	38	8	10	20	36	63	-27	34
20	Bradford City	38	5	11	22	30	70	-40	26

Arsenal 1 Liverpool 2

Saturday 12 May 2001

Dad's voluntary work had continued with the Long Eaton Sunday League and that year he put himself forward for tickets for the FA Cup Final again. So when Liverpool made it to Cardiff Dad gave the tickets to me, Daniel and another of Daniel's housemates who was a big rugby lad and as Welsh as Tom Jones and daffodils. Like Daniel his housemate supported Liverpool and as that year's Cup Final was being played at the Millennium Stadium in his hometown it only added to his occasion.

Derby had been beaten in the competition at Pride Park by Division One Blackburn Rovers after travelling to Ewood Park earlier to squabble over a 0–0 draw. Blackburn would finish that season promoted back to the Premier League after two seasons in the second tier, having been relegated from the top-flight just four years after being crowned champions in 1995.

At first I was not going to go to the Cup Final as, with the tickets costing £75, it was not something that I could afford at the time. When I raised this with Dad though he shunned my protests away and paid for both Daniel and I to go. While never frugal Dad was careful with money and he could have done a lot with that cash but I guess he recognised the ground that me and Daniel had made up together and the way in which football had been a bond between the two of us, and wanted to further the building of the relationship of two of his sons.

On the weekend of the match Mum, Dad and Ian travelled down to Bristol on the Friday night so we could get a head-start on the English invasion from Merseyside and London the following morning. Saturday arrived and we followed the directions to Daniel's housemate's family home in Cardiff where the two of them had stayed the night before. Satellite navigation systems had yet to be invented and so Daniel had scrawled the directions on a beer mat, which didn't fill us with confidence when we worked out that Daniel must have written them down while half-cut. Still, we found the location, complete with a parking space for us along a side street not far from the city centre.

Daniel was half asleep when we got there and we guessed that it had been a less than quiet Friday night for the pair of them. Eager to get going we didn't hang around for long, leaving the house and wandering excitedly towards the stadium, gradually mixing in with the crowd that started to build just as it does as it nears any sporting venue.

Supporters of both teams were out in force, waving scarves, flags and banners and turning the city streets into a carnival of red and white. Street sellers were making a killing with stalls of face-paints and hooters while the local shops were enjoying the upturn in trade. Fast food outlets were brimming with fans stocking up on burgers, fried chicken and chips, which made it easy for me to nip inside to use the facilities, even though they were meant for customers only.

After washing my hands upstairs in the toilets of Kentucky Fried Chicken I glanced at myself in the mirror. I would have given anything for it to have been me and my Dad going to the match, supporting our team in one of the sport's biggest matches but it had never happened. So far our glory had been limited to one-off victories against the big clubs with the odd promotion to leave us singing and waving our flags in the streets.

It was then that I noticed all four urinals occupied by Arsenal supporters, each with their current replica shirts meticulously washed and ironed for the day. Each stared straight ahead in perfect line with each other in a scene that had become synonymous with the North London club. I finished drying my hands and couldn't help but yell, 'Offside!' before legging it out of the door, down the stairs and into the street.

On the way to the ground we found a huge Walkabout bar full of supporters from both sides, with most not having tickets to the match. All seven of us enjoyed a beer together before me, Daniel and Gareth left to complete our journey to the ground, along with my Dad and Ian who didn't have tickets but who wanted to soak up the atmosphere anyway. Mum and Melissa stayed in the pub.

In spite of it not being Derby it was impossible to avoid the excitement that was building in the run up to the game. Stewards were shouting instructions directing supporters to the correct gates and vendors were calling out desperately to make final sales before the crowd were inside while odd chants would start up and carry on the slight breeze towards us. When it came to entering the stadium I turned to see Dad. Predictably his characteristic grin spread to his face before we all shook hands and went our separate ways.

The atmosphere outside had been incredible but once inside it was even more spectacular with Wales welcoming the English Cup Final with open arms. Unfortunately the game was edgy, as it so often is when the better teams are involved, and neither side wanted to give too much away.

After 72 minutes Freddie Ljungberg scored for Arsenal and in a game of few chances we were fearful of an Arsenal victory, however, with seven minutes remaining Michael Owen delivered his first of the afternoon before, five minutes later, slotting home the winner. The three of us were ecstatic and I celebrated the goal as if it was my own and even after being told to calm down by one of the spectators nearby we continued cheering and just ignored him.

After the match we headed back to the pub to meet with the others where there were more handshakes all round. Daniel and I were grateful of the occasion, which would represent another area of common ground for us to walk upon. Meanwhile Daniel's mate was in tears and constantly shaking the hand of my Dad and repeating, 'Thank you Mr Trembirth. Thank you Mr Trembirth.' like Kathy Burke playing Perry in a Harry Enfield sketch.

2001–02

By the summer of 2001 I was back in Long Eaton after returning from Bristol. The relationship that had tempted me south was perfect when it was long-distance but it didn't work with the two of us living together. Thankfully my family and friends were still around and I slipped almost seamlessly back into the routine that I had left the year before.

Rather than share a season ticket, me and my Dad had both come to realise that attending matches alone was a poor experience. Instead we started choosing matches that we could go to together, sitting next to each other as we had been through most of my life.

Every time I fell he had been there to catch me, along with my Mum, the pair of whom never chastised me for my attempts to break away and rather spent most of the time almost congratulating me for trying. The old adage that I had not failed until I stopped trying was wheeled out like an old footballing cliché but it was a cliché because it was true. I travelled through those years like a tightrope walker, trying new feats but always aware that I had that safety net to fall into if I came off the high-wire and subsequently I achieved and lived far better than what I would have were my parents not as supportive.

Dad seemed as eager as ever for us to go to games and when he asked me if I wanted to go to a match it conjured up the same excitement within me as it had when I was four years old. With me now having grown up though, as well as my mates, there was often a slight problem with Dad coming along.

In the pub one afternoon before a match against Everton, me, my Dad and the two Goodhall brothers were having a pint and a game a game of pool when Ryan piped up, 'Bob Hope's in bed with Cilla Black, and after having sex Bob Hope rolls over and says to our Cilla, "Will you hold on to my knob while I go to sleep".'

I was mortified. Despite being well into my 20s there were certain subjects that remained unmentioned in our home. But Ryan continued.

'Of course, our Cilla agrees and when he wakes up an hour later, they have sex again. Again, Bob asks Cilla to hold his knob while he goes back to sleep. After a few times, curiosity gets the better of our Cilla and she says to Bob Hope, "Bob, does it make sex better if I hold your knob after sex?" and Bob replies, "No love, it's just that the last time I shagged a Scouser, she ran off with my telly."'

Everyone was laughing, even my Dad, while I was wiping away the half pint of Guinness that I'd spat down that season's replica shirt.

Later when Dad went to the toilet I pulled Ryan to one side.

'Mate, what are you doing?' I asked, 'Telling that joke to my Dad?'

'Sorry Craig,' he replied, 'but I guess I don't see your Dad as your Dad, if you know what I mean, he's a mate.'

It helped that Dad could and wanted to talk to anyone, which went some way in explaining his marathon trips to the supermarket. When mates of either me, Ian or Daniel came round our house he could talk to them about their teams in the Long Eaton Sunday League and genuinely care about how they were doing.

That he had a wicked sense of humour helped as well. When Derby played at Aston Villa in a televised match, George Graham, the man who masterminded Arsenal's famous successes built on 1–0 victories was the half-time pundit. After slating Derby for our overcautious football Dad could take no more and suddenly quipped, 'Oh yeah, says George of the 4–3 megawins!'

It was easy to respect Dad's opinions on the games and it annoyed him intensely when great teams with great players came to Pride Park only for the crowd to boo them. He was right in saying that we wanted these great players to come, having spent many a year in lower divisions with only the odd cameo by Kevin Keegan to lighten the gloom.

As for Ian, Daniel and I, if we were watching a match on television and we were being critical of anybody Dad wouldn't stand for it. During an England match Daniel was criticising Darren Anderton throughout.

'Daniel,' Dad pointed out firmly, 'Darren Anderton has spent years playing in the Premier League and is an England footballer. How can you sit there and say he's rubbish? If you want to comment on a player, instead of slagging them off, try and find the best thing you can say about them.'

Daniel's response when Dad had left the room was, 'Well, the best thing I can say about Darren Anderton is, he's crap!'

In the years before we were born it was my Mum who had attended football matches with my Dad and they would often regale the three of us with stories about how they went to places like Stamford Bridge and Anfield. I guess when it started to get dangerous in the late 1970s though this pastime stopped. Now it seemed like Mum looked to football as something we did with Dad but she still had a keen interest, especially when England played, which was probably because we could all sit around the television as a family and watch together sharing the joy of victory or pain of a defeat.

Mum would often be stood ironing our clothes during these matches and on one occasion while the England team were attempting to break down a particularly difficult opposition Mum left us all speechless with the comment, 'If they brought on Beckham onto the right side of the pitch, this would allow Steven Gerrard to slip into the middle of the park where he's more effective and push forward more to support the attacking options.'

In October 2001 Jim Smith resigned as manager of Derby County, allowing assistant manager, Colin Todd, to take full reign of the club. Having guided Derby into the Premier League and making them a creditable force it was hard not to look back on his time with fondness in spite of the recent poor seasons of relegation struggles. Chairman Lionel Pickering, a lifelong Derby fan indebted to Smith for raising Derby's standing in the game offered the departing manager a role of Director of Football but either because Smith recognised it as a mere gesture or that Colin Todd felt that Smith's presence on the training ground would be a distraction the offer was not accepted.

Derby County 1 Chelsea 1

Sunday 28 October 2001

On Saturday 20 October I arrived home from Pride Park after having seen us draw against Charlton Athletic. Fabrizio Ravanelli had opened the scoring in the 15th minute and all looked rosy until Jason Euell equalised with 17 minutes to go. The draw left us in 17th place and digging in for what seemed like another season fighting off the drop.

Me and my Dad were talking about the match in the kitchen afterwards, with him making tea in much the same way as he always had done on a Saturday evening. Inside the living room I could hear Mum laughing at *You've Been Framed* but despite being a fan of watching hapless people bounce uncontrollably off trampolines and dogs on skateboards I preferred chatting to my Dad. I asked him if he was coming to watch us play Chelsea the following week but he said he was already going with my Mum.

I guessed that this was an opportunity for them to relive the past a little and so instead of going with them I went along as usual with the Goodhalls, meeting for a few beers before driving out to Derby. Another friend who had limited allegiance to the club but who had started attending a few games for a laugh came along too, which made four in the car.

Driving along London Road about half a mile from the park where we used to leave the car we spotted my Dad and Mum walking to the ground. As it was nearing kick-off they were walking quite fast but still had plenty of time to get there. Simon, who was driving asked if we should stop and give them a lift.

My Dad had met my Mum when she was just 17 years old and living with her parents in nearby Stapleford, which is commonly referred to as Stabbo. This, however, is less an abbreviation and more like a warning. The two of them had been married for over 30 years but looking out at them you would have thought they'd just started seeing each other, or courting as they said back then.

I'd never seen them together without them knowing I was there before and it was a magical sight. Both had the grin that I had seen on my Dad's face so many times, laughing at their attempts to get to the stadium on time, laughing at holding hands, laughing at being out and laughing at memories of days before they'd had children.

I didn't think they could get any happier than they were at that moment and certainly didn't want to break the spell and so I told Simon to keep on driving. I think that everyone in the car could see what I had seen in my parents that Sunday afternoon and agreed with the decision.

*****

On 3 November we visited Middlesbrough for our annual drubbing but this time lost by only five goals to one. Unsurprisingly we were still in the relegation zone at Christmas and further embarrassment came when Bristol came back to haunt me in the form of their Rovers when they visited Pride Park in the FA Cup third round. The team from the South West, who had been relegated to the fourth division in 2001, had needed two attempts to win both of their previous rounds, eventually overcoming Aldershot and Plymouth Argyle on their way to meet Derby.

Rovers' average attendance that season hovered around 6,000 fans, which was about the number of supporters that made the journey up to Derby that afternoon. It took the visiting striker, Nathan Ellington, just 14 minutes to find the back of the goal, who less than two weeks earlier had scored a hat-trick at home to Leyton Orient at the Memorial Ground, which saw Rovers climb to the dizzy heights of twentieth in the basement division.

Ellington scored twice more to secure another hat-trick as Rovers not only won but tore us apart, much to the delight of the travelling thousands who filled the South Stand behind the goal. A consolation from Ravanelli almost added to the embarrassment and we crawled out of the stadium fearing the media glare like vampires afraid of the sun.

Manager Colin Todd was left to sneak out of the club altogether after being sacked after only three months in full charge of the team. He departed from the club that he had represented so well as a player while I could only stand and watch as the former greats who my Dad revered were now cast aside to be remembered as poor managers.

In Todd's place came another former Rams player and one that I could actually remember seeing play, with John Gregory stepping up to the challenge. Success was immediate with a 1–0 win over eighth-placed Tottenham Hotspur and despite losing our next game at home to Sunderland, a convincing 3–0 win over Leicester, followed by a home draw against League leaders, Manchester United, had us believing of a great escape. However, just one win in the next eight games saw relegation confirmed at Anfield on Saturday 20 April against a Liverpool side who were then at the top of the League.

Sunderland 1 Derby County 1

Sunday 11 May 2002

In spite of relegation, me, my Dad and Uncle Paul decided to travel north to Sunderland's Stadium of Light to see the club's last game in the Premier League for the foreseeable future. Naturally we all believed that we would be promoted the following season with no let up in the optimism that was merely an extension of the frame of mind that had us believing we could avoid relegation right until the fat lady had started singing at Anfield.

Uncle Paul drove along the route that Dad and Mum had often driven me northwards during my years at university although this time the back of the car was not laden with all my clothes, pots and pans and boxes of food that Mum used to buy me before I embarked on another term.

Witnessing the old roads was like travelling through a motion picture of my past as we travelled up the M1, M18 and onto the A1 as it made its way on what was becoming a memorable road trip. The car radio was only background noise as we chatted constantly throughout the journey, as ever alternating between meaningful subjects like the problems in our lives and at other times reverting back to less important things like the problems with our club. It was often hard to distinguish between the two.

As we approached Ferrybridge Services the previous year's number one hit, 'Hero' came on the radio playlist, giving me and my Dad that day's first taste of Uncle Paul's one-liners,

'Where does Enrique Iglesias get his windows from? ...Enrique Iglesias' glaziers!'

We arrived in Sunderland several hours before kick-off and so parked up and found a quiet pub within which to pass the time. As we walked through the door in our Derby shirts we were met with strange glances and the odd sympathetic stare that I had come to expect after 20 years of supporting my club. Fortunately Dad was not recognised as the guy who had helped us defeat Sunderland at the Baseball Ground in December 1995 and we were served our pints of Cameron's without question.

As usual the conversation drifted onto matches that we'd seen, those that had burned themselves more severely in the memory either by being spectacularly terrible or monumentally victorious. As my Dad and Uncle Paul relived the golden era of the seventies I still managed to revel in the nostalgia and while it wasn't my history I still felt that by being a Derby fan I owned a part of it.

To the soundtrack of famous names that came forth like radio commentary of the past the visions kept alive through archive footage were replicated in our minds as we pictured the famous goals from players like Alan Hinton, John O'Hare, Roy McFarland, Francis Lee and Charlie George. Then there were the games that we'd been to together and our recollections of that trip through the clouds to Oldham spilled out and into the bar on the crest of laughter.

We also spoke about Plymouth, giving me the chance to ask Dad how close we had come to walking away for good and finding other things to do with our time. But he explained that, just like most football fans, we never get to choose which team to support and that often it is thrust upon us by location or we succumb to what the rest of the kids at school are into. 'Or by an eager parent!' I added.

It is very rare that anyone chooses their team based on the standard of football and to do so would be foolish. Looking back over the previous 20 years it was obvious to see how fortunes changed and how even those teams who were dominating the sport that year had spent their fair share of time disappointing the supporters who went along.

More often than not, come August and the start of the season our teams come to the front door like a rescued mongrel from the RSPCA and we have no choice but to take the lead and walk back to the ground. We might have talked about giving up, maybe even dreamed that we could although walking away from Derby County had never been an option for any of us.

At two o'clock we made our way towards the ground with Dad sporting a black and white jesters hat, complete with bells and making few friends with it being the colours of Sunderland's rivals, Newcastle United. That those home fans who took offence didn't recognise the fact that we ourselves played in black and white and that we might want to wear hats in those colours proved slightly pathetic.

With it being the last game of the season I wore a Hawaiian garland, which had somehow come into my possession on one drunken Saturday night in one of the major cities that we lived between. We also took a box of sponge cakes with us into the ground, which once inside were soon confiscated by stewards who told us with tongues firmly in their cheeks that it was an offence to enter the stadium with such items. Still, Dad saw this coming and had stashed a load underneath his hat, which were later devoured by the strangers who we shared that afternoon with.

In the stand we recognised the people who we saw week in and week out at Pride Park, even the lad who was caught crying on Match of the Day three weeks previously after the Liverpool game but their faces were all that we knew. Regardless of this lack of insight though we felt like friends and despite having nothing to play for we sang our hearts out all afternoon. It was like the last three seasons of fearing relegation had suddenly left us and the relief that came from actually knowing our fate was liberating.

Sunderland had only just avoided relegation themselves but despite ending the season in 17th place 47,989 supporters turned out to see their team. Kevin Phillips opened the scoring after just 17 minutes but conversely this only heightened our own desire to sing, which increased to ballistic when we later got a corner, sounding like we'd scored the winning goal in the Cup Final.

Finally we got our reward when Derby's Marvin Robinson equalised with 20 minutes to go, turning us into the sea of flailing limbs that I had come to love being a part of. Relegation was a certainty but despite that stab of regret when it was finally confirmed we had come to accept it and find that it didn't taste too bad after all.

Supporting Derby had always been a roller coaster ride and at that period of time we were simply falling from a crest. Come the following August we'd be back once more, back in familiar surroundings of Pride Park and cheering on our team that despite having different players and probably a different kit would always be Derby County.

The match ended 1–1 and we made our way out of the back of the stand after briefly applauding the effort of the players. That they had failed in their task was lost on us as we blindly showed our support, much in the same way that was common among supporters of the 11 teams who were relegated across all four divisions that season and the 80 who had failed to win anything at all.

The day wasn't over though and we still had to drive back home. Halfway back along the A1 we decided to look out for a pub where we could eat and came across the Black Horse Inn near Skipton-on-Swale. The gravel cracked beneath the tyres as we pulled into the car park while dusty lights burned from within and welcomed us. As hoped the bar was lined with a selection of real ales from which we ordered and sat down on tiny bar stools that resembled the seats you get in a photobooth.

Perusing the menu was easy and we decided on steak and chips although when the plates came out only a piece of steak and a mushroom were on each. Dad was just about to go and ask where the chips had got to when the barmaid came back with a platter the size of a baby's bath full of what Dad called 'proper chips' and placed them on the table beside us.

Again conversation flowed easy and it was becoming ever more clear that it wasn't the sport of football that mattered but the experience. Derby had ultimately failed but we had come just the same, not because we thought we'd win the match or somehow avoid our already confirmed relegation but because it formed a basis of somewhere to go and strengthened the bond with the people closest to you.

FA Carling Premiership 2001–02

Pos		Pl	W	D	L	F	A	GD	Pts
1	Arsenal	38	26	9	3	79	36	43	87
2	Liverpool	38	24	8	6	67	30	37	80
16	Bolton Wanderers	38	9	13	16	44	62	-18	40
17	Sunderland	38	10	10	18	29	51	-22	40
18	Ipswich Town	38	9	9	20	41	64	-23	36
19	**Derby County**	**38**	**8**	**6**	**24**	**33**	**63**	**-30**	**30**
20	Leicester City	38	5	13	20	30	64	-34	28

2002–03

Derby County 3 Reading 0

Saturday 10 August 2002

Before the first match of the 2002–03 season kicked off the Derby manager, John Gregory, had foolishly told reporters that you could tell you were in the second division when you had to play teams like Reading. Elm Park, which had been the club's home since 1896 may have been a dilapidated ground that had no roof to the toilets and weeds growing through the walls in the Reading End but by the time of this encounter they had moved to the new 24,000 seat Madejski Stadium. What was also lost on Gregory, who we almost named our new dog after, was that the club had actually been just 45 minutes away from the Premier League in 1995 when they were leading Bolton Wanderers at half-time by two goals to nil in that season's Play-off Final.

Gregory's words were initially proved right though and in front of 33,016 supporters, who were as surprised as each other to see so many, Derby cruised to a 3–0 win. The chant of, 'Champions' was being sung around the stands even before the final whistle and the promise of a quick return was looking like more than just bombastic bravado, until we visited Gillingham in the following match and lost 1–0 in front of 8,775 spectators.

Grimsby Town 1 Derby County 2

Saturday 17 August 2002

Our next fixture was another away match, this time at Grimsby Town who play their matches in the east coast seaside town of Cleethorpes. Despite the match being shown live on television, me, my Dad and the two Goodhall brothers decided to make the trip anyway. The kick-off was due in the evening so as not to conflict with the rest of the matches being played that day but we still went along early to enjoy a summer's day by the sea.

To me it was like being a kid again as we walked along the promenade, just as we had done as a family at holidays in Great Yarmouth and Newquay every year. Admittedly it wasn't Disney World or the Algarve but as children we needed nothing more than days in the biggest sandpit that nature could provide and evening trips out to the theatre to see acts like Cannon and Ball, Paul Daniels and Brian Conley.

We left the car in a side-street close to Blundell Park and wandered towards the beachfront where we came across a crazy-golf course and decided to have a go. As ever my Dad was fitting in with my friends while I was hoping Ryan didn't have any jokes about celebrities from Cleethorpes having sex with American comedians.

For the record Dad won the game of golf, which was not surprising when up against players of the calibre of Simon Goodhall. The older of the two brothers had taken his shot at the traditional rotating windmill only to hit the sail as it skirted the green Astroturf.

'What are the chances of that?' he lamented, before striking his ball once more only to see it hit the sail again.

'Two in two!' Dad answered without hesitation.

After a candyfloss and some seaside rock in the shape of a cooked breakfast it was nearing kick-off so we wandered back towards the ground but first stopped off for inflatable items from the beachside shacks that we could take to the game with us. Simon bought an inflatable alien, Ryan had a fish, Dad purchased a dinosaur while I bought a small inflatable dinghy. It was reminiscent of those days in 1989 as we strode into the Osmand Stand, which built in 1939 was probably not named after Donny.

Formed in 1878, Grimsby Town were created after members of the local Worsley Cricket Club expressed a desire for something to do in the winter months, which is a euphemism for needing an excuse to stay away from the wife. This desire to be away from home extended as far as Christmas Day when along with neighbours Hull City the two became the only professional teams given official permission to play on 25 December because of the demands of the fishing industry.

The home side took the lead on 37 minutes with a strike from Darren Barnard who, despite being born in Germany, played 22 times for Wales in a career that included Chelsea and Bristol City. Derby soon equalised though with Adam Bolder scoring just before half-time and again halfway through the second half. Derby clung on to victory in front of just 5,810 supporters, which was 5,811 if you counted Simon's alien.

*****

Inconsistency marred those opening matches that season with Derby winning five and losing six of the first 11 League games. The experience hadn't put us off going though and if anything me and my Dad were travelling to more away grounds than ever. Maybe it was the great day me, my Dad and Uncle Paul had enjoyed at Sunderland the previous season or the fact that despite moving away to study at university and a year in Bristol my life's journey had somehow seen me still living at home with my parents at 27 years old and Dad thought I needed a bit of fresh air now and again.

By Christmas we were down in 13th position and those earlier dreams of an instant return to the Premier League echoed embarrassingly through the stands of Pride Park. Grimsby Town arrived on Boxing Day intent on revenge and won 3–1 while Reading served up a slice of humble pie to go along with John Gregory's Christmas turkey when they beat us 2–1 on 28 December, climbing into sixth place while leaving us languishing in 17th.

We travelled to third division Brentford in the FA Cup and lost by a single goal to nil while a draw at home to Gillingham the following game saw voices of discontentment raised among the Derby faithful. The Rams responded with wins against Stoke City and Rotherham but then went seven games without victory, leaving us in twentieth position and not the sort of form you want to be in when facing your bitter rivals when they themselves occupy the dizzy heights of fifth.

In March 2003 I moved out of home again, this time to share a house in Nottingham with two friends I knew through the first job I'd secured since moving back from Bristol, which involved overseeing the installation of electricity meters. I'd managed to stick this out for a year, which was a testament to the people who worked there as the job was far from interesting.

By October 2002 I'd actually found a career, teaching road safety education in schools around Nottingham, but I was still in touch with some of those who I'd left behind.

The two times I had left home before only to return, led me to thinking that my family home was some kind of Hotel California where you could check out any time you liked you just could never leave, but I still attempted to move again. My new home was on a row of terraced houses in the Meadows area of the city, which believe it or not is the English translation of Las Vegas. Rather than the opulence of its namesake in the United States though the Meadows in the East Midlands had developed a negative reputation among most people in the city and almost everyone else in the region. As ever it is the misbehaviour of the few that scar a place with a bad name.

The day after I moved I heard a knock at the front door and cautiously I went into the corridor to look through the window at the top of the door. Instead of being confronted by a gang of marauding youths it was an elderly lady who lived on our street. Assuming she was being chased by some local hoodlums I opened up the door but instead of running in screaming she showed me a wallet in her hand.

'I found this in the street and didn't know who it belonged to,' she explained, 'and as I didn't know you I thought that it might be yours.'

That act of thoughtfulness plus the fact that the rent was ridiculously cheap and the house was only a couple of miles from my office in the city made it a great location to live. The only downside though was that my room was at the top of the house, built into the roof with a single window set out against the tiles like a birdhouse. Notts County's Meadow Lane was just over the main road and their crowd could easily be heard talking to each other on matchdays but worse was that to my right I could make out the red cantilever structure of the Trent End at the City Ground.

On the Wednesday after I moved in, on the same day as allied forces invaded Iraq, Derby were due to play Nottingham Forest. The game coincided with that most imperfect of combinations: Forest on fire while we were having what could generously be considered as 'an off-day', which in fact had been lasting for months. Derby were thrashed by three goals to nil and to coin a phrase from Len Shackleton we were lucky to get nil.

Both sides remained in their respective places in the League but things didn't get better for the Rams. Manager, John Gregory, was suspended for what the Board called 'gross misconduct', although they would not go into any detail as to what it was that the manager had done and left supporters to start their own rumours based on what the bloke down the road who lives next door to the newsagent who sells papers to the mother of the son who cleans the changing rooms overheard. That Gregory was later to win an out-of-court settlement in April 2004 makes it seem that he was probably not misconducting himself grossly after all.

Gregory was replaced as manager by George Burley who had been sacked by Ipswich Town the previous October. This was just two years after winning the Manager of the Year award in a move that had football fans united in harrumphing, 'Well there's gratitude for you!' Burley had guided Suffolk's finest side into the Premier League and brought European football to Portman Road for the first time since Bobby Robson had left the club to manage the England team, but chairmen can be fickle like that.

While our results got better we were also thankful that those teams below us in the table were just as bad as we were and a good return of three wins and three defeats in the next six games saw us climb to 18th. Supporters were voting with their feet though and when we played Millwall on 16 April only 21,014 supporters were in attendance, over 12,000 less than that which had witnessed our first match of the season back in August.

Walsall 3 Derby County 2

Saturday 26 April 2003

Our last away match of the 2002–03 season was at the Bescot Stadium, Walsall. Instead of almost 50,000 supporters who me, my Dad and Uncle Paul had sat among the previous year this time there was less than 10,000.

Despite most of the season being spent at the wrong end of the table relegation was never an issue and we arrived in the West Midlands with the avoidance of a second successive demotion seeming like a success.

Walsall were founder members of Division Two when it was formed in 1892, founder members of the Third Division North in 1921 and founder members of Division Four in 1958. Seemingly more concerned with starting new Leagues than climbing high Walsall had spent the entirety of their history outside of the top-flight.

This time only me and my Dad made the journey to the game, which was considerably shorter than the trip we had made to Sunderland but was just as enjoyable. With two games to go we were 11 points ahead of Brighton and Hove Albion who occupied the final relegation spot and who would ultimately be relegated along with Sheffield Wednesday and Grimsby Town.

Although in 19th place in the table Walsall were also sitting comfortably 10 points clear of the relegation zone and so the match took on a relaxed atmosphere. Walking among the home support beforehand felt like wandering to the park in Long Eaton for the carnival. The previous season the Saddlers had finished just two points from being relegated and it was apparent that nobody was really missing the excitement that this must have generated.

With the comparison of this venue with that of last season firmly in our minds our discussion turned to what typified a ground rather than a stadium. It was similar to how we used to try and distinguish 'classic' films from 'epics' with Dad surmising that the only difference was that 'classics' were in black and white while 'epics' were in colour. When pressed on where sepia-toned films lay, his answer was that, 'they never made great films in that era.'

Being on row B it was easy to find our seats and we settled down for one of the most relaxing matches either of us had seen. The Derby players seemed just as relaxed and it took only three minutes for Walsall's Brazilian striker, Junior, to open the scoring, prompting Dad to remark that it was a good job the seniors weren't playing.

At half-time me and my Dad were looking around the ground and uncharacteristically Dad found himself looking at the negatives instead of what was good about the area.

'I mean,' he asked, 'who would live in Walsall? If you had a chance to live anywhere in world, why on earth would you choose to live in Walsall?'

After ranting further, only stopping briefly to sip the scalding tea that was almost melting the plastic cup in his hand a woman behind us, despite being decked in Derby scarf and replica shirt commented, 'Actually mate, I live in Walsall.'

Six minutes into the second half Dad was quietened further when Junior scored again and despite Simo Valakari grabbing one back for Derby, Junior went on to get his hat-trick and ensure that, despite an 83rd minute strike from Ravanelli, the home side were victorious and rose above the Rams to 17th to rub salt into our wounds.

*****

At the end of a season where we had promised ourselves so much the players delivered so very little and lost 24 matches, the most in the division apart from Grimsby who finished bottom. Before the last home game of the season against Ipswich Town, Brian Clough, the Middlesbrough-born manager who had made the Rams the best team in the country back in the seventies was given the freedom of the city. During the game the Derby players gave the Suffolk side the freedom of Pride Park and they cruised to a 4–1 victory.

Whereas before I had been worried that Derby's demise would result in an end to mine and Dad's relationship with the club, by the end of the 2002–03 season I had seen enough dross to realise that nothing would come between us and our team. The wars of attrition had actually bought us together and as comrades from some long ago battle we continued our pilgrimage to the ground like veteran soldiers to Ypres.

Nationwide Football League Division One 2002–03

Pos		Pl	W	D	L	F	A	GD	Pts
1	Portsmouth	46	29	11	6	97	45	52	98
2	Leicester City	46	26	14	6	73	40	33	92
16	Burnley	46	15	10	21	65	89	-24	55
17	Walsall	46	15	9	22	57	69	-12	54
18	**Derby County**	46	15	7	24	55	74	-19	52
19	Bradford City	46	14	10	22	51	73	-22	52
20	Coventry City	46	12	14	20	46	62	-16	50
21	Stoke City	46	12	14	20	45	69	-24	50
22	Sheffield Wednesday	46	10	16	20	56	73	-17	46

2003–04

England 2 Liechtenstein 0
Wednesday 10 September 2003

With our suntans barely faded the long-suffering supporters of Derby County were left disappointed by an opening day defeat at the hands of Stoke City. By the time England played Liechtenstein in a World Cup qualifying match a month later we were still without a win.

It was a testament to Dad that he didn't interfere when Ian started supporting Forest and Daniel turned towards Liverpool and while he was the first to intervene if we were erring towards danger he was also aware that we had to choose some paths ourselves. Because of our relationship with Derby County it could easily be perceived that I had a special bond with my Dad but the truth was that he was equally supportive of my brothers in their various pursuits. As a result of this, all three of us had graduated from university but were successful in different ways.

Resigned to the fact that all of his three progeny would never support his team Dad asked us all if we wanted to go and see England play instead. Why we had never had the idea before can only be guessed at but we all took to the suggestion with the same fanaticism that we had previously reserved for our own clubs.

Dad picked me up from work in the centre of Nottingham, taking the opportunity to visit someone at the Nottinghamshire Football Association across the road from my office so that he could use their car park and then drove out of the city to collect Ian and then continuing on to meet Daniel from the school in the Clifton area of the city where he taught maths.

Daniel was in a staff meeting and was running late and emerged from the building, stripping his tie off as if he was about to turn into Superman and as soon as he was in the car his shirt was off, which he replaced with an England rugby jersey. With us all getting into the spirit of the occasion Dad headed north to Old Trafford where the match was due to be played while Wembley stadium was being redeveloped.

We made good progress and arrived into Manchester with plenty of time to spare, so much so that by the time we parked up we still had chance to go to a JD Wetherspoon's pub near the ground for a drink. All evening Dad's grin was never far from his face as Ian and Daniel entered the usual conversation that me and him had shared with their own examples of footballing success and failure.

Old Trafford was huge in comparison to Pride Park and the City Ground and dwarfed everything around it. Whereas elsewhere supporters streamed towards the grounds in an orderly fashion here we swarmed round like ants, each trying to find the right turnstiles to get into while inside we dispersed to our separate sections, some in the gods while others nearer to the touchline.

Our seats were in the lower tier of the South Stand and as such we could have been watching the match at Pride Park, apart from the fact that we were being gazed upon by thousands of other fans who seemed to disappear way up into the autumn sky.

I was used to the crowd at matches singing as one, chanting together and cheering on in unison but here, maybe because it wasn't a club side or maybe because the sheer size of the place separated each section you could hear pockets of noise spring up among the thousands.

They say that there is never an easy game in international football but Liechtenstein at home should never raise the fear of blood in anyone other than Andorra. Still, at half-time the score remained 0–0 and we were thinking that our early predictions of goals in their hatfuls would have to be readdressed.

With players of the highest calibre that England had to offer like David Beckham, Frank Lampard, John Terry, Steven Gerrard, Michael Owen and Wayne Rooney on display it was easy to be absorbed by the football on the pitch but for me, my Dad and my brothers there was as much off it to enjoy. Supporting our different teams may have driven us apart but only in the way that we wouldn't attend matches together. Regardless of which team we supported all three of us still had that bond of knowing that a Saturday night could be made or ruined by what had happened at our respective clubs that afternoon.

England manager, Sven-Göran Eriksson, must have done something during the interval as it took Michael Owen just a minute into the second half to open the scoring. Wayne Rooney added a second six minutes later and England ended the game winning 2–0. There was enough time for one more beer before we headed back to the car and as Dad dropped me off his smile advertised the fact that by watching a live football match all together some sort of ambition had been met.

*****

Derby's first win that season came against Walsall on 13 September. Derby manager, George Burley, was obviously impressed by Junior's hat-trick at the Bescot Stadium the season before and had signed the Brazilian in August. He then opened his Derby account against his former club.

We lost just one match out of the next six, seeing us rise up to 16th but after losing the next four we dropped back down to 21st place in the table where we continued scrapping around towards the end of 2003. Crowds were averaging 20,000 with the swathes of empty black seats a testament to how far we had dropped, which had never been a problem on the terraces when people could spread out and create the illusion of a full house in grounds that were two-thirds full.

Rotherham United 0 Derby County 0

Saturday 13 December 2003

Everyone has those aunties and uncles that they call Auntie and Uncle, which are actually your Mum and Dad's mates rather than related. We would visit ours on Friday nights or go on holiday with them when we were growing up but when I moved away from home I started seeing them less. My Dad and Mum still remained friends with them though and so we knew about it when one of their daughters started seeing a professional footballer from the village near Nottingham where the two of them grew up.

Since Garry Birtles astounded the locals of Long Eaton by playing in two European Cup Finals everybody in the town seems to know a footballer but these claims are usually tenuous and laughed out of the pub. This was one reason why I used to avoid telling everyone that Mum was a colleague of England international Mark Draper's mother at the accountants where she worked although it didn't stop me telling the story about when Draper first went to play for Rayo Vallecano in Spain.

On arrival Draper looked up the term, 'pass' in a Spanish dictionary only to come up with the word 'pass' as in 'certificate of authorisation' and apparently spent the first few months at the Estadio Teresa Rivero in Madrid running around the pitch shouting, 'DRIVING LICENCE!' to his baffled teammates.

Far from being a seasoned professional and household name the mystery footballer who my parents were told about turned out to be a reserve player at Rotherham United, which was certainly unlikely to secure bragging rights in any pub before matches. I didn't know then that Shaun Barker would go on to play first team football at Millmoor before moving to Blackpool and eventually sign for Derby County in 2009.

By 2003 Barker was making his first few steps on the rungs of his career at Rotherham, prompting me and my Dad to travel the short distance up to the town when Derby played them in December that year. In reality the journey was similar to that which we took to Sheffield United, made better by the fact that you didn't actually have to go to Sheffield.

Before the game Dad made some excited phone calls and arranged for us to get into the players' lounge after the match, which is possibly the pinnacle of every football fan's sporting life if they support teams that never win anything. As ever Dad was true to his word but unfortunately the players' lounge at Millmoor turned out to be a Portacabin at the back of the Railway End of the ground and after the match me and my Dad were the only ones in there.

Shaun walked in with a huge grin on his face after being made man-of-the-match. Derby were looking in control and sure to take the lead at some stage when one of the Rotherham centre-backs went off injured, requiring Barker to move into the middle from his position on the right. Derby didn't get a sniff after that and while he kept the Rams forwards at bay he also created havoc by launching long throw-ins into the box.

Inside the relative warmth of the Portacabin the three of us talked about football but soon drifted onto other subjects. Dad's intuition with people meant that he appreciated that Shaun probably didn't want to talk about football all the time, in much the same way as he would not have appreciated talking about grinding aeroplane engine blades down to the required specifications immediately after a shift at work.

In the end me and my Dad didn't stay long and were embraced by the winter night of the town. Supporters who had stayed for a drink after the match were heading out of the pubs where they would probably walk into a family life similar to that which we enjoyed. Meanwhile others stayed inside with the community of the pub offering some sort of substitute to a home life.

It was easy to be grateful for my family who remained close even though we no longer shared the same home. If Derby were playing at Pride Park on the Saturday I would often travel back to Long Eaton on the Friday and stay over, going out with friends or just staying in with my Dad, Mum, Daniel, and Daniel's girlfriend, who he had met at university and who had moved in with my parents when they had both graduated.

I seemed to have finally struck the fine balance of being able to leave the family home but still retain the string of support that all of us forever need. That I was still in the position of going to football matches with my Dad in much the same way as I had done since I was four years old was testament to this. It was always apparent that wherever I was the safety net was still there beneath me.

*****

Derby's form remained dire and by early January we were out of the FA Cup and in the relegation zone. The only saving grace was that early progress at Nottingham

Forest had been deserted and they were only one place above us in the table. Two wins in two saw us leapfrog our rivals and it was shaping up as a tussle among the two teams to see who would be relegated. As Ian and I were living in different homes it meant that any duelling with newspapers was avoided, and the fact that we were 28 and 31 years old also prevented this.

One win in the next six matches saw Derby back in the relegation zone while Forest had risen to 19th. It was difficult to see where the points were coming from but the eternal positivity that exists within each football supporter remained. But it was under this cloud of a lowly position combined with our worst period of football in recent years that Dad was presented with the chance to fulfil a lifelong ambition.

Derby County 1 Rotherham 0

Saturday 13 March 2004

On 13 March 2004 Rotherham visited Pride Park Stadium. We met in the pub as usual and this time Daniel was coming along, and as Shaun Barker, the player who me and my Dad had met up with after Derby had played at Rotherham the previous December was playing, so was Ian.

Dad never once said anything about Ian and Daniel supporting other teams but I got the feeling that he was disappointed that matchdays could have been better as a family rather than with just the two of us. I asked Mum once why they didn't just make Ian become a Derby fan but her answer was that you have to let your kids make their own decisions. Thinking back to my own initiation though I couldn't help wondering with a wry grin not dissimilar to my Dad's whether I had had that chance.

The fact that my brothers and I all supported different teams went someway in making us immune to the seething hatred of other teams, including Forest that I have witnessed in grounds across the country. Admittedly when I see the opposition score and hear that distant cheer at the far end of the ground I want to dive right in and kick a few shins but this feeling soon leaves me and I return to sanity and the same understanding that was shown to me throughout my life by my Dad.

Back in 1990 Forest had beaten Coventry in a League Cup semi-final and Dad had cheered as loudly as Ian in support of the Reds. At that time, however, my own tolerance was yet to build.

'You've been in a mood ever since Forest won that match!' Dad complained to me later and I looked at him in a way similar to that which Caesar looked up at Brutus when he stabbed the Roman Emperor for stealing his salad recipe.

All too often Derby's success was paramount to making me delighted and this was swiftly followed by the pleasure generated by Forest's misfortune. Dad on the other hand always had the happiness of all of his sons to override anything that football had to offer and to him if Ian was happy then he was happy.

Since our trip to watch England play Liechtenstein in September Dad wanted to go one better and as we walked out of the pub that Saturday afternoon in March 2003, 23 years after his youngest son had been born, he turned to one of my mates and said, 'At last I've got all my lads to a Derby game.'

Watford 2 Derby County 1
Tuesday 16 March 2004

We had beaten Rotherham but this had done nothing to ease our fears of relegation and a midweek match against Watford pitched us against another team near the foot of the division. Vicarage Road was not a ground I had been to before and with rent in the Meadows being so cheap I had quite a lot of disposable income at the time and so decided to go.

Travelling to Watford in midweek was one of those matches that sets you apart from other supporters. Visiting clubs within a 40-mile radius on a Saturday afternoon is commonplace, whereas driving down the M1 after work when the clouds threaten snow and when a ladder falls from a Jewson van in front of you and almost knocks you off the carriageway, is one of the games you put down on your footballing cv.

Dad was going to the theatre in Nottingham with Mum, Daniel and Daniel's girlfriend so it was just me and Simon Goodhall who took the trip. Watford always seemed within easy reach but after an hour we had still not reached Northampton and we both nervously gazed at the clock on Simon's dashboard.

We had left relatively early with the plan to park in Watford in enough time to find a pub for dinner before the game. None of the regular pubs looked inviting though and so we opted for the safe and recognisable option of a Wetherspoon's. As it was steak night, with an 8oz rump and pint for less than five pounds the choice was not so bad, although it was far from the standard that we had received on coming back from Sunderland.

Some games attract a larger following for no apparent reason and so a strong away support can only be the work of something machiavelian. That night was one of those occasions when people just came as if attracted by some simple sports-ground built by Kevin Costner. Before the game I felt like I was in an episode of This is your Life as I bumped into old friends, relatives and work colleagues who had all made the random journey that evening.

The Derby contingent numbered almost 3,000 and the early roar of those travelling fans urged the team to make the perfect start as Paul Peschisolido took just 10 minutes to open the scoring. We needed the goal, we really did, and the relief and joy was immense, so much so that the cheering in our Vicarage Road Stand went on for an age. This was what being a football fan was all about, that moment of sheer exhilaration when the ball hits the back of the net and signals a goal of the upmost importance.

At that moment I was so happy, singing into the cold Watford night with our voices rising on exhalations of steam pouring out from beneath the roof of the stand. Only sport can ignite such excitement in such a split second. But then sport can take it away. Just nine minutes later Watford equalised and then went on to win the match in the second half with a 53rd minute strike from Gavin Mahon.

I wasn't expecting a win but we had been teased by the opening goal that led us all to believe that we would be ok and that relegation was a demon that just rested in the shadows. The truth was that it was omnipresent that night, lurking in every doorway of the unfamiliar town as we made our way back to the car.

As soon as I'd put the seatbelt on my mobile started to ring, as if whoever was calling was giving me time to close the result before returning to the land of the normal.

The phone had been given to me by the Carlisle United fan I had met at university and the Kylie Minogue cover was his idea. I was told it was so bad it was good and when I set the phone to vibrate, Kylie seemed to dance so I'd kept it. Tonight though even that failed to cheer me up and when I saw it was Ian ringing, my disappointment turned to anger as I pictured him calling to gloat. He didn't say anything about the match though, he just said, 'When you get back, come home.'

With roadworks on the M1 this was easier said than done and according to those people who I had seen before the match the traffic was a nightmare for the 3,000 supporters from the East Midlands. It took them several hours to get back but for some reason as the carriageway narrowed from three lanes to one, when we drove home the traffic seemed to ease through and we progressed in good time.

Simon dropped me off at my parent's house, which had me reminiscing at the time me and my Dad had walked back from the game in 1987 that had made us champions of Division Two. I walked up to the front door and looked up into the clear dark night as the ghosts of dead stars blinked back. The snow had failed to come but the night was still bitterly cold.

The two-hour drive back had failed to clear my foul mood that always accompanied a defeat and when my Mum opened the front door I was already expecting the usual solemn face that greeted me, which she always owned when Derby had lost.

I looked at her to say we'd lost the match, but she just held my shoulders and said, 'We've lost your Dad.'

*****

Most people understandably associate heart disease with an unhealthy lifestyle but it can also act indiscriminately and at random, like God taking a shot but getting the wrong man.

Dad's 10km runs and half marathons had developed into the full 26 miles and four times throughout the 1990s my Dad had completed the London marathon. He was very athletic, especially for his age and had been out running along one of the lanes that stretch from Breaston to Long Eaton just short of the level crossing that used to take me and him to Derby, between the breaker's yard and the riding school, when he suffered a heart attack. He was only 54.

While we often hope for a quick and painless death these wishes do not take into account the people who we will leave behind, the people who one moment have a devoted father who has given us such fond memories only to have them disappear. Dad's death was instant but the devastating effects on our family woke us every single day and then continued.

From that moment our loss would rise repeatedly in memory of him when future milestones like bringing the girl home who I was destined to marry, buying our first home together and getting engaged were all accompanied by the fact that I missed him so much and would continue to do so forever.

Daniel was only 24 when we lost Dad and would miss out on having the man who would have been so proud of him offering him that winning smile that spurred us all on to bigger and better things. And when Ian had children there would be times when advice and support that only a father can pass down to his son would be absent.

I also mourned the loss to my Mum who had to endure hours, which must have dragged like days waiting for me to get home on the night of 16 March just so she could tell me the sad, sad news. I was as distressed that she had lost her husband as I was at the fact that I had lost my Dad.

Until that moment our family had existed in a realm of relative bliss with none of us aware of how fragile life could be. The option of a check-up at the health centre seemed like a waste of the doctor's time but had he known how his death would affect his family Dad would have been down the clinic every morning.

In the days afterwards people came to pay their respects and also offer stories of the man he was, coupled with warming anecdotes of when they had last seen him. A good friend who Dad knew from working at the Long Eaton Sunday League told us how he and his wife always used to see Dad running along the streets without recognition but on that last occasion Dad had caught their eye and waved. That was also when my mate told me what Dad had said when leaving the pub before the Rotherham game just three days before his death, about having his three lads at Derby at last.

Derby County 4 Nottingham Forest 2

Saturday 20 March 2004

Me and my Dad had tickets for the match but I wasn't going to go. Mentally I closed down and rolled myself like a hedgehog so that nothing else could hurt me. Negative things in my life that had seemed so desperate suddenly became relatively acceptable compared with this and if I did think about relegation, catching something on the local news between endless cups of tea or in the papers I felt only a wave of something akin to nostalgia as I could only recall what it once felt like to care about football.

Mum asked me if I was going to the match and I flatly refused. Later I said I'd only go if Uncle Paul was to have Dad's ticket, knowing that Paul was on holiday and that it wouldn't happen. Later still Ian, who had sat the other side of our Dad on that day in November 1979 when the people stood up and cheered and the lights changed said that if I wanted to go then he would come along. It was an option.

I'd spent the whole week at what my mates still referred to as my Mum and Dad's before catching themselves and becoming silenced with embarrassment. So after deciding to go to the match after all, Ian and I drove to pick up the tickets from my house in Nottingham. We then continued back along the A52 to Derby, parked up at Alvaston Park and walked along the River Derwent to Pride Park Stadium.

At the back of the stand before the game I bumped into Ryan Goodhall and to his credit he was trying to stem the flow of tears just like James England had tried on the phone when he called earlier in the week. I'd said to Mum on that Tuesday night that there wasn't one person who knew Dad that wouldn't be absolutely gutted at what had happened and I was right.

It wasn't just my loss. The running club who Dad ran for renamed their sportsperson of the year award after him. And now any 10-year-old kid stumbling into the changing rooms of our local park where we played in the paddling pool and ate ice lollies in summer, and rode our bikes among the trees in winter will see a plaque just below the one commemorating its opening, and that other great man of Derby County Football Club, and see:

In Memory Of

Tony Trembirth

for service to the

Long Eaton Sunday League

1973–2004

For that first match without Dad we could have been playing to half a stadium against Wimbledon, Bradford or Crewe but the local Derby secured a full house of 32,390 supporters and made an event of it. The fact that Forest were also threatened by relegation added to the atmosphere and both sets of supporters rose to the occasion.

It wasn't just the supporters either. Our team who had spent most of the season fighting off relegation surged forward to secure a lead in just the fourth minute with a stunning move that swept along the pitch. After 28 minutes we extended our lead, as Paul Peschisolido chased a hopeful ball forward and scored one of the strangest goals seen in the stadium's short history.

Before the match the wind had blown strongly around the stadium, spinning around the stands and uprooting banners and litter into the sky. Supporters pulled their coats tighter in defence at the cold and wandered with heads bowed to the safety of the concourses beneath the stands. Inside it was the same with scarves and flags blown in all directions as the wind spun wildly, trying to get out of the ground.

As Peschisolido advanced, the Forest goalkeeper, Barry Roche, was favourite to reach the ball first but instead it got caught in the wind, hit the ground and bounced wildly away from him, which forced him to slice his clearance towards the Derby forward. It was as if some invisible foot had intervened to set-up our second goal and the striker side-footed the ball easily into the open net.

Ian and I were at the other end of the pitch and just saw the ripple of the goal before feeling everyone around celebrating wildly, uncontrollably, an exquisite goal that I used to dream of. Instead of cheering though I stood there and let Ian hold me as I failed to stem my tears.

The match ended with Derby winning by four goals to two but mercifully both teams avoided relegation at the end of the season.

As me and my brother sat in the car after the game queuing to get out of the car park and back to Mum, it was up to the commentators on the radio to tell us what had happened.

Derby's second goal had come after the ball hit a plastic coffee cup to make it bounce into the path of Peschisolido. The following morning the newspapers agreed and so did all 30,000 Derby supporters, all of who claimed that it was actually their coffee cup which set up the goal.

But after the miracles I'd seen watching Derby County with my Dad, the mascot appearances against Orient and Oldham and the seat tickets to see Kevin Keegan play at the Baseball Ground. Getting tickets for the FA Cup Final in 1986 and then convincing a manager of cub football to leave me on the pitch at my own Cup Final so that we could win the trophy. After bypassing the queues for Portsmouth and shouting Derby on to the Division Two Championship in 1987, the silhouette of Daniel at the foot of some huge terrace at Burnley and my Dad holding the ball against Sunderland to go top of the League in 1995, to me it will never be a coffee cup that set up our second goal that afternoon.

Printed in Great Britain
by Amazon

33373665R00111